P9-DUR-746

WITHDRAWN
From Heritage University Library
Heritage University Library
3240 Fort Road
Toppenish, WA 98948

Class Struggle and the New Deal

Studies in Historical Social Change

SCOTT G. McNALL AND JILL S. QUADAGNO, EDITORS

Social Change in the Southwest, 1350–1880, Thomas D. Hall

Class Struggle and the New Deal: Industrial Labor, Industrial Capital, and the State, Rhonda F. Levine

Class Struggle and the New Deal

INDUSTRIAL LABOR, INDUSTRIAL CAPITAL, AND THE STATE

Rhonda F. Levine

University Press of Kansas

Published by the University Press of Kansas (Lawrence, Kansas 66045), which was organized by the Kansas Board of Regents and is operated and funded by Emporia State University, Fort Hays State University, Kansas State University, Pittsburg State University, the University of Kansas, and Wichita State University

Library of Congress Cataloging-in-Publication Data

Levine, Rhonda F.
Class struggle and the New Deal : industrial labor, industrial capital, and the state / Rhonda F. Levine.
p. cm. — (Studies in historical social change)
Bibliography: p.
Includes index.
ISBN 0-7006-0373-5 (alk. paper)
1. United States—Economic policy—1933-1945. 2. Social conflict—United States—History—20th century. 3. New Deal, 1933-1939. I. Title. II. Series.
HC106.3.L398 1988 88-17183
338.973—dc19 CIP

Printed in the United States of America
10 9 8 7 6 5 4 3 2 1

The paper used in this publication meets the minimum requirements of the American National Standard for Permanence of Paper for Printed Library Materials Z39.48-1984.

FOR ROSE ESTHER LEVY
my appreciation for the past

FOR JEREMY ROBERT LEVINE-MURRAY
my hope for the future

CONTENTS

PREFACE

The conjoined impact of the 1970s world economic downturn and the persistent business slump in the United States engendered a serious reassessment of the 1930s Great Depression and the lessons that it might contain for contemporary policy makers. The apparent inability of Keynesian techniques to provide a lasting solution to business cycles has stimulated radical departures from the prevailing economic orthodoxy. So-called supply-side economics—with its emphasis on strict monetary controls, savings and investments, private entrepreneurship, and a rollback of state regulations—suddenly emerged as the practical panacea that would arrest and reverse the business downturn. The fortuitous coincidence of this fiscal neopopulism in mainstream economics and the neoconservative political resurgence under the Reagan presidency coalesced in a common quest for a broad, all-encompassing paradigm that would displace welfare-state liberalism with an antistatism laissez-faire standard. This neoconservative backlash has not only challenged existing state-sponsored social programs but has also questioned the very premises upon which welfare-state liberalism was founded in the first place. Stripped to its essence, neoconservative ideology has not only instinctively targeted the Roosevelt administration's New Deal reforms as the basic foundation for the postwar Democratic party's liberalism but has also placed the blame for the persistent 1970s–1980s "stagflation" on the historical legacy of the New Deal's "Big Government" predilections and anti-big-business rhetoric.

The Roosevelt administration's New Deal recovery program originated in a specific historical conjuncture in world history and politics. The New Deal and the historical legacy that it spawned marked a decisive watershed in the structural relationship between the entire trajectory of capital accumulation and what, loosely speaking, can be termed state interventionism. For the first time in United States history (with the possible exception of the World War I era), top-level state officialdom wrested political authority for the executive branch to actively adjudicate conflicts between labor and capital and between fractions of capital, to establish economic priorities and provide the profitable incentives for businessmen to leap at the chance to realize them, to tinker with macroeconomic trends through the judicious use of fiscal and monetary mechanisms, and finally, to establish the programmatic foundation for an envelope of economic security for those who were unable to achieve it through their own devices.

The New Deal was anchored in its particular program for industrial recovery, the National Industrial Recovery Act (NIRA), which became the cornerstone of the entire industrial-recovery program. These elemental features of the New Deal can be understood *sui generis.* Yet more importantly, a detailed analysis of the New Deal industrial-recovery program can illuminate a broad range of perplexing questions that were just as appropriate at the time of the Great Depression of the 1930s as during other periods of severe business decline. The analysis of the New Deal industrial-recovery program can provide a starting point for uncovering the structural limits to political decision making during a period of severe economic decline. During all economic crises, analysts have come forward with solutions to the economic impasse. For state officials, elected representatives, and bureaucrats, political solutions to economic crises seem not only historically possible but also conceptually unproblematic. The underlying aim of the historical investigation of the New Deal that I undertake in this book is to establish the factors that governed the concrete prerogatives of policy makers in the Roosevelt administration. This explanation of the material and historical preconditions for the New Deal industrial-recovery programs has serious implications for theories of the capitalist state in general and for the determinants of policy making in particular.

This book originated as a doctoral dissertation. There are a number of people whom I would like to thank for their constructive comments at the early stages of my research. Melvyn Dubofsky and Melvin M. Leiman helped me to clarify historical and economic material respectively. James A. Geschwender not only offered helpful comments during the initial stages of writing but he also has supported the process of transforming what was then a dissertation into what is now a book. Comments made by Perry Anderson, Suzanne de Brunhoff, and Manuel Castells were particularly instructive in the process of revising this manuscript for publication. Manuel Castells was especially supportive of my research, and his continual faith in my work helped me in sustaining the stamina necessary to revise, and revise again, until the project was completed.

I am especially grateful for comments by Larry J. Griffin, Scott G. McNall, and Jill S. Quadagno. Larry Griffin's comments helped me to sharpen my argument at various places in the manuscript. Although we disagree on a number of matters, his critique has sharpened my appreciation of the strengths and weaknesses of this book. I owe more than a mere thanks to Scott McNall and Jill Quadagno. Their comments were not only indispensable during the final stages of writing, but their enthusiastic support and guidance made the final stages of completing the manuscript an experience I will always treasure. Such collegial support is a rarity in today's academic marketplace.

Numerous archivists and librarians at the National Archives, the Tamiment Institute, the Franklin D. Roosevelt Library, the George Arents Research Library, the Jackson Library of Business, the Hoover Institution on War, Revolution and Peace, the Bancroft Library, the AFL-CIO Library, and the International Longshoremen's and Warehouseman's Union Library were especially helpful in locating material pertinent to my research project. A grant from the Eleanor Roosevelt Institute helped finance my numerous trips to the FDR Library. The manuscript collection held at the FDR Library proved invaluable for my understanding of the complexities surrounding the policy-making process.

My very special thanks go to Margaret Abbott and Thelma Mayer for their secretarial assistance in the final preparation of this book. I am particularly grateful to Thelma Mayer, who never seemed to lose her patience with what might have seemed like endless revisions.

Finally, I wish to thank my family. My parents, Rae and Frank Levine, have been supportive of this project from the beginning. Martin Murray offered constructive criticism throughout the writing of this book, and although I am not always willing to admit it, I do appreciate the time and energy he spent with me going over various drafts. Last, but certainly not least, I wish to acknowledge Jeremy Robert Levine-Murray. Although his birth did indeed throw me off my original timetable for completion, his good-natured temperament provided me with the incentive to finish a project that I began long before he was conceived. I am quite confident that Jeremy, along with others in my family, is as relieved as I am that this book is finally completed.

CHAPTER ONE

The Capitalist State, Class Relations, and the New Deal

The Great Depression of the 1930s represented an unparalleled economic crisis in the United States. The "boom years" of the 1920s were characterized by tremendous industrial expansion both in scale and scope, the rapid concentration of social wealth, and an unequal modus vivendi between capital and labor in which the former subjected the latter to an accelerated pace of production. In retrospect, visible signs of the impending economic crisis abounded. Nevertheless, the confident optimism in business cycles that was shared almost universally came to an abrupt halt with the stock-market crash in October 1929. By 1932 the plummeting price of overvalued stocks had brought a decline of more than 38 percent in national income, more than five thousand bank failures and eighty-five thousand business bankruptcies, and an unemployment rate of 23.6 percent of the civilian labor force.[1] Representatives of small-scale capitalist firms—nonmonopoly capital—placed the blame for the profit squeeze and the expanded rate of bankruptcies among small-to-medium-sized manufacturing firms on the increased concentration and centralization of capital—monopolization—in the principal branches of industrial production. Consequently, they sought relief from the federal government in the form of revitalized antitrust legislation that would renew competitiveness and profitable opportunities and hence restore economic stability on the basis of a free-market ideology. In contrast, the representatives of large-scale capitalist firms—monopoly capital—argued quite vociferously that huge capital investments in manufacturing plants were responsible for the heightened economic prosperity of the 1920s. Hence, the domination of a few large firms in ever-expanding industry was certainly not the source of economic woes; it might even be the solution for them. If economic difficulties did exist, they were caused by unreliable markets. Monopoly capital sought state aid in stabilizing the market by calling for an easing of the antitrust laws and for the self-regulation of industry through price fixing and profit control.

As unemployment continued to rise during the early years of the depression, wages fell, and the hours of work increased for hundreds of thousands of employed workers. Total wages within the industrial sector had fallen some 20 percent by June 1930, and real weekly earnings of those employed in manufacturing and mining had declined by 15 to 30 percent.[2] Unemployed workers sought federal aid in relief for unemployed families as leftist political groups became more active in the struggle for relief and unemployment insurance. Employed workers concentrated on defensive goals: resisting wage decreases and demanding wage rates that would support their families. Leaders of organized labor called on the federal government to institute some sort of industrial-planning measure that would benefit workers.

The Hoover administration did virtually nothing either to restore business confidence or concretely to relieve the suffering of the impoverished and the bankrupt, believing instead that tinkering with recurrent business cycles would only exacerbate an already difficult situation. Holding on to a laissez-faire ideology, the Hoover administration declared that the depression was temporary. The result of economic recklessness, it could be overcome through voluntary measures adopted by leaders of the banking, business, labor, and agricultural communities.

The 1932 presidential election and the victory of Franklin D. Roosevelt indicated the general discontent and the overwhelming repudiation of a state administration that based its policies on laissez-faire ideological premises. As soon as Roosevelt had taken office in March 1933, his administration attempted to put into motion plans and programs for industrial economic recovery by first concentrating on a policy that would alleviate antitrust provisions, regulate production, and control prices to stimulate investments. The National Industrial Recovery Act (NIRA) stood as the centerpiece of this grandiose scheme to overcome industrial economic decline. Through the "codes of fair competition," representatives of firms within a particular branch of industry would come together and establish price- and production-control guidelines for their industrial branch. In exchange for an implicit promise of cooperation with management, the Roosevelt administration assured industrial labor that it would set minimum wage standards and maximum hours of work through specific codes of fair competition and that it would also, through section 7a of the NIRA, guarantee industrial workers the formal rights to join unions of their own choosing without management reprisals. The Roosevelt administration theorized that regulated industrial competition, in tandem with a more-or-less guaranteed standard of living, would assure the conditions of economic recovery.

The formulation of the NIRA appeared to coordinate the perceived interests of both industrial capital and industrial labor within an overall joint project to generate economic recovery. Labor leaders confidently surmised that the provisions of NIRA's section 7a provided the type of protective shield that would guarantee formal rights to form unions and to bargain collectively. It soon became evident, however, that they had misread the signals. Employers, remaining wary of the provisions of section 7a, nevertheless welcomed state-regulated price controls and production-output codes. Monopoly capital received the much-desired lifting of antitrust provisions. Nonmonopoly capital thought that it received protection from monopolies and that it could now remain competitive in the industrial market.

Contrary to its design, the NIRA did not effectively stimulate economic recovery, it failed to adjudicate the already delicate competitive relations between monopoly and nonmonopoly capital, and it never convinced an otherwise suspicious organized labor movement that the newly created triumvirate—the partnership between capital, labor, and the state—was in its best interest. The NIRA's performance did not match its promise. While the codes of fair competition were designed to benignly coordinate the market in the interest of both monopoly and nonmonopoly capital, they actually contributed to the increased concentration and centralization of capital. Consequently, large firms found themselves in a much more favorable structural position to obtain larger market shares and to expand in size and scale. Small-to-medium capital was unable to withstand the competition. Hence, the NIRA codes of fair competition served to heighten the conflicts between fractions of monopoly and nonmonopoly capital. Moreover, the refusal of many employers to abide by the labor provisions in section 7a meant that organized labor was unable to recruit membership without conflict and confrontation. Rebuffed on the shop floor and believing that the Roosevelt administration had ignored their plight, units of industrial labor in the yet-to-be-organized basic, mass-production industries adopted new strategies and tactics to match their perceived enemies. Strike activity took on new proportions as industrial workers demanded the right to organize and join unions of their own choosing. In the face of rising working-class unity coupled with determined militancy, the industrial capitalist class appeared to lose momentum and to retreat into internecine squabbling.

The concatenation of rising labor militancy and of the erstwhile convenience that was uniting the emergent industrial union movement with the Democratic party brought together a unique convergence of social forces. In order to slow the rising tide of labor militancy and class unruliness, the Roosevelt administration enacted the National Labor Relations Act (NLRA) in June 1935. The NLRA, by guaranteeing industrial labor the right to join unions of their own choosing and to engage in collective-bargaining arrangements with employers, gave industrial labor the much-desired state machinery to enforce labor's right to organize independent unions and to protect industrial workers from employers' refusals to engage in collective-bargaining agreements with unions that were elected by a majority of workers. Moreover, this legislative enactment altered the course of the class struggle. Through the NLRA, the industrial union movement had acquired a special legal standing with both industrial capital and the state administration. In addition, organized industrial labor found a "political voice" through the medium of the Democratic party within the national political arena.

On the capitalist front, nonmonopoly capital criticized the New Deal industrial-recovery program for fostering monopoly growth, whereas monopoly capital increasingly became disenchanted with the apparent prolabor policies of the Roosevelt administration. Intracapitalist conflict increased over the "monopoly" issue, and the divisions within the class provided barriers for structural changes within the state apparatus, such as the reorganization of the executive branch. Yet, by the end of the 1930s, the industrial economy was recovering from the worst effects of the depression, primarily because of war-related production; large-scale corporate capital had come to dominate key state agencies; and industrial labor had entered into an unequal relationship with industrial capital at the level of the state. In brief, the political and economic order by the end of World War II was fundamentally altered from what it had been at the outset of the depression. Not only did the trajectory of capitalist development in the United States take a different course, but also the relationships between industrial capital, industrial labor, and the state became regulated by new structural forms.

In retrospect, the economic crisis of the 1930s presented three obstacles to the accumulation of capital in the United States: (1) too high a rate of exploitation, which resulted in problems of profit realization; (2) unregulated competition, which led to problems of investment; and (3) a political structure that was not conducive to the imperatives of the accumulation process. The New Deal industrial-recovery program produced three important political consequences: (1) the unchallenged political hegemony of monopoly capital; (2) the diffusion of labor militancy into a general ideological consensus for capitalist rule; and (3) the incorporation of organized industrial labor into the national process of political bargaining. How did these political consequences aid in overcoming obstacles to the accumulation of capital? To what extent did New Deal policies provide political and resulting economic conditions that were favorable to the growth and expansion of monopoly capital in particular and of United States–based firms in general, despite capitalist opposition to many of these policies? How can the formulation, as well as the implementation, of New Deal policies be explained? In short, how can we explain the particular New Deal response to the economic crisis of the 1930s as manifested in the United States? A central task of this book is to answer those questions.

New Deal Historiography and Problems of Conceptualization

With few exceptions, mainstream historiographical debate over the character of the Roosevelt administration's New Deal policies has focused narrowly on a single line of intellectual inquiry: namely, can New Deal policies be interpreted as a compendium of "radical innovations" that fundamentally altered the future course of "state/economy" relations or, alternatively, as essentially "conservative strategies" that were designed to restore economic stability without greatly modifying the status quo?[3] Those who can be classified in the "radical innovations" camp have contended that the New Deal project represented highly innovative government-sponsored programs that signaled an unparalleled departure from the prevailing attitude governing the role that state bureaucracies ought to perform. William E. Leuchtenburg, perhaps the premier New Deal historian, argues that the "radically new departure" of the New Deal—which was marked by the expansion of the federal government, the development of a federal relief system, and unionization for the industrial working class—makes the 1930s one of the most significant periods in United States history.[4] Conversely, those writers who can be classified in the "conservative strategies" camp have emphasized that New Deal programs were fundamentally aimed at the preservation of the capitalist order. While agreeing that the New Deal produced significant changes, Barton J. Bernstein nevertheless concludes that the New Deal "failed to solve the problems of the depression, it failed to raise the impoverished, it failed to redistribute income, it failed to extend equality and generally countenanced racial discrimination and segregation."[5] For Bernstein, the "liberal" aims of New Deal policy makers produced "conservative" results.

Despite the apparent diversity of these alternative approaches, conventional historiographical accounts of the New Deal locate the problematic within a common frame of reference. To begin with, they tend to take as their starting point the attitudes, presumptions, intentions, and goals of the policy makers themselves. They then debate the "success" or "failure" of New Deal policies from the common perspective of the stated intentions of policy makers, thereby ignoring the structural context within which decision making, political persuasion, and compromise took place. In describing the manner in which policies were formulated, most New Deal historians take for granted the boundaries of state intervention and rarely question the limits that economic processes might place on political decision making. To argue that New Deal policies were either a success or a failure in bringing about economic recovery or that they represented either radical innovations or conservative strategies assumes that in counterfactual terms, a different set of *political* circumstances could have provided a different response. What is obscured in such an analysis is the underlying economic processes that are manifested in those very political relations.

Many of the theoretical presuppositions that inform conventional historiographical debates over the New Deal are hidden from view. Nevertheless, to a great extent the problem of conceptualization within New Deal historiography rests on the very set of theoretical assumptions that underlie the analysis of the capitalist state. Almost without exception, mainstream debates over New Deal policies have relied upon what can be termed pluralist or instrumentalist conceptions of the state. In the pluralist view, the state functions as a neutral arbitrator. Pluralists tend to focus on the immediate activities of politicians and self-defined interest groups and on the pressures that they bring to bear individually and collectively on legislative bodies. Shifting coalitions of political participants demand state policies, and they are rewarded according to relative need. Such a view of the state leads these historians either to make broad claims about evolutionary changes without focusing on the conflicts and tensions of the day or to concentrate on interest-group formation and intragroup conflict without understanding the impact of economic processes or political structures that govern these immediate relationships.[6] To argue that the NLRA was the result of pressure groups that operated within the legislative process fails to explain the impact of extraparliamentary struggles that segments of the industrial working class waged on the shop floor for union recognition.

In addition to New Deal historians who operate from a pluralist perspective, a number of New Deal historians have approached their analysis of New Deal policies through the prism of an instrumentalist conceptualization of the state.[7] In the instrumentalist view, the state becomes a powerful weapon in the hands of a relatively small number of groups which possess a disproportionate share of the power to enact policies that would be to their own benefit. Instrumentalists argue that these groups are able to shape policy and to satisfy their economic objectives to an extent that is contrary to the "public" interest. Most analyses of New Deal policies from an instrumentalist conceptualization document the coincidence of interests and the coincidence of individuals in both government and the industrial business community. Whereas pluralists would argue that New Deal policies were a result of a government that was responsive to the interest of all citizens in strengthening the political and economic order, instrumentalists would argue that the economically powerful capitalist class pressured the federal administration to enact policies that would be to their benefit alone.[8]

Those New Deal historians who operate under the explicit or implicit rubric of an instrumentalist view of the capitalist state acknowledge that the dominant classes in capitalism wield considerably more influence in terms of the formulation of state policies. This recognition—that propertied classes almost invariably coalesce into powerful interest groups that not only attempted to shape New Deal programs but also implanted their own particular imprint on the policy-making process—stresses the significance that economic-class relations have on the formulation of state policy. These insights have offered an important corrective to those authors who uncritically ignore the differential in class power between labor and capital and, instead, review New Deal policies as if they had occurred in a vacuum wherein the "common good" was always the prime value governing the policy-making process. However, those who operate within an instrumentalist framework often tend to rely upon a "conspiracy" model, assuming that the dominant classes enjoyed a more or less unmediated representation in the formation of New Deal policy. The assumption that a class-conscious monolithic capitalist class has the foresight to manipulate state policy in such a fashion as to further its own interest and to counter labor unrest oversimplifies the nature of class relations, on the one hand, and fails, on the other hand, to account for divisions within the capitalist class itself. For example, to argue that enlightened capitalists pressured politicians to consciously design New Deal labor policy in such a manner as eventually to create the conditions for a relatively self-disciplined labor force fails to explain capitalists' resistance to the provisions of these very policies.

Both pluralist and instrumentalist analyses of the state assume a separation between the internal laws of capital accumulation and governmental activity. In so doing, New Deal historians ignore the structural relationship between the state and the process of capitalist development, regarding the relationship between "state" and "economy" as one of technical manipulation. What is therefore missing from the analysis of New Deal policies is an understanding that while state activity might attempt to provide the conditions for the uninterrupted accumulation of capital, the nature and the course of capital accumulation will condition the effects of state intervention and will place limits on political decision making.[9] By perceiving the state either as an object (in the instrumentalist view) or as a subject (in the pluralist view) that acts upon the laws and the motion of capitalist development, class conflict—both at the level of the state and at the point of production—is concealed, thereby overlooking the manner in which the economic division of labor might provide the basic elements of state activity.[10] In short, pluralists take capitalist property relations for granted. They tend to treat as unproblematic the source of differential power relations and the origins of vested interest groups, and consequently they fail to examine the complexities of macrohistorical change. Instrumentalists, on the other hand, recognize the significance of property relations as a source of political power yet fail to distinguish between intentions, interests, values, the behavior of members of the state administration, and recognizable objective relations between the state apparatus and the process of capital accumulation.

State Theory and the New Deal

The publication of Ralph Miliband's *The State in Capitalist Society* and the ensuing debate between Nicos Poulantzas and Miliband marked the beginnings of a renewed theoretical interest in the relationship between the capitalist state apparatus and the process of capitalist development.[11] The general tensions between "instrumentalist" and "structuralist" conceptualizations of the capitalist state have produced a new field of literature that goes well beyond the theoretical frameworks used by New Deal historians.[12] While Poulantzas and Miliband circumscribed their controversy within a selected range of topics, the debate itself inspired a multitude of separate lines of inquiry that extended well beyond the original confines and, in fact, created new terrains for both theoretical and historical investigations. In particular, the renewed controversy over the 1930s economic crisis in the United States and the attendant New Deal recovery program has raised a new set of questions that have shifted the state debate beyond the generalized framework of "instrumentalism" or "structuralism."[13]

In the structuralist perspective, the state is located within the confines of the social relations of capitalism. Poulantzas argues that state policy can best be understood as arising from the basic class contradictions of capitalism. Contrary to instrumentalist accounts, the class antagonisms between labor and capital are not the only defining characteristics of capitalism. For Poulantzas, the capitalist class itself is divided internally. The internal conflicts of the capitalist class arise from the fact that units of capital are in constant competition with one another. The separation of capital into competing units of accumulation, isolated from one another and working against one another, is a necessary component of the accumulation process. These class contradictions and class conflicts, which arise from the nature of capital accumulation, are embedded within the very structure of the state and, as such, provide structural limits or boundaries to state activity. According to Poulantzas, "Class contradictions are the very stuff of the State: they are present in its material framework and pattern its organization; while the State's policy is the result of their functioning within the State."[14] Because the state is relatively autonomous from any given class or fraction of a class, Poulantzas argues that state policy is able to mediate between conflicting fractions of the capitalist class and to channel working-class discontent within limits that are compatible with the overall accumulation of capital. The precise manner in which this mediation takes place is dependent on the balance of class forces represented throughout the state.

Poulantzas's contribution to a theory of the state has directed social scientists in the United States to analyze the New Deal in terms quite different from those originally posed by New Deal historians and, in the process, to advance an alternative formulation of the state that purports to more adequately explain New Deal recovery programs. Drawing on Poulantzas's claim for the significance of class contradictions in shaping state policy, Fred L. Block's emphasis on "class struggle" to explain various New Deal policies appears to challenge the instrumentalist view that capitalists directly shape state policy.[15] Block finds a separation between those who are directly involved in the accumulation process and those who are involved with the management of the state. The central constraint on political decision making for state managers is "business confidence." Hence, because the narrow fractional interests of capitalists might cause them to be unaware of the overall political and economic climate, state managers are forced to respond to overall political and economic trends in such a fashion as to preserve the existing order. As such, state managers, especially in times of crisis in regard to business confidence, will make concessions to the working class in an effort to stimulate social peace and harmony. State managers, because of their position within the state, are capable of transcending the narrow economic interests of various fractions of the capitalist class, incorporating working-class pressures into state policy, and still preserving the basic political and economic order that assures their own particular position of power. In contrast to Poulantzas's view of the relative autonomy of the state, Block posits the *total* autonomy of state managers. Block's analysis might very well seem plausible in explaining why concessions were made to industrial labor both within the NIRA and through the NLRA. Labor policy can be explained as the result of both working-class pressures for such reforms and the willingness of state managers to grant such concessions at a time when capitalists' veto power was particularly weak. Although Block's analysis might seem quite plausible and although his attention to the immediate political actors of the day is quite instructive, he nevertheless fails to analyze the complexities of the political constraints on the state managers themselves. In essence, Block views state managers as members of a distinct and separate social class who gain their power within the hierarchical organization of the state. This view now assumes that state managers are superrational, and are able to juggle and mediate conflicts of the day into a rational program that will guarantee the strengthening of existing political and economic relations. In this fashion, Block has not moved decisively from an instrumentalist perspective. Moreover, Block seems to suggest that state managers have the foresight to direct overall economic and political development because of their particular position within the state and that they therefore engage in voluntary activity that will preserve capitalism. However, just as capitalists at the point of production cannot impose their class program on the working class with impunity, state managers cannot impose their policies independently from ongoing processes of social reproduction and transformation. As such, Block's analysis of state managers cannot adequately explain why the NIRA was so short-lived or why efforts at executive reorganization that originated among some state managers were blocked by others.

Whereas Block expands on Poulantzas's notion of the significance of class contradictions, Theda Skocpol and her associates draw on the significance of state structures in explaining New Deal policies. However, unlike Poulantzas, whose focus is on state structures as embedded with class contradictions, Skocpol centers her analysis on the administrative and bureaucratic capacities of the organization of the state. For Skocpol, it is not class conflict or struggles that condition state activity; rather, the structure and activities of the state profoundly condition the ability of classes to achieve certain levels of struggle, organization, and representation.[16] By arguing that all existing conceptualizations of the state fail to consider the specificity of party and state structures, Skocpol conceptualizes the state as being independent from the social relations of capitalism and proceeds to analyze the specificity of the structure of the state.

Claiming that her "state-centered" approach best explains the formulation and implementation of various New Deal policies, Skocpol focuses on the fragmentary character of the United States state, the weak national administrative structure, and the nonprogrammatic structure of political parties as the root for explaining the limits to New Deal policies.[17] While there is no denying these aspects of the state in the United States, there is little explanation of the forces that shaped the structures to begin with. By arguing that the determinants of state response to the economic crisis of the 1930s is traceable to the United States national administrative arrangements, governmental institutions, and political parties, Skocpol and her associates obscure the impact of inter- and intraclass conflict on the very structure of these arrangements.

By arguing that state policies are shaped primarily by the development of state and party structures, "organizations that have their own historical trajectories and cannot be taken for granted or reduced to manifestations of the current array of social forces," Skocpol and Kenneth Finegold proceed to analyze the fate of the NIRA in terms of the administrative weaknesses of the agency that was designed to implement the act.[18] While correctly pointing out these administrative weaknesses, Skocpol and Finegold, in their haste to dismiss competing explanations, ignore the importance of the underlying economic processes that shaped the structures of the state in the first place.

In order to unwind Skocpol's (and her associates') argument, it is necessary to evaluate how she defines the terrain of analysis and how she understands existing frames of reference.[19] For Skocpol, the Great Depression of the 1930s signaled an economic crisis in the United States. The two striking indices of this economic crisis for Skocpol were high and persistent levels of unemployment and stalled business activity, measured by underutilized productive capacity. To be sure, Skocpol's crisis was a capitalist crisis in that it entailed reduced profits, laid-off workers, and declining demand. The "solution" to the economic crisis was centered in the expanded demand for war materials that occurred during the late 1930s.

Skocpol's argument conforms more or less to the standard historiographical interpretations. The problem, however, is not so much what she says but what she omits. The economic crisis of the 1930s was a worldwide depression. It signified an "organic crisis" in that it entailed structural contradictions in the overall mode of capital accumulation and in that it required a restructuring of the mainstays of the entire productive/reproductive edifice.

The specific difference that distinguished this economic crisis was the specific relationship between three overlapping structural barriers to expanded accumulation: (1) an exceedingly high rate of labor exploitation, which was manifested in low levels of consumption on the part of the working class and resulted in problems of profit realization; (2) unregulated competition, which led to problems of investment; and (3) an antiquated matrix of state apparatus, which did not reflect the changing balance of class forces. In short, the dominance of large-scale corporate capital on the economic terrain was not matched by the political practices of a centralized dominant apparatus of the state.

Skocpol does not acknowledge that the "organic crisis" of the 1930s was a crisis of accumulation that both destroyed capital, by eliminating high-cost and extraneous producers, and restored capital on a new footing, by rewarding low-cost producers and by accelerating the growth of large-scale corporate capital. This process of structural selectivity occurred "behind the backs" of the social actors who were enmeshed in the immediate reality of day-to-day politics. Skocpol's narrow and incomplete conceptualization of the economic crisis permits her and her associates to pose the problem of New Deal recovery measures in terms of the conscious intervention by state bureaucrats and of the administrative means by which to carry them out. In general, Skocpol argues that various New Deal policies, such as the NIRA, "failed" to bring about the intended economic recovery because of the administrative weaknesses or the lack of state capacity to bring them about. This "success/failure" autonomy merely assumes what must be proven. Capital accumulation is a contradictory process. Capitalist growth and recovery certainly meant enormous profits for some, yet it also entailed financial ruin for others. No single New Deal policy could have satisfied all capitalist interests.

In their "state-centered" approach to explain New Deal policies, Skocpol and associates ignore the process of capital accumulation and the internal barriers and contradictions that it engenders. Thus, the structural limits to state policies are glossed over. In her attempt to prove that the state has an organizational and bureaucratic autonomy of its own, Skocpol operates under a set of undeclared and unsubstantiated assumptions. Thus, she is able to "prove" what has already been assumed: (1) the state has a true essence, an undifferentiated homogeneity; (2) the state enjoys the capacity to act; and (3) state managers are vehicles for the formation of the state's policy and are the personification of the state's capacities and powers.

Skocpol's task is made easier because she conflates two levels of analysis that should be kept distinct and of concepts that actually have different social meaning. Specifically, Skocpol collapses the analysis of the institutional ensemble that constitutes the capitalist state's apparatus with the evaluation of the historically specific political regime under Roosevelt. Equally important, she treats the Roosevelt administration, the state, the government, and even Roosevelt's advisors more or less without differentiation. This means that she oscillates between levels of analysis; she analyzes deep structures, which have their own distinctive rhythms, and reform proposals, which have their own biographical origins within the internal frame of reference. The result is a confusing set of critical commentaries that do not go to the heart of how a capitalist state actually works.

The methodological and analytical problems of Skocpol's "state-centered" approach are made even more pronounced if one looks carefully at the manner in which she eliminates existing frames of reference.[20] By categorizing all Marxist and neo-Marxist theories of the state as similar, Skocpol overlooks the fact that these various arguments, under the rubric of "instrumentalism" and "structuralism," employ very different languages, different structures of presentation and exposition, and distinctive objects that place them on very separate terrains. In addition, Skocpol and associates at times selectively and even unfairly reconstruct their arguments. One illustration of this "reconstruction" is the unexplained omission of Poulantzas's later works from Skocpol's treatment of what she labels "political functionalism." A composite picture of Poulantzas's work does not lend itself, as Skocpol would lead one to believe, to the specific characterization as the type of "born-again" Parsonian structural functionalism in Marxist garb.[21]

In particular, Skocpol fails to appreciate Poulantzas's distinction between the general characteristics of the capitalist state and the specific characteristics of political regimes. This distinction enables one to argue that the structural relationship between the capitalist state and the process of capital accumulation is carried forward, distorted, and blocked by the actual relations of class forces. The relations of class forces, in turn, are reflected in political parties, state administrations, and state structures. Moreover, Poulantzas specifically argues that the state is *not* a functionally integrated monolithic whole but, rather, that it is constituted by class contradictions.

An Alternative Class-Centered Approach

Because mainstream New Deal historiography has operated within the theoretical framework of pluralist or instrumentalist approaches, these conventional studies have been hampered by a frame of reference that tends to oversimplify the complex relations between social classes and the capitalist state. Yet what about the alternative formulations? In his critique of instrumentalist accounts, Block theorizes the autonomy of state managers. By proposing that state managers ought to be conceived as historical subjects, he simply reverses the instrumentalists' problem. For instrumentalists, the principal object of inquiry centers on the discovery of historical evidence that points to the interpretation that the ruling class—as historical subject—is able to wrest control over the state apparatus and to wield it as a weapon against their opponents in order to impose their class will by fiat. Despite provisions about business confidence, Block merely reverses the position of the instrumentalists: state managers become historical subjects rather than the ruling class, without altering the basic frame of reference. Skocpol et al. simply carry Block's line of reasoning to its logical conclusion. According to this formulation, state managers are not only conceived of as historical subjects; they also appear to be almost unimpeded in their deliberations except by existing bureaucratic structures. In essence, the bureaucratic structures and administrative arrangements have been relieved of any class content, class controversies, or conflicts. Bureaucratic structures appear as *sui generis* sets of rules and procedures governing the process of decision making and policy implementation. "One cannot take the state as an unproblematic given or reduce it to one of its multiple determinations," Bob Jessop has warned.[22] Skocpol et al. have ignored this admonition. Consequently, their analysis of the New Deal has been largely confined to a narrow scope of interpretation of political decision making.

The work of Poulantzas serves as a starting point for a comprehensive theory of the capitalist state that decisively breaks with mainstream pluralist conceptions and oversimplified instrumentalist positions. Nevertheless, critics of Poulantzas, such as Block and Skocpol, have argued that concepts advanced by Poulantzas suffer from "structural abstractionism," making it difficult to generate hypotheses for historical research. Despite the harsh tone contained in these assaults on Poulantzas, they are generally based on a caricatured reading of Poulantzian texts and not on an evaluation of Poulantzian theory as applied to specific historical conjunctures.[23] By theorizing general characteristics of the capitalist state, as Poulantzas does at the outset, the particular aspects of the state in historically specific conjunctures can indeed be analyzed. Although all states share certain common characteristics, every state and every political regime is historically unique. This implies that an analysis of state activity means much more than merely examining administrative and bureaucratic arrangements. Operating within a Poulantzian frame of reference, Jessop suggests that an adequate analysis of state activity can be founded on the specific qualities of the capitalist mode of production, can attribute a central role to the limits imposed by the accumulation process on class forces, can establish the relationship between the economic and political without reducing one to the other or treating them as autonomous from one another, and can allow for historical differences in forms of representation, intervention, and internal structures.[24] Because state responses to economic crisis are based on the political repercussions of the crisis, it follows that an analysis of the specificity of New Deal policies must take into account the balance of class forces and the dynamic of class struggles.

In an effort to adopt the Poulantzian frame of reference to an analysis of a particular historical conjuncture, Jill S. Quadagno has focused attention upon the Social Security Act of 1935—an important part of the New Deal social-welfare program—through the prism of a class-centered theory of the capitalist state.[25] By operating at the level of the specific historical conjuncture, Quadagno is able to translate somewhat weighty abstractions, adopted from the major contributions of Poulantzas's work, into manageable propositions that provide an alternative framework for evaluating New Deal policy debates. Through the judicious use of concepts such as monopoly and nonmonopoly capital and class fractions, Quadagno concludes that "the state mediates between various interest groups who have unequal access to power, negotiating compromises between class fractions and incorporating working class demands into legislation on capitalist terms."[26] More importantly, Quadagno has stressed that the historical investigation of New Deal policies—and by implication, state decision making in general—must operate at a number of levels of abstraction simultaneously in order to appreciate the complexity of the translation of political power into economic power. In her words, "political structures simply cannot be analyzed as autonomous entities but must be considered in terms of their underlying economic dimensions."[27]

Accepting the Marxist premise that capitalism is a contradictory system and that the primary social classes of labor and capital are in an antagonistic relationship to each other, the class-centered approach presented here takes as its starting point a set of propositions:

1. The capitalist state is internally divided by its location within the social relations of production. Because the state is located within the contradictions of capitalism, the state itself is a product of class contradictions. According to Poulantzas: " . . . the State is through and through constituted-divided by class contradictions. . . . Contrary to conceptions that treat it as a Thing or a Subject, the State is itself divided. It is not enough simply to say that contradictions and struggles traverse the State—as if it were a matter of penetrating an already constituted substance or of passing through an empty site that is already there."[28]
2. As a consequence of the forces that continuously separate capital into distinctive competitive and antagonistic units, the capitalist state is the political terrain for the adjudication of fractions of capital. By being relatively autonomous from various class fractions, state policy serves to mediate between units of capital by attempting to politically unify an otherwise disorganized capitalist class. Moreover, as a consequence of the antagonistic relationship between labor and capital, the capitalist state becomes the arena for assuring a consensus for capitalist rule. State policy simultaneously attempts to unify an otherwise disorganized capitalist class and to channel working-class struggles within elements compatible with capitalist social relations of production, thereby short-circuiting independent working-class political organization;
3. State policies always reflect, in Poulantzas's words, "strategic compromises."[29] Although state policies attempt to maintain class rule by providing the conditions for profitable accumulation, state policies are formulated or implemented, not according to a preestablished functional harmony, but in and through the struggle of antagonistic classes. The particular formulation and implementation of a specific policy are shaped by the nature and the dynamic of the class struggle in the particular historical time and setting.

Categories such as monopoly capital and nonmonopoly capital, fractions of capital, and relative autonomy form the conceptual apparatus through which to initiate an analysis of specific historical conjunctures. By "bringing classes back in," the class-centered approach side-steps one-sided analyses that reduce a complex process of variable determinations into a unilinear explanation for the formation and implementation of policy.

The Argument in Brief

The major thesis of this study is that the exigencies of the balance of class forces and uninterrupted accumulation of capital limited political decision making and the formulation and implementation of New Deal policies. The manner in which the New Deal industrial-recovery program attempted to maintain and further conditions for profitable accumulation was shaped by the dynamic of the class struggle in the United States during the 1930s. Based on the careful examination of the manuscript collections of Franklin D. Roosevelt and his advisors and of other pertinent governmental documents, I argue in this study that class forces shaped both policy formulation and outcomes. The state is not a rational organization of political power with its own historical trajectory; rather, it is constituted by the contradictions of class society. The seemingly ad hoc fashion in which various New Deal policies were formulated had less to do with existing administrative and bureaucratic arrangements, or the fragmented character of the United States state apparatus, than it did with the nature of class relations in the United States.

A reassessment of the New Deal industrial-recovery program from a class-centered approach sheds light not only on the manner in which New Deal policies were formulated and implemented but also, and perhaps more importantly, on the extent to which New Deal policies provided conditions for a new phase of capital accumulation. The origins and implementation of New Deal policies under the Roosevelt administration represented a bold program of national economic recovery during a period of significant economic collapse, political turmoil, and ideological dissensus. Seen retrospectively, New Deal policies appear to exhibit a certain coherent logic. Yet from the perspective of those policy makers who designed and implemented them, the various policies and programs appeared as a series of ad hoc, almost desperate measures that were designed to defend temporarily against further economic decline and political rebelliousness.

Put broadly, various New Deal policies, designed to restructure the political and economic order, existed in abstraction. Yet the practical possibilities of implementing a particular policy are limited not only by the specific balance of class forces but also by a more complex set of circumstances inherited from the past. The Roosevelt administration inherited a complex set of circumstances that circumscribed its historical possibilities. The world depression that had ravaged business operations for more than three years had exposed deep structural contradictions in the accumulation process. These obstacles to the accumulation process included: (1) too high a rate of labor exploitation, which resulted in problems of profit realization; (2) unregulated competition, which led to problems of investment; and (3) a political structure that was not responsive to the imperatives of the accumulation process.

When Roosevelt took office, the industrial working class was becoming increasingly restive. Unemployed workers engaged in street demonstrations and marches to demand federal relief and some form of unemployment insurance, while employed workers resisted decreases in wages and increases in the hours they were expected to work. Industrial capitalists themselves were hopelessly divided over the causes of the Great Depression and possible ways to solve it.

The shift in the balance of class forces engendered a chaotic situation in which capitalists—who themselves were increasingly being fragmented both economically and politically—were gradually losing the iron grip that during the 1920s boom period they had enjoyed over the working class in general and the increasingly restive industrial working class in particular. The various mechanisms through which capitalists had subjected labor to their discipline during the previous decade gradually became unraveled as the depression wore on. The resulting class tensions threatened to add even further to the economic chaos during Roosevelt's first term in office. By the middle of the 1930s, the growing round of strikes was the most visible sign that the industrial working class had actively intervened to determine the future course of industrial production. This intervention of the working class meant that whatever policy was pursued for economic recovery was hindered not only by the structural reality of the accumulation process but also by the activities of the industrial working class that interrupted the capital-accumulation process.

Rather than representing a coherent blueprint that by conscious design established an overall plan for economic recovery, the Roosevelt administration muddled along, tinkering with various programs—making every effort to force compromises between antagonistic interests wherever possible and simply imposing a solution when adjudication seemed impossible. The NIRA was formulated not only to overcome obstacles to accumulation but also to politically organize a fractionated industrial capitalist class. The inclusion of section 7a was an afterthought; it was only included as an effort to sidetrack the Black Thirty Hour bill and to make concessions to industrial labor simultaneously. The Black Thirty Hour bill called for the prohibition of interstate shipments of goods produced by labor that was working more than six hours a day and five days a week. Roosevelt believed that the Black bill was too rigid, that it was perhaps unconstitutional, and that it would lead to an actual drop in purchasing power because of the lack of minimum-wage provisions. The best strategy for administrating opposition to the Black bill was seen to consist of presenting a better proposal for stimulating both recovery and employment. Contrary to its design, the implementation of the NIRA only stimulated disunity among industrial capitalists and militancy among industrial labor.

Rising labor militancy combined with a significant realignment of the Democratic party, which had a strong working-class base, to stimulate the implementation of state policies that made crucial concessions to industrial labor, such as the NLRA. The class recomposition of the Democratic party, in addition to labor legislation that was favorable to segments of the industrial working class, served to diffuse labor militancy, directing the leaders of the newly emergent industrial-union movement to accept, by the end of the decade, a general consensus in support of the existing political and economic order.

The disunity among industrial capitalists persisted throughout the 1930s, as many industrial capitalists criticized a variety of New Deal programs. Yet the Roosevelt administration—because it represented the balance of class forces—attempted to put into motion plans for economic recovery that reflected compromises not only between capital and labor but also within capital itself. As a result of criticisms of nonmonopoly capital concerning the performance of the NIRA, the Temporary National Economic Committee (TNEC) was established to investigate the growth and repercussions of monopoly growth in the industrial economy. Although TNEC documented the prevalence of monopoly growth, nonmonopoly capital was not able to alter the process of the concentration and centralization of capital. However, the conflicts within the industrial capitalist class over the best strategy for economic recovery did reveal to the Roosevelt administration that the bureaucratic structures inherited from previous administrations were inadequate to accomplish the tasks necessary to implement New Deal policies. These organizational forms constituted a structural impediment that hindered the nature and the type of recovery strategy that was historically possible. As a consequence, the Roosevelt administration was compelled to adjust, improvise, and tinker with the existing framework while it simultaneously attempted to create new structures. This process was not formalized until the administrative reorganization proposals of 1938/39.

Whereas nonmonopoly capital was not able to stimulate changes in the accumulation process, the industrial-workers' movement was able to do so. The trajectory of capitalist development took a different course as a result of the upsurge of workers' militant activities during the 1930s. Labor militancy in demanding and using collective bargaining made it possible to overcome large-scale capital's resistance to a fundamental reorganization of wages and consumption. Nevertheless, it was monopoly capital that was able to adjust to these working-class gains. Monopoly capital not only passed on to consumers the wage gains and benefits acquired by workers (both nationally and internationally); it also used collective bargaining as a way to ensure labor peace. In the process, monopoly capital was able to dominate crucial state agencies. Increased state economic intervention aided not only in the regulation of competition but also in further investment outlets. The obstacle to capital accumulation posed by too high a rate of exploitation was temporarily resolved through the institutionalization of collective bargaining and the incorporation of significant industrial unions into the national process of political bargaining. Problems of unregulated competition were temporarily resolved through state policies. The political structure was altered to correspond more closely with the imperatives of the accumulation process by having monopoly capital dominate key agencies and by having the industrial-union movement incorporated into a clearly subordinate position vis-à-vis monopoly capital on the political terrain. The incorporation of the industrial-union movement into the national process of political bargaining and into a more cooperative relationship via collective bargaining with monopoly capital, the resulting ideological consensus for capitalist rule, and the unchallenged political hegemony of monopoly capital—all combined to produce the conditions for a new phase of capitalist development. By attempting to resolve class conflicts and antagonisms, New Deal industrial policies simultaneously created new structural conditions that regulated the objective conditions for capital accumulation and the conditions under which future struggles would be waged.

The class-centered approach that I take here is premised upon the recognition of the multilayered determination of New Deal policies. At the specific historical conjuncture (1933–39), the combination of uninterrupted capital accumulation on a world scale, symbolized by the Great Depression, the growing rift between capital and labor on the shop floor, and conflicts within the industrial capitalist class limited the available political options and circumscribed the choice of recovery policies and their implementation. Seen in this light, pluralist approaches are far too simplistic because they assume the "neutrality" of the state administration. Instrumentalist approaches are seriously misleading because it is difficult to conclude, on the basis of the historical evidence, that the Roosevelt administration set out to preserve capitalism through a conscious plan. Moreover, Block's approach is inadequate, because it not only assumes a basic homogeneity of capitalist interests but also ignores how the intervention of the working class—not of a conscious political sort—actually hampered economic recovery by interrupting production in the mid 1930s. Finally, the state-centered argument of Skocpol et al. offers a one-sided approach to the investigation of the New Deal. The implementation of New Deal programs was certainly impeded by the existing bureaucratic and administrative arrangements, but these arrangements themselves should be understood in terms of their underlying class content.

In explaining the New Deal industrial-recovery program from a class-centered approach, this book is organized upon three separate levels of analysis: (1) an analysis of the tendencies within the process of capital accumulation and their manifestations; (2) a concrete analysis of class forces and class struggle; and (3) an analysis of state policies as a reflection of and a response to class forces and class struggle, and the process of uninterrupted capital accumulation. Chapter 2 outlines the structural tendencies of the process of capitalist development in the United States prior to the 1930s; it highlights the general and specific characteristics of both the accumulation process and class forces that led to the particular nature of the crisis in the United States. Chapter 3 examines the specificity of the crisis and the impact that it had on industrial labor and industrial capital. In particular, this chapter traces the manner in which the structural barriers to capital accumulation that surfaced during the 1930s served to heighten the contradictions of United States capitalist development, to crystallize the contradictions between industrial labor and industrial capital, and to exacerbate conflicts within the industrial capitalist class. Chapter 4 analyzes in detail the formulation and implementation of the NIRA. The central concern of this chapter is to illustrate the manner in which the state administration attempted to offset economic decline, to overcome obstacles to capital accumulation, and simultaneously to unify the capitalist class and make concessions to organized labor leaders to offset the potential of independent political practices of the working class. This chapter is intended to further illustrate that the policy-making process is one of contradictions and that the state is not a rational organization of political power or a political organization that merely reflects economic class relations. Chapter 5 examines the process of intracapitalist conflict and how the state administration attempted to make concessions to nonmonopoly capital while monopoly capital was gaining political dominance. Chapter 6 provides an analysis of the struggle for industrial unionization and the consequent changes in the state's labor policy. Chapter 7 traces the development of cleavages within the labor movement and the development of the Congress of Industrial Organizations (CIO) and its relationship with the Democratic party. Moreover, this chapter also examines the process whereby organized industrial labor was incorporated into the national process of political bargaining. Chapter 8 focuses on attempts at reorganization of the state apparatus and the marginalization of militant workers vis-à-vis the dominant political parties. This chapter illustrates that these two developments, which themselves arose from the dynamic of the class struggle and were not predetermined in a functionalist or rational fashion, helped to lay the foundations for the postwar economic and political order.

CHAPTER TWO

The Process of Capitalist Development: Capital, Labor, and the State, 1890–1929

> It is inevitable that the business of the country shall be done by very large companies which reach back to the source, and, taking the raw material, carry it through the necessary processes to the finished state.
>
> —*Henry Ford and Samual Crowther*

> Developments in the status of labor are not a function of economic change alone. The history of the position of labor in modern industry had been a record of interaction among social, economic and political forces. . . . Changes in the position of labor thus reflect, in addition to economic conditions, developments in the technique and management of industry; in established social, economic, and political institutions; and in influential currents of opinion.
>
> —*Leo Wolman and Gustav Peck*

The tremendous expansion of industrial production in the United States between the 1890s and 1929 had embedded within it contradictions that were specific to the process of capitalist development in the United States.[1] This historical process of the unfolding of the ensemble of social relations that constituted the conditions for continual and uninterrupted capital accumulation necessitated what David M. Gordon, Richard Edwards, and Michael Reich refer to as a new "social structure of accumulation."[2] The rapid industrial accumulation from the 1890s to 1928/29 entailed changes in the structure of the class struggle between labor and capital. The growth of large-scale industrial enterprises required the introduction of massive labor-saving machinery and gave rise to mass-production industry. These two factors had a fundamental impact not only on the labor process and the organization of production but also on the position of workers vis-à-vis capitalists within the capitalist production process. Moreover, the changes in the logic of accumulation made essential a new pattern of state involvement in the national economy. An examination of these particular tendencies of the process of capitalist development will highlight the general and specific characteristics of both the accumulation process and class forces that help explain the particular nature of the 1930s economic crisis in the United States and the specificity of the state response to that crisis.

The concrete historical development of capitalism on a world scale involved accelerated accumulation following the 1870–90 depression and lasted until World War I. The general phase of accelerated accumulation from approximately 1890 until 1913 was followed by a long period of decelerated accumulation and relative stagnation from the end of World War I until the beginning of World War II. The upswing phase was characterized by the generalization of monopoly competition, accompanied by a rise in the productivity of labor, which resulted in a rise in the rate of surplus value. The downswing phase was characterized by declining profits, gradually decelerating accumulation, decelerating economic growth, and increasing difficulties with the realization of surplus value. This downswing provoked the disruption of world trade, the increase in workers' class struggles in Europe, the reinforcement of the victory of the Russian Revolution, and the narrowing of the capitalist world market.[3]

By the end of the nineteenth century, the tendency toward large-scale industrial production, with fewer firms dominating a larger share of the industrial market, was evident in the United States. This process of concentration and centralization of capital was occurring in basic industry—especially the so-called newer industries of steel and mass-produced consumer goods such as the automobile. The United States deviated from the general world pattern of decelerated capital accumulation in the period following World War I, and large-scale corporate capital experienced a profit boom.[4] This was partially because of the absence of a working-class movement able to counter the organization, mobilization, and collective action of the capitalist class. Unlike their counterparts in Europe, American capitalists were able to isolate and crush any militancy on the part of the workers' movement that potentially challenged capitalist control.[5] Moreover, the expansion of industrial production in the United States during the 1920s was aided by the rapid introduction of labor-saving devices and a steady increase in the rate of exploitation. A rough indicator of the rising rate of exploitation is that in the manufacturing industries, real value added per worker rose 75 percent between 1919 and 1929, whereas real wage rates increased by approximately 47 percent for the same period.[6] The introduction of labor-saving machinery altered the labor process and the organization of production in a way that facilitated the intensive exploitation of labor.[7] These changes provided the preconditions for the rising rate of exploitation that is required for the expanded reproduction of capital under conditions of a declining world market.

The growth and expansion of large-scale industrial production altered the organization of industry, the forms of competition between firms, and the social relationships at the point of production. Monopoly capital accumulated rapidly after World War I as a result both of the greater rate of exploitation of the industrial labor force and of the merger of firms within various branches of industry.[8] Monopoly capital was able to concentrate on long-range profit plans as their survival was no longer threatened in the short term. By the end of the 1920s the capitalist class was increasingly becoming differentiated between fractions of monopoly and nonmonopoly capital. Although monopoly capital had become increasingly dominant within the industrial accumulation process, it had not permeated critical decision-making centers within the state apparatus.

Even though the state apparatus had been altered in such a fashion as to expand its administrative capacities to correspond with the changing nature of economic activity on the national level by the 1920s, the new social structure of accumulation that was required by the changing nature of economic activity waited until later.[9]

The Tendency toward Concentration and Centralization of Capital

The process of capitalist production and accumulation in the United States had produced a greater tendency toward the growth of monopoly capital as early as 1860. The Civil War stimulated the accelerated growth of large-scale industry through demand for war materials. This required more efficient and larger factories, the investment of more capital, and the consolidation of firms. In the period following the Civil War, declining prices and intensified competition encouraged the growth of large-scale industry. In 1847 there were 82 industrial conglomerates with a capitalization of $1 billion; in the three years 1898, 1899, and 1900, eleven conglomerates were formed with a capitalization of $1.14 billion; and the largest conglomerate of all, the United States Steel Corporation, was formed in 1901 with a capitalization of $1.4 billion.[10]

By the 1880s American manufacturing firms were beginning to grow by way of mergers. Mergers essentially involved having a number of individually owned firms join together to form one national enterprise. By the 1890s the number of mergers was increasingly rapidly—the main motive being the control of price and production schedules for a particular branch of industry. In addition to mergers, many industrial firms grew by building national and global markets and extensive purchasing organizations and by obtaining their own sources of raw materials and transportation facilities.[11] In both cases, growth in the size of firms coincided with the massive introduction of machinery, attempts to keep down the cost of production, and a greater rate of labor productivity.

Between 1860 and 1870 the total value of manufactured products increased more than 100 percent, from $1.9 billion to $4.2 billion; in the following decade the increase was less, a mere 25 percent, from $4.2 to $5.4 billion; ten years later the value of manufactured goods had increased again, this time by 75 percent; and by 1900 the total value of manufactured products amounted to $13.0 billion, almost 40 percent more than in 1890 and about seven times as much as in 1860.[12] Between 1860 and 1894, U.S.-based firms greatly increased the output of manufactured goods. The increase in the amount of capital invested in manufactured goods was even more rapid than the increase in the value of manufactured goods. Jurgen Kuczynski argues that the "means of production—machinery, buildings, etc.—became relatively more and more expensive as compared with labour power, and played an increasingly greater role."[13] Between

1860 and 1900 the rate of growth in the value of manufactured goods was outstripped by the amount of capital invested in manufacturing industries.

In general, by the end of the nineteenth century, the development of industry and the increase in manufactured output had helped make the United States an "industrialized power" within the world arena. The opening up of a vast United States domestic market, along with forces of competition, helped to produce large-scale industrial enterprises in the United States. Between 1860 and 1900 the industrial sector of the labor force grew much more rapidly than other sectors, particularly agriculture.

Between 1867 and 1900 there was the growth and expansion not only of older industries but also of what have frequently been called newer industries. In manufacturing, steel played an important role. In 1867, 1,643 tons of steel ingots were produced, and thirty years later, 7,156,957 tons were produced.[14] Basic industry developed rapidly, especially in the period 1897 to 1919. Between 1899 and 1919 the number of wage earners in manufacturing almost doubled, and the value of products increased almost sixfold.[15] The growth in manufacturing output coincided with the growth of manufacturing establishments. Between 1899 and 1919 the value of the product of each manufacturing firm increased fourfold, and the number of workers increased 53 percent. Table 1 illustrates the long-term trend from 1859 to 1919 in the growth of manufacturing establishments.

Not only did manufacturing firms tend to grow in size, but smaller firms also tended to decrease in importance with respect to their output. Firms with an annual output of less than $20,000 each declined in their percentage of the total with respect to the number of firms and wage earners and the value of the product. Those with an annual output of $20,000 to $100,000 declined in their percentage of the total with respect to wage earners and the value of the product. Contrary to this tendency, firms with products of $1 million or more increased notably in their percentage of the total with respect to the number of firms and wage earners and the value of the product. The 10,414 such establishments in 1919 amounted to only 3.6 percent of the total number but employed 56.9 percent of the wage earners and manufactured 67.8 percent of the products according to value.[16]

The process of concentration and centralization of capital within the industrial sector of the United States met with few obstacles in the post–World War I period. Between 1919 and 1928 more than 1,200 mergers were recorded in manufacturing, involving a net decrease of more than 6,000 independent firms by the end of 1928 and some 2,000 more by the end of 1930. Furthermore, more than 4,000 public-utilities firms were absorbed in the same period before 1929, and nearly 1,800 bank mergers caused the disappearance of an unrecorded but probably larger number of banks.[17] In addition, by 1919, chain stores were selling 27 percent of the food in the United States, 19 percent of the drugs, 30 percent of tobacco, 27 percent of clothing, and 26 percent of the general mer-

Table 1. Growth in Manufacturing Establishments, 1859–1919

	1859	1899	1904	1909	1914	1919
Average value of product	$13,429	$54,969	$68,433	$76,993	$87,916	$125,157
Average number of wage earners	9.34	20.49	25.30	24.64	25.51	31.36

Source: Harold U. Faulkner, *The Decline of Laissez-Faire, 1897–1917* (New York: Holt, Rinehart & Winston, 1951), p. 155.

chandise. By the end of 1929 the 200 largest business corporations possessed nearly half the corporate wealth of the United States, 38 percent of the business wealth, and 20 percent of the total national wealth.[18]

The Rise of Mass Production and Changes in the Organization of Production

The growth of large-scale industrial enterprises coincided with the massive introduction of machinery and the rise of mass-production industries. Between 1919 and 1929, capital per worker jumped by 36 percent.[19] Although mass production had been implemented in some industries as early as 1870, it did not become widespread until after World War I. In general, mass production was based on the standardization of parts and interchangeable mechanisms, and it required technological and organizational innovations, the availability of adequate capital, and a home market large enough to absorb the product.[20] Hence, the introduction of mass-production industries required certain changes in the organization of production itself, with corresponding changes in the labor process and the conditions of labor for the working class.

Mass-production techniques first appeared in industries that processed liquids or semiliquids, such as crude oil. These techniques came later in a number of mechanical industries but appeared more slowly in the metal-making and metal-working industries. Mass production meant that an increase in output for a given unit of labor, capital, and materials was accomplished through the development of more efficient machinery and the development of a more organizationally suitable design of manufacturing procedures that were required to synchronize flows and supervise the work force. Mass-production techniques led to an increase in the ratio of capital to labor, materials to labor, energy to labor, and managers to workers for each unit of output. These techniques made possible a much-greater output at each stage in the overall process of production. Machinery was placed and operated so that several stages of production were integrated and synchronized technologically and organizationally within a single industrial establishment. As a result, the speed of production was faster at each stage than if each stage of production had been carried on in separate establishments.[21] By 1900, inventions and technology had reached a point at which standardization and rapid production could come together. This situation was based on the development of the machine-tool industry and the improvement of such machine tools as lathes, grinders, boring mills, drill presses, planers, and milling machines. Although hundreds of new machines were developed and thousands of improvements were made, the great advance was based on the development of a new high-speed carbon steel.[22] By 1900 the industries making machinery employed 414,000, or 8.8 percent of all workers in the United States. By 1919, workers employed in machine-making industries increased to 11 percent of the total labor force. The production of machinery had increased more rapidly than the total manufacturing output. By 1919 the machine-tool industry was producing new and complex machinery of automatic and multiple design. In addition to increased productivity, capitalists introduced the electric motor to machine tools, giving them greater power, speed, and flexibility and at the same time providing portable, power-driven hand tools. Electricity also made important contributions in the assembly of metal parts after electric welding was invented in the 1880s.[23]

Once the machine-tool industry had reached a stage where interchangeability of parts had become practical for even the most complicated machinery, large-scale industrial capitalists concentrated on the assembly aspect of production. The rapidly growing automobile industry and the Ford Motor Company, in particular, were preeminently suited for experimentation in assembly techniques. During its early years the industry was largely involved in assembling parts that had been made in various machine shops and collected at an assembly point. Ford had implemented the moving assembly line by 1913. By the 1920s, when the automobile industry was the leading industry in the United States with respect to the value of its products, Ford introduced improved methods in order to deliver work at a predetermined speed that would accomplish a small and specialized task. With assembly lines and subassembly lines and specialization by individuals and crews, mass-production techniques reached their peak.[24] The net effect of the assembly line for capitalists was a reduction in labor time and labor costs.

Large-scale capital focused its attention upon the advantages of mass production during World War I and the corresponding push for wartime production. In the preparation of war materials, many capitalists narrowly specialized their factories and organized them for single purposes.[25] Massive innovations in mass-production techniques were introduced in the years following World War I. Not only were models standardized but also sizes, lengths, and thicknesses: the varieties of paving brick were reduced from 66 to 4; of sheet metal, from 1,891 to 261; of range boilers, from 130 to 13; of invoice, inquiry, and purchase-order forms, from 4,500 to 3. During a period of ten years, the Department of Commerce could report that under its guidance, more than one hundred plans for standardization had been adopted in as many industries and that the estimated annual saving to the manufacturers involved was $250 million. Standardization made possible further mechanization, made it easier to replace parts, and permitted the integration of allied industries.[26]

Standardization was accompanied by a new capitalist interest in industrial research. In the words of Louis Hacker: "The entrepreneurs of the twentieth century were less willing to depend upon chance and the work of individual erratic genius to blaze new trails for them and furnish outlets for their great accumulations of capital."[27] Industrial research, carried on within corporations such as General Electric and American Telegraph and Telephone Company, enabled large-scale corporate capitalists to develop new materials and new industrial processes.[28]

The rise of mass-production industries and the corresponding changes in the organization of production had a profound effect on the productivity of labor. The introduction of machinery on an ever-increasing scale meant that more goods were being produced with less labor time. Labor productivity rapidly increased between 1914 and 1927, especially in basic industry: 55 percent in iron and steel, 178 percent in automobiles, and 292 percent in rubber tires. As Louis M. Hacker and Benjamin B. Kendrick put it:

> In other words, the same number of men working in the plants of United Steel Company, Bethlehem Steel, and Youngstown Sheet and Tube, were turning out half as much steel again, working the same hours a day in 1927 as they had been in 1914; the same number of men in the Ford and General Motors plant were turning out almost three times as many automobiles in 1927 as they had been in 1914; the same number of men working in the Akron and Toledo factories were turning out four times as much rubber tires in 1927 as in 1914.[29]

In terms of the interest of capitalists, the benefits of mass production required both a home market that was large enough to absorb the products produced and a labor force that cooperated with the capitalist drive for profit. As I shall illustrate, the "cooperation" of labor came as a result of changes in the labor process and the ability of industrial capital to thwart the unionization of industrial workers during the 1920s. These two factors combined to keep the overall wage bill for industrial capital quite low. Ironically, the attempt of capital to increase the rate of exploitation of labor contradicted the requirement that there be a home market capable of consuming products and thereby enabling the realization of profits. This contradiction was to surface by the end of the 1920s, and it created obstacles to the further expansion of industrial production.

Changes in the Labor Process and the Relations of Production

The economic crisis of the late nineteenth century stimulated the larger and more mechanized firms to increase the rate of exploiting labor by speeding up operations. The speed of operations became of prime importance because the higher the productive capacity of a given plant (i.e., the more products that are turned out in a given time), the more quickly can capital be turned over, and the lower is the unit cost of the output, thus increasing the competitiveness of a particular firm.[30] It is no coincidence that in the late 1890s Frederick Winslow Taylor first introduced the concept of "scientific management." Scientific management grew out of the capitalist imperative not only to speed up operations, but also actually to gain greater control over the labor process. This capitalist imperative was a result of increasing competition, the rise of labor-saving machinery, and changes in the organic composition of capital since the end of the nineteenth century.

Scientific management involved a detailed study of the time that a given piece of work should take. These studies then determined the rate at which workers were paid on the basis of how much work they accomplished in a given amount of time.[31] Although scientific management was never fully implemented throughout the industrial sector, it did entail the transfer to management of skill and experience that the workers possessed. Not only were workers separated from the tools and instruments of production, but they also lost control over their own labor and the manner of its performance. This knowledge in the hands of management enabled managers to be active in organizing the labor process according to the direct interests of capital.[32] In the words of Alfred Sohn-Rethel:

> The new division of mental and manual labour must not be confused nor assumed identical with the fundamental one, dating from classical antiquity, now mainly rooted in the intellectual nature of science, although there are of course links and changes in the practice of science which reinforce these links. But the division directly involved in the managerial authority over the monopolistic labour process is one between technical and organisational intelligentsia and the manual work-force. As this division springs from the foundations from which monopoly capitalism itself arises, the stability of monopoly capitalism vitally depends on the relations between these two forces, the mental and the manual, remaining safely divided. Should the division be changed into the alliance, the authority of the management would be in jeopardy. Acting in unison, the direct producers could dispose of the capitalist management and take production into their own control.[33]

Time-management studies and the role of management in ensuring a particular amount of output in a given time meant that the status of foremen and shop superintendents deteriorated and gave way to gang bosses, inspectors, and time-study men. This concentrated all the powers necessary to ensure capitalist control over the labor process and production in general. Scientific-management techniques sought to recompose the organization of work in such a way that each worker's relationship to the production process would be exclusively mediated by individual efficiency norms, rather than by work-group solidarity. In short, labor was not only subsumed economically to capital—by the act of having workers sell their labor power to the capitalist—but also physically and technologically.

Another important effect of these new management techniques was the continual deskilling and fragmentation of labor itself. Although this element became more noticeable with the introduction of mass-production techniques between 1880 and World War I, scientific-management techniques had the consequence of dividing the work process. According to Michel Aglietta, scientific management

> was a capitalist response to the class struggle in production in a phase when the labour process was composed of several segments, each organized on mechanical lines internally, yet whose integration still depended on direct relations between different categories of workers. The insufficient mechanical integration of the different segments meant that constraint had to be exercised by way of rules fixing the output norm for each job as well as the nature and order of the movements to be performed. . . . The aim of this separation and specialization of functions was to combat the control over working conditions that the relative autonomy of jobs in the old system could leave the workers.[34]

Mass production consolidated the mechanical integration of the work process through the electrification of the factory and the introduction of the conveyor system. The new assembly line virtually eliminated the possibility of traditional forms of job control, or "soldiering." Concurrently, the resulting deskilling of large sectors of the industrial work force tended to further unify and homogenize the working class as a mass of machine operators. As early as 1919, with the growth of workers employed in factories and the rise of mass-production industry, capitalists devised new methods not only to control workers' activities, but also, to a lesser degree, to control workers themselves. Capitalists continually faced the necessity of restructuring the production process both to reduce unit costs and, even more compelling, to retain capitalist control over the class struggle. Many capitalists were forced to realize that in order to control the factory and its labor force, more was needed than changes and improvements in the physical setting, better methods of communication, and financial or social incentives to increase production—it was also necessary to deal with the workers as a group.[35]

The intensification of mass-production techniques during World War I was significant for the form of class struggle that was to take place during the interwar years. The labor shortage during the war, as well as later unemployment rates resulting from technological displacement, led many workers to resist capitalists' power advantage on the basis of industrial collectivity as opposed to craft-style organization. As Claus Offe states so clearly, "In the absence of associational efforts on the part of workers . . . workers would simply have no bargaining power that they could use to improve their conditions of work or wages, because each individual worker who started to make such demands would risk being replaced either by another worker or by machinery. . . . The formation of unions . . . is . . . a response to the 'association' that has already taken place on the part of capital, namely, in the form of the fusion of numerous units of 'dead' labour [machinery] under the command of one capitalist employer."[36] The development of industrial unionism led many capitalists and state administrators to enact various forms of labor legislation as well as private welfare programs in an effort to diminish the potential unity of working-class interests and to weaken the organizational capacity of industrial unions. In some instances, this took the form of company unions or employee-representation plans. The ultimate impact of this form of "personnel management" was that managers increased their control over production, which resulted in extended capitalist control over the worker. Moreover, the campaign to bust unions in the 1920s, "The American Plan," was successful enough to virtually eliminate gains made by labor during World War I.[37]

The Capitalist Exploitation of Labor

Simply put, the capitalist exploitation of labor refers to the process by which labor produces value for the capitalist (translated into profits) over and above the value (translated into wages) that the worker receives to reproduce his own labor power. The rate of exploitation refers to the ratio of the time that a worker spends producing value for the capitalists to the time the worker spends producing value that comes back to him in terms of wages. The extensive exploitation of labor is accomplished through a lengthening of the working day and/or the speeding up of the pace of work. The period of capitalism that is characteristic of extensive exploitation predates the introduction of mass-production techniques and labor-saving machinery. The intensive exploitation of labor is accomplished through the introduction of labor-saving machinery. The introduction of large-scale machine production during the early years of the twentieth century marked the shift from the extensive exploitation of labor to the intensive exploitation of labor within the industrial sector.[38]

Concomitant with the increase in labor productivity as a result of labor-saving machinery was the intensification of work that is referred to as the speed-up in the auto industry and the stretch-out in the textile industry. During the

1920s in particular, the rising rate in the exploitation of industrial labor was due to both intensive and extensive exploitation. The productivity of labor in manufacturing, for example, increased by 4.7 percent between 1899 and 1919, but it increased by 53.5 percent between 1919 and 1927.[39]

As productivity rose during the first quarter of the twentieth century, so did money wages for workers. Although money wages rose steadily from 1890 to 1913 and increased between 1919 and 1928, real wages remained rather stable between 1890 and 1919 and increased only slightly between 1919 and 1928. A study comparing money and real wages for various manufacturing occupations found that real wages rose slightly between 1890 and 1918. Money wages in 1919 were more than 80 percent higher than in 1914, yet real wages had not increased by more than 5 percent.[40] During the 1920s, despite the great increase in worker productivity, the real wages of industrial workers increased slightly if one takes into account differential wage rates of skilled and unskilled workers, differentials within branches of industry, and the geographical location of employment. The slight increase in real wages for industrial workers did not, however, keep pace with the physical productivity of the time. The general lag in real wages helped to account for the rising profits of sectors of the industrial capitalist class and was a contributing factor to the rise in stock-market value.[41] In spite of a slight increase in real wages, the relative economic position of the industrial worker during the 1920s declined. Real wages lagged behind those of managers and executives, and most real wages clearly lagged behind profits and dividends. Inequality in the distribution of income increased at a rapid rate between 1920 and 1929.[42]

With the introduction of labor-saving machinery and with a decrease in the cost of production, the average hours of the work week declined somewhat from the late 1890s to 1929.[43] However, the average hours per week for full-time workers differed from branch to branch of industry and differed between unionized labor and nonunionized labor, with unionized labor averaging less hours of work per week. The average hours worked per week declined in manufacturing industries by roughly 5 hours between 1914 and 1928; the average was 50 hours by 1929. The largest reduction in hours worked per week occurred in the iron-and-steel industry, where the nominal week was 66 hours in 1913, 63 in 1920, and 54 in 1926.[44]

As the volume of production and the output per worker increased during the first two decades of the twentieth century, so, too, did the number of workers employed within the industrial sector; the percentage increase of industrial workers from 1899 to 1919 was 103. Yet, during the 1920s, a period of greatly expanding productivity, there was actually a 2.9 percent decrease in the number of industrial workers employed. Furthermore, the cost of labor, or the amount paid in wages in manufacturing industries, increased by 878 percent between 1889 and 1919 and by only 11.4 percent between 1919 and 1925.[45]

With the introduction of labor-saving machinery on an increasing scale since the end of the nineteenth century and with the increase in the number of wage earners in industrial establishments, the level of unemployment and the number of permanently unemployed also grew. World War I exacerbated the problem of unemployment when thousands of persons left rural areas and farms to seek industrial employment. Even during the years 1923 to 1926, years in which industrial capitalists were making great profits, the estimated annual rate of unemployment in the manufacturing, transportation, building, and mining industries exceeded 9 percent, compared to an average of 7 percent in 1899. Advances in technology and corresponding changes in the organization of production led to old industries dying out and new industries coming to dominate the market, with workers not necessarily moving from one industry to another. The competitiveness of the market and the constant competition between capitalists stimulated industries not only to constantly change the labor process to produce more but also to produce more at a lower cost. The 1920s witnessed both a great expansion in new industries and a shift in location in search of a cheap supply of labor. Major shifts in the constitution of industry meant that increasing numbers of workers had to discard their old skills and crafts and seek new means of employment—usually involving less skill. In a sample of displaced workers from numerous trades, less than a third of those who found jobs returned to their old industries, while the rest found work in new industries. A small proportion did a similar type of work in new industries in which they were employed. Another study in the clothing industry revealed that only one-fifth of the displaced cutters were able to find work in their former occupation. In both cases, a substantial proportion of the workers who were studied suffered long periods of unemployment, exceeding in some instances one year's time.[46]

The Changing Composition of the Labor Force

Shifts in industrial production, the growth of large-scale corporate capital, and the introduction of mass-production techniques all combined to have profound consequences for the labor force in the United States. Along with changes in the nature of work performed, there were changes in the distribution of the working population and shifting occupational patterns. As the percentage of the total labor force that was employed in agriculture steadily declined between 1890 and 1929, the percentage of the total labor force that was employed within the industrial sector steadily increased. In 1900 the number of farm laborers and farmers was roughly equivalent to the number of wage earners. However, by 1920, farmers and farm laborers accounted for 25.5 percent of the total labor force, whereas industrial wage earners accounted for 42.4 percent.[47]

The mechanization of industry affected the composition of the industrial work force, not only in terms of employment possibilities and job availability but also in terms of skilled and unskilled occupations. By the late 1920s in the machinery industry, 20 percent of the workers were unskilled, 55 percent were semiskilled, and 25 percent were classified as skilled workers. In the automobile industry between 1912 and 1923, less than 15 percent of the workers were skilled, and the number of semiskilled machine tenders and assemblers had been increasing since 1923. The number of skilled workers who were needed to meet production quotas decreased.[48]

Between 1870 and 1930, changes in the composition of the work force in basic industry were under way. In 1870, 22 percent of the gainfully employed were dependent upon employment in manufacturing and construction; in 1920, 30 percent. Increased labor productivity made it possible for this relatively small increase in factory employment to support a great increase in industrial production. The increase in output per worker between 1920 and 1930 was not accomplished, however, by an equally rapid increase in industrial employment. Consequently, there was a relative shrinkage in manufacturing employment and a decrease in the numerical importance of manufacturing and mechanical industries. In the mining industry in 1870, 1.5 percent of the total labor force was necessary to meet production requirements, and by 1920, the proportion of those gainfully employed in mines and quarries had increased to almost 3 percent of the working population. As in manufacturing, by 1930, fewer workers were needed as a result of the reorganization of the labor process itself. In sum, in 1870 about 75 percent of the gainfully employed were engaged in the production of physical goods, whereas in 1930 only about 50 percent of the labor supply was so required.[49]

Outside of basic industry the major occupational groups to show a steady growth after the end of the nineteenth century were the combined categories of trade and transportation, which included those workers engaged in moving, storing, and selling goods. With the rise of mass-production industry after World War I, it is no surprise that more workers were required in the distribution of goods as well as in the clerical and technical side of distribution. Between 1870 and 1930 those who were engaged in trade, transportation, and communications had more than doubled their numbers relative to the total work force.[50]

The shifts in the general occupational distribution of the labor force were concomitant with changes in the nature of work within the various occupational categories. Although the mechanization of coal mines lagged behind that of iron and nonferrous metals, the extension of mechanical methods in underground operation led to an absolute decline of more than 100,000 in the number of workers employed in the mining industry and a relative decline of 0.7 percent in the extractive occupations as a whole during the 1920s. Changes in the operation of production following World War I also meant qualitative changes in manufacturing and mechanical trades. The great expansion in manufacturing took place between 1870 and 1910, when the number of people in these trades increased from less than 2,750,000 to 10,250,000 and continued to grow to 13,750,000 in 1920. The nature of labor for the factory worker changed dramatically. In the shops and factories, old jobs became obsolete and new ones appeared; old tools and methods became inadequate, and thousands of former handicrafts were first converted into auxiliary tasks to machine operations in semiautomatic production and then into machine operations. In the building trades, capitalists introduced new methods of production and technology and thereby reduced the amount of handwork done by construction workers.[51]

The specific characteristics of industrial expansion in the United States between the 1890s and 1929 resulted in a more nationally integrated industrial market and a more homogenized industrial labor force.[52] Yet, this result did not happen in a conflict-free environment. Capitalists in general did not merely impose new production techniques and alterations in the labor process on a docile working class, and large-scale capitalists did not assume dominance within the industrial sector without concerted opposition from smaller-scale industrial capitalists. The patterning of a new social structure of accumulation, required by the changing nature of industrial development, was, in the final instance, directed by the trajectory of the class struggle in the United States, a struggle that was itself situated within the context of changing class relations.

The Dynamic of the Class Struggle

The Struggle over Control of the Labor Process

The changes in the labor process since the late 1890s, especially the development of scientific management and the development of mass-production techniques, were not implemented merely by having capitalists impose their will on the working population. Rather, any change within the capitalist labor process was met with constant struggle from workers in an effort to maintain some control over the work process. Workers attempted to use craft unions to maintain as much control as possible over the day-to-day organization of the labor process, although by the 1920s the attempt seemed futile.

David Montgomery points out that there were essentially three levels of formal and informal organization which workers developed at the end of the nineteenth century in an effort to maintain control over the work process.[53] The first level was the functional autonomy of the craftsmen resting on their knowledge, which made them self-directing at their tasks and enabled them to supervise one or more other workers. Functional autonomy was enforced externally by strikes and slowdowns and, within the union, by either expulsion from the union or by ritual castigation carried out by dissatisfied craftsmen. The second level was the union's work rules. Work rules sought to regulate, although not eliminate, the practice of subcontracting whereby craftsmen hired helpers to assist them in production; this often involved various piece-rate schemes of petty exploitation. The third level was the mutual support of diverse trade in rule enforcements and sympathetic strikes. Montgomery's analysis of strikes indicates that craftsmen were forging important connections across locales and industries in order to enforce work rules or win union recognition. Montgomery's analysis of workers' attempts to control the labor process at the end of the nineteenth century helps to situate the rise of scientific management. Scientific management was not merely an evolution in management thought associated with the rise of mass-production industrial techniques but also a response to changing relations between capital and labor.

The craft unions of the late nineteenth century could not resist the encroachment of scientific-management techniques during the first few decades of the twentieth century primarily because they ignored the masses of unskilled, semiskilled, and, especially, immigrant workers. However, unions were extremely hostile to scientific-management techniques; the strike at the Watertown Arsenal in 1911 occurred in response to the introduction of them. Various American Federation of Labor (AFL) affiliates, led by the Molders Union and the International Association of Machinists, initiated intense lobbying efforts in Congress. The lobbying proved to be a successful attempt to pass legislation forbidding the use of federal appropriations to pay any manager who was employing time-study devices or to provide incentive bonuses to employees at army and navy arsenals.[54] Local union leaders, through testimony before congressional hearings, remained adamant in their opposition to the efficiency experts.

However, by the end of World War I, the AFL leadership had become less hostile to scientific-management techniques and had become more cooperative with efficiency managers. The war itself had much to do with the new cooperation. The war meant continual production and a certain amount of concessions to labor so that production would continue uninterrupted by strikes and walkouts. The labor movement was strengthened by the combination of the government's emphasis on production, its policy of union recognition, and the sharp drop in unemployment as a result of the increased levels of production. The rapid rise in union membership provided striking confirmation of the beliefs of those members of the scientific-management community who advocated cooperation between management and labor unions. Increased production provided the material conditions for mechanization in key branches of industry. The rapid expansion of the scale of production created new positions for both semiskilled and skilled workers and provided conditions in which craftsmen could improve their status and earnings even while mechanization was proceeding at a rapid rate. The appointment of conservative trade-union officials to wartime production boards meant that trade-union leaders worked alongside the proponents of scientific management.[55] Although trade-union leadership may have been amenable to the new methods and forms of management in the decade following World War I, the rank and file in various ways opposed systems of speed-up and changes in the loss of control of the labor process. Whether through strikes or slowdowns, working-class resistance did take place after World

War I in opposition to the devices of scientific management. In fact, Brian Palmer argues, the resistance of the working class prior to World War I was what gave rise to the more sophisticated modes of managerial control.[56] After World War I the strikes that were waged by skilled workers and members of trade unions were conducted in an effort to maintain the little control they still retained over the work process. Although unskilled and semiskilled workers joined in the strikes, the strong craft-mindedness of the unions and the emphasis on skilled workers contributed in some ways to the defeat of strikes; skilled workers in steel and coal would often be willing to return to work in response to an offer of higher pay or the threat of losing their skilled and privileged position within the work force.[57]

Union Struggles and Antiunion Policies

Capitalist control over the labor process has provided a necessary precondition for industrial expansion since the late 1890s. Labor unions, however, have presented a direct threat to capitalist hegemony on the shop floor.[58] Labor unions provide workers with the organizational apparatus to combat capitalist attempts to further exploit labor in pursuit of higher profits, lower costs, and greater productivity. It is no surprise, therefore, that the expansion of industrial capital during the early decades of the twentieth century coincided with the concerted efforts of employers to stop the unionization of the labor force.

As early as 1903 the National Association of Manufacturers (NAM) provided employers with the leadership to launch a concerted effort to stop unionization and the implementation of the closed shop. With ample resources to engage in a propaganda campaign against unions, the NAM convinced many that the open shop was un-American and that strikebreakers were American heroes.[59] By convincing prominent members of both political and academic realms about the danger of unions, the NAM was able to strengthen the ability of small producers and local residents in particular to resist unionization and to weaken union sentiments among portions of the working class.[60] Although left-wing political organizations attempted to unify new immigrant workers with native workers through mass strikes during the early decades of the twentieth century, the use of martial law and political repression of left-wing organizers sought to cripple the trade-union movement and make more pronounced the splits within the working class between immigrant and native workers and between skilled and unskilled workers in the newly emerging mass-production industries.[61]

The trade-union movement, although it suffered significantly from antiunion attacks during the years before World War I, was able to flourish during the war years. The war created emergency conditions that required a well-disciplined labor force, thus causing both governmental officials and many industrial capitalists to endorse unionization in an effort to produce more war goods. As a result, the union movement emerged from World War I with an enlarged membership, full union treasuries, a temporary governmental guarantee of the right to collective bargaining, and numerous state agencies for adjustment and arbitration that adopted the principles not only that wages should be sufficient to support a family but also that they should rise with the cost of living.[62] Although the union movement was stronger after World War I than it had been before, unions led by the AFL made little headway into the basic mass-production industries, such as steel and automobiles. Moreover, many of the new union members were located in munitions and metal-working plants that were demobilized at the end of the war. More importantly, collective bargaining, imposed by the government upon employers, was perceived as primarily a wartime necessity.

Employers launched the "American Plan" after the war as a countermovement to the unionization drives of industrial workers. The American Plan meant, in essence, no worker self-organizations. Providing the leadership for the movement, the NAM put forth a massive literature campaign that linked unionization efforts to pro-Communist activities, making the connection between being a union member and being un-American. The sentiments that unions posed a threat to political institutions, to law, and to order were disseminated through a massive literature campaign of the 1920s that reached not only industrial employers, particularly small- and medium-sized industrial capitalists, but also politicians, clergymen, college professors, and the general population through newspapers and pamphlets. By 1929 the publicity department of the NAM reported that coverage of NAM stories had increased 100 percent in actual space covered and 50 percent in the number of clippings and columns received over the previous year. In addition to the propaganda campaign, the NAM actively lobbied for antiunion policies in the legislative realms, endorsed or condemned political candidates on the basis of their position on unions, and advocated employee representation plans as a way to impede the independent organization of workers.[63]

The educational pamphlets of the NAM were perhaps the clearest indication of the arguments against unions and the methods by which appeal was ascertained. A pamphlet in 1927 concerning the reasons for the open shop argued:

> As members we favor the open shop because:
> (1) Rules governing plant operations are not made by men who have neither moral nor financial interests or responsibility in the success of the individual establishment
> (2) It does not, by arbitrarily limiting the number of apprentices or workers who will be permitted to join unions, reduce the number of skilled workers available to industry
> (3) Closed shop rules which restrict the amount of daily output do not apply
> (4) It is possible to pay workers according to ability, securing greater production per dollar of wages than is possible under the closed shop. Lower

production costs bring wider markets and larger sales. This benefits the worker by increasing the continuity of employment
(5) Plants are seldom, if ever, shut down because of sympathetic strikes and jurisdictional disputes
(6) Agreements by groups of employers with closed shop leaders to deprive other employers or business . . . are not possible. We believe that all employers should support these advantages of the open shop and energetically oppose efforts of the American Federation of Labor and its constituent unions to impose the closed shop production system of bygone centuries upon American industry. As American citizens we favor the open shop because it best represents and protects fundamental American ideals.[64]

The union movement had neither the resources nor the unity of membership to combat the antiunion offensive of industrial capital during the 1920s. The steel strike of 1919 is indicative of the power of capital to defeat unions in the years following World War I. The strike itself was called after the chairman of U.S. Steel refused to meet with union leaders to discuss the abolition of the twenty-four hour shift, one day's rest in seven, wage increases, and the eight-hour day. Labor espionage agencies reported union leaders to steel's management and strove to create disunion and discouragement among the rank and file. Mounted state troopers rode their horses through the steel towns of western Pennsylvania, dispersing striking workers with clubs and pushing people off the sidewalks. The sheriff of Allegheny County issued an order that no meetings or gatherings of more than three people could be held. The United States Senate sent an investigating committee whose members reprimanded steel employers at the same time that they spoke out against the so-called Red leadership of the strike. The press was hostile to the strikers. After four weeks, workers had few resources to live on; the steel corporation was the only source of wages and survival for many of the workers. By January 1920 significant numbers of workers had returned to work, and the strike was called off.[65] With no financial or other support from nonstrikers, U.S. Steel, with the aid of local officials and with public sentiment in its favor, was able not only to defeat the strike but also to prevent any other strong union drives in the steel industry for the entire decade of the 1920s.

The struggles of workers during the 1920s, although not waged in vain, were severely defeated by capitalists. Between 1922 and 1926 there was a total of 1,164 industrial work stoppages involving 688,538 workers.[66] By 1929 all of labor's wartime gains had virtually been wiped out. Union recognition and collective bargaining, which were under the protection of the state administration, had become things of the past by the mid 1920s. Moreover, the capitalist offensive against unionization compounded the internal constraints of the labor movement—the growing disunity between skilled and unskilled workers and a growing nativist reaction to immigrant workers.[67] By the end of the 1920s, industrial capital had succeeded in forging disunity among industrial workers and in retaining its hegemony on the shop floor.

The State of the Leftist Opposition

The victory of the workers' revolution in Russia heightened the threat of workers' organizations for U.S. capitalists in the years following World War I. Although the organized Left never posed a direct challenge to the capitalist control of the labor process or to capitalist relations of production, capitalists and state administrators paid particular attention to any development of a class-unified leftist political movement in the United States. The strong antiunion capitalists, specifically represented in such groups as the NAM, the Chamber of Commerce, and the National Civic Federation, were symbolic of attempts to destroy any potential movement that may have emerged to challenge capitalist control.

The outright political repression of radicals predated World War I. It was during the so-called Progressive Era that for the first time, laws were passed that made illegal the advocacy of anarchy. Although anarchists and other leftists within the trade-union movement were the primary target of the anarchist laws between 1900 and 1917, these laws became the models for later repressive legislation. The anarchist laws of 1902/3 were the first sedition laws since 1798 and the first laws in the history of the United States to provide penalties for simply belonging to a political organization. According to Robert J. Goldstein, the laws of 1902/3 provided the model for: (1) the criminal-syndicalism laws passed by many states from 1917 to 1920 to outlaw the Industrial Workers of the World and again from 1947 to 1954 to outlaw the Communist party; (2) the 1917/18 Federal Wartime Espionage and Sedition Acts, which outlawed all criticism of the government and were used to harass the Socialist party; (3) the 1917, 1918, 1920, 1940, 1950, and 1952 immigration laws, which were used to exclude and deport members of the Industrial Workers of the World and the Communist party; and (4) the 1940 Smith Act, which outlawed advocating or belonging to groups that advocated the overthrow of the government, for all citizens, even in peacetime. Whereas the use of private repression was used during the nineteenth century to quell labor militancy, state and local repression came to the forefront during the early years of the twentieth century and was followed by federal repression on a massive scale during World War I and the immediate postwar years.[68] The tremendous amount of political repression severely weakened the leftist opposition in the United States during the 1920s.

Leftists, leftist political groups, and labor groups were fiercely persecuted during the war and the immediate postwar years (1917 to 1920). Vigilante raids on radical meetings were common. Leaders of leftist political groups were indicted, arrested, and imprisoned. Shiploads of foreign-born leftists were deported.[69] The Industrial Workers of the World (IWW) came under attack both during

World War I and immediately thereafter. During World War I, many IWW members went on trial and many went to prison for acts of alleged treason and betrayal. After the war, the public surveillance of IWW members continued, and federal troops stayed on duty in Arizona and Montana where they cooperated with mine owners and local authorities in curbing IWW activities. Naval and army intelligence infiltrated spies into the IWW locals and sent agents to the 1919 IWW convention in Chicago. The western states used previously enacted criminal-syndicalism statutes to inaugurate their own prosecutions against IWW members as federal prosecution abated.[70]

Although political repression during World War I severely damaged the IWW and the Socialist party, a rising tide of radicalism and labor militancy developed during the immediate postwar years, which increased federal political repression tremendously. In September 1918 Eugene V. Debs, the leader of the Socialist party, was persecuted under the federal sedition act and was sentenced to ten years in prison. The so-called Red scare of 1919 was a business and governmental response to the threat of growing radicalism within the labor movement. Socialist-party newspapers were banned from the mails, and elected representatives of that party were denied seats in state and federal legislatures. The climax of the Red scare was the Palmer raids of January 1920, in which somewhere between five and ten thousand people, believed to be alien members of Socialist and Communist organizations, were arrested in more than thirty cities around the country. The raids virtually destroyed local Communist organizations. The decline of the Red scare early after the 1920s indicated that political repression had accomplished its goal—namely, the intimidation of the labor movement and the decimation of the leftist political opposition.[71]

Although the IWW never developed into a class-based political party, its clearly stated Socialist objectives were a major threat to capitalists—especially in light of the victory of the Russian Revolution in 1917. Organized Socialist and Communist parties during the 1920s also posed a potential threat to capitalists. The IWW faded, but the Socialist party and, to a greater extent, the newly formed Communist party continued to organize workers, to raise demands, and to offer political support for political prisoners. Unlike its European counterpart, the labor movement in the United States did not, during the years following World War I, take a class unified position; and leftist political groups—faced with severe political repression—had little impact on the direction of the political struggle of the working class.[72] Electoral politics are a crude measure of leftist political activity at best, but leftists made a poor showing during the decade of the 1920s. The Socialist party's candidate received 902,000 votes in the 1920 presidential elections. The Socialist party's presidential candidate received 268,000 votes in 1928, more than one-third of which came from New York. The Communist party's presidential candidate received only 48,000 votes.[73] Although the Left did not present any particular electoral threat to capitalist rule, leftist political groups posed a challenge in the field of labor control during the immediate postwar years through union organizational efforts. For example, Communists were able to exercise some influence on left-wing trade unionists through the Workers' party (synonymous with the Communist Party of America), through its umbrella organization of the Trade Union Educational League and, later in 1925, through the International Labor Defense League. Communists played an important role in the steel strike in 1919 and in the meat-packing industry during the early postwar years; but internal factional fighting, political repression, and the "power of capital" prevented Communists from having much widespread working-class appeal before the 1930s.[74]

Intracapitalist Rivalry

Although capitalists found unity in their opposition to unionization drives among industrial workers, they were nevertheless torn by conflict over the nature and the consequences of the large-scale industrial enterprise. The expansion of manufacturing and industrial production in the United States after 1890 meant that some firms were expanding at the expense of others. The rapid technological innovations and the introduction of labor-saving devices made some firms more competitive in the market. Smaller firms generally did not have enough capital to invest in machinery, so they lost out in the drive for profits in the twenty or so years prior to World War I. In 1893 and 1894 the number of manufacturing concerns that declared bankruptcy was 3,422 and 2,832 respectively. The liabilities of these bankrupt manufacturers totaled $176 million in 1893 and $67 million in 1894. The largest proportion of manufacturing failures was found in those regions of the United States in which industrialization was occurring at a tremendous rate and the level of competition was highest.[75] The high degree of competition within the industrial sector of the United States coincided with the drive to invest in regions outside the jurisdictional boundaries of the United States. In the 1890s, manufacturing and industrial capitalists formed the NAM in an effort to maintain their competitiveness within the capitalist market. Members of the NAM primarily represented nonmonopoly capital—businessmen drawn from the generally less profitable small- and medium-scale firms in the more competitive industries in which labor costs could not so readily be reduced.[76]

The development of the NAM is significant insofar as it represents the combined effort of small- and medium-scale manufacturing capitalists to join together to bring political pressure on the state administration to make policy favorable to U.S.–based manufacturing firms and to protect the competitive position of small- and medium-scale manufacturing enterprises during a period of the growing concentration and centralization of capital. Similarly, the United States Chamber of Commerce, also formed in the late nineteenth century, entailed promoting the interests of U.S. capitalists. The Chamber of Commerce was broader based than the NAM although the Chamber operated on similar platforms and in a like manner.

Nonmonopoly capital found support among middle-class reformers in the opposition to large-scale corporate strategy. The antitrust campaign was the vehicle through which small- and medium-scale capitalists attempted to curb the extension of monopoly growth. By joining with middle-class reformers, nonmonopoly capital was able to pressure the state administration to monitor collusive pricing agreements and mergers, thereby threatening the profitability and the future existence of large-scale corporate capital. The growing divisions within the capitalist class allowed the state administration to gain a greater degree of autonomy from large-scale corporate capital, thus permitting greater influence from nonmonopoly capital.[77] From the point of view of nonmonopoly capital, antitrust legislation meant the breaking of "unfair" competitive practices carried out by the industrial monopoly capitalists and the regulation of the economy so that small- and medium-sized firms could be competitive in the drive for profits.

The antitrust campaign, with its potential for curbing the growth of monopolies, was halted during the war years. Because reformers now were more concerned with the war effort and because large-scale corporate capital, as well as small- and medium-sized capital, was profiting from the wartime economic boom, public sentiment, particularly from nonmonopoly capital, was deflected by the war away from the hazards of large-scale corporations. Moreover, the partnership between corporate capital and the state during the war made any governmental action against the interests of monopoly capital unlikely. By the end of the war, monopoly capital had decisively thwarted the opposition to its growing dominance on the economic terrain. The antitrust laws and the actions of the Federal Trade Commission, which was mandated to investigate unfair competition, proved inadequate to curb the expansion of monopoly capital. In the years 1915 through 1928, 13,193 charges of unfair competition were filed with the Federal Trade Commission. The great majority of these were dismissed after further inquiry. Of the cases that went to trial, 546 resulted in dismissal, 857 in cease-and-desist orders, and 350 in stipulations to offending parties that they would stop practices held to be contrary to law. Moreover, 75 antitrust cases were started between 1925 and 1929, of which 37 were settled by consent decrees, 13 were settled by pleas of guilty or nolo contendere, and 12 were dropped.[78]

The Political Scene

The changing nature of industrial production and class relations during the first decades of the twentieth century impacted on internal changes of the state apparatus. In turn, changes within the state impacted externally on both capital and labor. The alterations within the state as well as the changing relationships between classes and the state, while significant, were nevertheless insufficient to assure conditions for the continual profitability of capital and the cooperation of labor in a changing economic environment.

The new form of industrial economic activity and the emerging social structure of accumulation necessitated a state apparatus that was able to supercede the particular interests of various fractions of capital, adjudicate between the antagonisms of labor and capital, and simultaneously assure conditions for the profitable accumulation of capital. Stephen Skowronek has illustrated how the internal arrangements of the national government and the power that political parties had on local state governments provided barriers to the transformations of the national state apparatus in the late nineteenth century.[79] The electoral realignment of the 1890s altered the national electoral configuration in such a fashion as to delimit the competitiveness of national electoral politics and to open the way for major reforms within the institutional ensemble of the state apparatus. Whereas prior to 1896 both Democrats and Republicans could gain majorities in districts in the North and West, the electoral realignment produced a sectional alignment of a Republican North against a Democratic South. As a result, the Republican party gained majority status in the Congress and more frequently than before was also the party of the president. While representing the northern industrial interests, the Republican party was also able to appeal to industrial workers and immigrants in its platform for progressive reform and antimonopoly rhetoric, especially under the Theodore Roosevelt administration. Except for the Democratic victory during World War I with the election of Woodrow Wilson, the Republican party was the dominant party in the United States until the 1932 presidential election.[80] In a nutshell, after the 1896 realignment, the favorable partnership between the presidency and Congress created initiatives to strengthen the power of the presidency by rising above party politics and by proposing administrative reform in the structure of the national government. Nevertheless, what form such changes were to take did not reach a consensus. The pressures for an expansion of state activity to regulate and stimulate production as well as to provide services that were required by a new social structure of accumulation did lead to internal changes within the institutional ensemble of the state, yet were not transformed sufficiently to correspond with the impending necessity of an accumulation process that was dominated by monopoly capital.

World War I, with its domestic mobilization, was what forced the state into not only regulating but also stimulating production. For example, the growth of the automobile industry during the 1920s and the rise of trucks as major carriers required the improvement and extension of highways in the United States. The Highway Act of 1921 provided almost $1 billion for the federal grants-in-aid program for road construction throughout the United States. In addition, the Department of Commerce, from 1921 to 1928, greatly enlarged its services to businessmen, especially by encouraging the organization of trade associations and the elimination of wasteful or unnecessary competition. Furthermore, tax policies of the period were intended to place light burdens on the wealthy in order to encourage investment in new productive industries.[81]

As state activity aided in the accumulation of industrial profits, it did not do likewise in supplying benefits for the working class. With the Republican party in office, the political repression of leftists encountered a new surge, the trade-union movement was crushed for all intents and purposes, and the working class in general experienced a relative decline in its standard of living. By the 1920s the Republican party was able to subsume its progressive elements, and reform was no longer a party slogan. The nomination of Alfred E. Smith as the Democratic party's presidential candidate in 1928 signified a substantial shift in midwestern rural areas to the Democratic party's ticket. Although Smith lost by a landslide and Hoover clearly had the majority of the electorate behind him, the Smith ticket provided the conditions under which large segments of the urban working class could be brought back into the Democratic party for the first time since the election of 1896.[82] The anti-Catholic campaign of many Republicans also brought the urban areas and some blacks back into the Democratic party. Smith was a Catholic, and the Ku Klux Klan had previously enjoyed a positive impact on the Democratic party in the South. But the nomination of Smith signaled a transformed Democratic party, and blacks saw a vote for Smith as a vote against the Klan. This slight shift in class affiliation was to reach its peak in the 1932 presidential election.

In brief, the Republican party's dominance during the early years of the twentieth century provided the context in which changes within the state apparatus began to match the requirements of a new social structure of accumulation. Yet, these changes were not sufficient to assure the regulation of economic activity that took into account the ongoing antagonist relationship between labor and capital, as well as the continual rift between large-scale corporate capital and small- and medium-sized capital. Not able to adjudicate between monopoly and nonmonopoly capital during the early years of the depression, thereby making policies that pleased few if anyone, the Republican political regime gave way to a Democratic party that was willing and able to take the necessary steps to consolidate a political structure that more evenly matched the requirements of the changing accumulation process.

The Accumulation of Capitalist Contradictions

Labor and production conditions that existed prior to World War I were intensified during the 1920s. The general conditions involved (1) the increased growth of large-scale industry, probably best exemplified in the merger movement of the 1920s; (2) the rapid introduction of mass-production techniques that had further implications for the capitalist organization of the labor process; and (3) the new form of capitalist exploitation of labor. The development of scientific management itself was a response to the existing organization of the labor process which was not suitable for production in large-scale industry, and it provided the preconditions for a higher rate of exploitation that was necessary for the expanded reproduction of capital in a phase of capitalist development in the context of a declining world market.

None of this was met by any class-unified workers' opposition. This is not to say, however, that workers did not resist the speed-ups and stretch-outs. Rather, it is to argue that workers were not successful in curbing the growth of monopoly corporations and, therefore, in preventing consequential changes in the social relations of production. Between 1907 and 1917 there were political campaigns to reform labor conditions which did gain strength. This movement developed to a great extent outside of militant trade unionism. It succeeded in getting state governments to pass a series of ameliorative laws: nearly every state established a minimum wage for laborers, some states prohibited children from doing night work as well as certain dangerous or strenuous tasks, and forty states fixed maximum hours for women. The restriction of working hours for men continued to be blocked by insurmountable obstacles; only railways, among major industries, after countless accidents and the intervention of the federal government which wanted to avoid a general strike, adopted the eight-hour day in 1917. World War I and war production strengthened the position of workers and generalized the eight-hour day and the forty-four-hour week, although this was soon dropped at the end of the war.[83]

A number of developments in the United States followed the growth of monopoly capital and associated changes. The growth of monopoly capital from the end of the nineteenth century was most dominant within the manufacturing branches of industry—especially the new mass-production branches of the basic industries of steel, rubber, and automobiles. Consequential changes in the organization of production resulted in a greater productivity of labor and a decrease in the number of wage earners necessary to produce a given unit of output. However, greater percentages of wage earners were employed in large-scale enterprises at the same time that smaller-scale firms were being either combined with larger corporations or eliminated. The growth of large-scale enterprises meant the disappearance of smaller-scale firms that did not have enough capital to invest in machinery that would have allowed them to remain competitive. Many smaller-scale enterprises could not keep down their costs of production and were, as a consequence, absorbed by the larger-scale enterprises. Moreover, state economic activity—for example, the standardization of parts for machinery, the formation of employer associations represented within the state apparatus, and state tax policies—aided in the accumulation of monopoly capital.

The conditions of labor changed during the period under review in the following way. The introduction of mass-production techniques greatly reduced the ability of labor to control the day-to-day organization of the production process, and it further deepened divisions between mental and manual labor. Workers were not only separated from the tools of production, but they also lost control over their own labor and the manner of its performance. The hierarchical nature of the control of the labor process entailed the development of managerial authority and undermined the former status of the foreman. Managers now directly oversaw the production process which solidified the control of capital over the labor process. The deskilling of labor stripped the worker of any potential control over his own work tasks. These changes within the capitalist labor process were concomitant with the change from the extensive exploitation of labor to the intensive exploitation of labor.[84] The greater productivity of labor and the production of relative surplus value increased greatly—especially during the 1920s. The small advance in real wages for portions of industrial workers was not enough to offset rising unemployment, and it created a home market that was not large enough or affluent enough to absorb the surplus value being produced. This problem of consumption caused problems of accumulation in the latter part of the 1920s which led eventually to a devalorization of capital.

The trade-union movement during the period under review was not strong enough to counteract the great profits being realized by industrial capitalists. Although the labor movement and workers in general did make wartime gains, these gains were short-lived, and capitalists were able to abort any attempt at massive union organizing. Part of the problem with the expansion of the trade-union movement derives from the organizational strategies of the AFL and the failure of any leftist political movement to make headway among the masses of workers. The AFL was formed on a craft basis, and it managed only to organize narrow fringes of the working-class population—generally, skilled workers. The massive introduction of machinery and the deskilling of workers created a context within which unions could make little headway in mass-production basic industry. Political repression served to divide the working class, making leftist political groups ineffective against the assaults of capitalists. Consequently, capitalists were able to launch a general antiunion campaign and to take the offensive on the political as well as the economic front. A number of craft unions were forced to disband, while the courts paralyzed the actions of those that remained.[85] In part, the transformations of the labor process were not well enough articulated within the demands of the labor movement, and the Left was not strong enough to have a far-reaching impact on the movement at a time of general "prosperity."

The course of capitalist accumulation and the associated dynamic of the class struggle led to contradictions that are specific to the process of capitalist development in the United States. Monopoly capital accumulated at an astonishing rate as a result of the greater rate of exploitation of the industrial work force. Conditions that are favorable to the private accumulation of capital corresponded with a redistribution of wealth to the advantage of the upper layers of the capitalist class between 1920 and 1929. The top 1 percent of the population increased its share of the total national income from 12 percent to 18 percent; the top 5 percent, from 24 percent to 33.5 percent. Total income in the form of profits, interest, and rent increased by 45 percent, whereas the real wages of factory workers increased by only 2 percent. As a result, between 40 percent and 45 percent of all households were not able to participate in the market for new consumer durable goods.[86]

Growth in the concentration and centralization of capital within the industrial sector did not correspond with the necessary reorganization of wages and consumption, the regulation of competition, and an alteration in the political structure that was necessary for the new imperatives of the accumulation process. The centralization of capital required a reorganization within the industrial sector because of the massive destruction of capital as a result of a large number of business failures. This required the establishment of "new relations of competition because the destruction of one sector of industrial capital reduces the total mass of capital involved in production and gives all sections of capital new possibilities of valorization."[87] However, the need for regulated competition was blocked by a political apparatus that was not able to transcend particular fractional interests of capital. Monopoly capital, while dominant within the economic sphere, had yet to secure political dominance. The manner in which the state favored monopoly capital was established through a complex process in which state institutions underwent "changes whereby certain dominant mechanisms, modes, and decision-making centres [were] made impermeable to all but monopoly interests, becoming centres for switching the rails of state policy or for bottling up measures taken 'elsewhere' in the State that favour[ed] other fractions of capital."[88] It was the trajectory of the class struggle during the depression years that guided the process of change that the new social structure of accumulation required.

CHAPTER THREE

The Crisis and Its Impact on Labor and Capital

> When nearly 70% of American industry is concentrated in the hands of 600 corporations; when not more than four or five thousand directors dominate the same block; when more than half of the population of the industrial east live or starve, depending on what this group does; when their lives when they are working, are dominated by this same group; and flow of capital within the economic system is largely directed by not more than 20 great banks and banking houses, . . . the individual man or woman has, in cold statistics, less than no chance at all.
>
> Your government will go rapidly to the left, either because it is led, or if not that, because it is driven, and we have only just begun to do the underlying thinking on which the next set-up will have to be based.
>
> —*A. A. Berle*

THE SPECIFICITY OF THE CRISIS IN THE UNITED STATES

The New York stock-market crash in October 1929 and the succeeding world economic crisis of the 1930s gave the appearance that capitalist development in the United States, as well as capitalist development on a world scale, was on the decline.[1] Both foreign capitalists and American banks withdrew enormous cash reserves from the New York money market after the stock-market collapse; this caused serious losses to individual investors and a decline in industrial production, commodity prices, and world trade. Moreover, the stock-market crash in New York brought about a decline in bank credit and consequently caused bank failures around the world. World production decreased, and the aggregate number of unemployed workers in the advanced capitalist regions of the world was estimated at the end of 1929 at some ten million and had reached twenty million by the beginning of 1931. A large-scale liquidation crisis followed a gradual price recession, and the demand for new investments in all parts of the world diminished. Large quantities of stocks were placed on the world market at a time when the demand for these goods was restricted. The inevitable result was a rapid decline in world prices and world trade. Between 1929 and 1932 the trade of the entire world declined by approximately 61 percent.[2]

As in all periods of crisis, the world economic crisis of the 1930s marked a crucial phase in the development of capitalism in the United States. A distinguishing characteristic of a capitalist crisis, in contradistinction to an economic downturn or a business cycle, is that accumulation cannot continue unless barriers to accumulation are overcome. The solution to a capitalist crisis, therefore, implies a basic transformation in the relationship between classes, between fractions of capital, and between classes and the state.[3] As such, crises of capitalism perform an organic role in the reproduction of capitalist social relations of production by providing the occasion for the restructuring of the social relations of production that are necessary for the expanded reproduction of capital.

The impediments to capital accumulation in the United States were not exogenous factors that interfered with the accumulation process; they were generated by the process of accumulation itself since the end of the nineteenth century. The contradictions of U.S. capitalist development became acute with the New York stock-market crash and the succeeding economic depression. Although the world economic crisis affected almost every country of the world, the crisis was especially severe in the United States because of the specificity of U.S. capitalist development. In particular, the economic depression revealed three basic obstacles to capital accumulation in the United States: (1) too high a rate of labor exploitation, which resulted in problems of profit realization; (2) unregulated competition, which led to problems of investment; and (3) a political structure that did not fully reflect the changing balance of class forces.

The capitalist prosperity of the 1920s came to an abrupt halt with the 1929 stock-market crash; the results were bankruptcies for capitalists and massive unemployment for workers. Capitalist competition since the end of the nineteenth century had led to the development of large-scale industrial firms and an increase in the amount of capital invested per worker. During the 1920s alone, capital per worker increased by 36 percent, while real value added per worker increased by almost 75 percent.[4] With real wages remaining relatively stable during the 1920s, problems of profit realization resulted from the heightened rate of exploitation. With the realization problems occurring in the context of heavy speculation, the stock-market crash and the ensuing depression were especially severe, as obstacles to accumulation were coupled with financial failures and the collapse of the credit system.[5] It had been possible to counteract previous tendencies towards economic crisis in the United States by opening new markets and by expanding the number of firms via the great "industrial" frontier. However, the crisis of the 1930s occurred after the completion of basic industry and the closure of the industrial frontier and in the context of a collapsed world market. As such, the course of capital accumulation and the future of capitalist development in the United States depended upon a reorganization of wages and consumption and the regulation of competition between monopoly and nonmonopoly firms.

The very pattern of political and economic relations that had led to the crisis and the heightened class struggle that is characteristic of all crisis periods constituted a series of obstacles that took more than a decade to overcome. Through a combination of class strategies reflected in state policies and individual strategies by separate capitalist firms that were attempting to maximize their own profits, the impediments to the accumulation process were temporarily resolved, and the accumulation process was continuing in new forms by the end of World War II. However, it was the dynamics of the ongoing struggle between labor and capital, as well as the conflict between the various fractions of capital, that directed the particular response to the crisis and the mode of its temporary resolution.

The heightened rate of exploitation during the 1920s was partially made possible because of the fragmentation of the working class, nativist reactions to ethnics, and the tremendous amount of political repression and deportations of militant workers. As such, the trade-union movement and various leftist political groups entered the depression in a weakened state and were unable to muster enough political clout to play a major role in guiding the path to economic recovery during the early years of the depression. Using hindsight, we can see that the major political battles during 1929 and 1933 over the direction and course of capitalist recovery were waged, not between labor and capital, but within the capitalist camp.

The Crisis and Capital

The general capitalist prosperity of the 1920s came to a brief but significant halt with the stock-market crash of October 1929 and the ushering in of the Great Depression. In the seven years prior to the fall of 1929, industrial productivity and national income had both risen more than 40 percent. Between 1929 and 1932, however, national income declined by more than 38 percent, and the number of unemployed had risen, at its peak, to approximately 15 million. The massive deflationary effect of the decline of income and the curtailment of all forms of private-investment expenditure and consumption were followed by the collapse of the financial infrastructure, typified by the failure of more than 5,000 banks.[6] During the years 1930 through 1932 there were some 85,000 business failures in the United States, and the market value of stocks on the New York Exchange declined from $87 billion in October 1929 to $19 billion in March 1933. The index of physical output in manufacturing dropped from 58 in 1929 (1947–49 = 100) to 30 in 1932.[7]

Bank insolvencies during the first few years of the depression led to corporate difficulties. Corporate profits, which reached a high of $9.6 billion in 1929, declined rapidly, and in 1932 U.S.–based corporations reported losses of $3 billion.[8] In an effort to decrease the overall wage bill, industrial capital responded to this economic crisis by "laying off" a considerable portion of workers while simultaneously forcing the remainder to work longer hours. The firing and laying off of workers resulted in a decline in consumption which partially was reflected in the decline of business activity by more than 30 percent in 1930.[9]

The economic crisis caused great reductions in activity for housing and heavy industry, in particular. There had been 937,000 housing starts in nonfarm areas in 1925; by 1929 the number was 509,000; by 1932 it was 134,000; and by 1933, a mere 93,000. Income in the construction industry declined from $3.8 billion in 1929 to $800 million in 1933. Steel output, 56.4 million long tons in 1929, was 13.7 million in 1932, a three-year decline of more than 75 percent; 1,161 locomotives were produced in 1929, 123 in 1932, and only 7 in 1933. The automobile industry, the most "prosperous" of the "new industries" of the 1920s, was also hard hit by the economic crisis. The factory sales of motor vehicles, which were 2,790,000 in 1929, were down more than 75 percent to 617,000 in 1932. The output of bituminous coal, which was used to produce more than half of the mechanical energy in the United States, declined by 43 percent in just three years. The wholesale price index went down by a third from 1929 to 1932. Prices for farm products also declined; as a result, farm prices in 1932 were less than a third of those during 1919. Agricultural income declined from $8.3 billion in 1929 to $3.3 billion in 1932. The *New York Times*'s composite stock declined by more than 90 percent, from 312 in September 1929 to 13.7 in 1932. New issues of corporate securities totaled $9.4 billion in 1929 but only $380 million in 1933—a reduction of some 96 percent.[10]

Initially, most industrial capitalists perceived the economic crisis as a normal downturn in the business cycle, which was beneficial in the long run for overall business activity. The president of the National Association of Manufacturers (NAM) argued that the depression was nothing to panic about—at least seventeen similar depressions had occurred during the previous 120 years. In January 1931 a spokesperson for U.S. Steel argued that the peak of the depression had passed in December 1930.[11] The position of the Hoover administration was similar to the general consensus of the business community: the depression was temporary; its worst aspects were an outcome of "economic recklessness" and could be overcome by having leaders of the business, banking, labor, and agricultural communities adopt voluntary measures. When the depression continued and business did not "pull itself up by its own bootstraps," the Hoover administration began to focus on the international sphere and the world market, for both the causes and the consequences of the crisis within the United States.[12]

By late 1931 the depression was worsening. The European financial crisis of 1931 took its toll on U.S. banks that had foreign holdings. More than 2,000 banks with liabilities in excess of $1.7 billion failed between the spring of 1931 and the winter of 1932. Business failures increased, reaching 2,000 a month in the spring of 1932, then rising to 3,500 a month a year later. By the end of 1931, capitalists as well as state administrators were no longer speaking about the beneficial nature of periodic downturns in the business cycle; they were forced to face the severity of the depression. By late 1931, various capitalists had begun to propose schemes for economic rationalization which called for some sort of governmental institutionalized assistance to the capitalist class.[13]

Economic rationalization proposals ranged from outright national economic planning—originated mainly by economists—to stabilization schemes—proposed by different fractions of capital—which were rooted in corporate and trade-association experience and would be guided by the trade associations as opposed to governmental agencies. However, all plans for stabilization, whether originating from capitalists or intellectuals, were flatly opposed by President Hoover, who rejected such proposals as an "unacceptable violation of the American System."[14] In September 1931 Gerard Swope, president of the General Electric Company, privately presented to Hoover a scheme for stabilizing industry and employment and then publicly presented it to a dinner meeting of the National Electrical Manufacturers Association. Hoover called the plan unconstitutional and later labeled it as nascent socialism or fascism.[15] Swope's plan called for the self-regulation of industry through price fixing and profit control, some minimal compensations for workers in an attempt to prevent labor discontent, and an easing of the antitrust laws. The plan called for a greater cooperation between trade associations and the state machinery and a dismissal of the fears of monopoly and competition in order that greater stabilization might be achieved in the depressed atmosphere of the time.[16] Swope's plan reflected the fractional interest of monopoly capital.

Swope's plan drew reactions from all fractions of the capitalist class as well as from state officials. Capitalists who were not active in trade associations and small-scale capitalists, in particular, perceived the plan as being a call for the end of the free-enterprise system. However, Henry Harriman, president of the Chamber of Commerce and head of the New England Power and Light Company, in December circulated a modified version of the Swope Plan among members of the Chamber of Commerce who supported some sort of business planning and cooperation and a lifting of the antitrust laws.[17] Although it appeared that significant portions of the capitalist class, specifically monopoly capital, were in favor of some sort of industrywide stabilization measure to be enforced by the federal government, the Hoover administration stood firmly opposed to such a measure, and no legislation of economic stabilization ever reached the Congress prior to 1933 when the Roosevelt administration came to dominate Capitol Hill.

The stabilization schemes that were proposed by different fractions of the capitalist class forced Hoover, in December 1931, to turn to new measures for economic recovery. Hoover, convinced that the key to recovery lay in the restoration of the banking system, called upon banking leaders to propose plans to aid failing banks. The lack of response from the banking community left it to Hoover and the federal government to take the leadership. One of the most dramatic proposals of the Hoover administration was to call for the establishment of the Reconstruction Finance Corporation (RFC), which was to become one of the chief agencies for the expansion of credit during the depression. Congress enacted the law that created the RFC in January 1932. The stated intent of the

RFC was the federal guarantee of loans to furnish credit during the depression to banks, insurance companies, building-and-loan associations, and other financial institutions that were in difficulty and otherwise would not be able to obtain the necessary loans.[18] The greatest beneficiaries were banks and trust companies, which got three times as much money as did the railroads, the next largest classification of claimants. Smaller disbursements were made to building-and-loan associations, mortgage loan companies, relief and work relief, and insurance companies; even less was granted to a variety of agricultural credit agencies. By the end of Hoover's term, small- and medium-scale capitalists, governmental officials, and portions of the working class all attacked the RFC, calling it a bread line for big business at a time when direct relief to the unemployed was being systematically refused.[19] The Hoover administration's one attempt to offset further economic decline and restore economic normalcy failed.

The Crisis and Labor

From 1929 through 1932, unemployment rose, wages fell, and the hours of work were increased for hundreds of thousands of workers. In 1929 approximately 3.2 percent of the civilian labor force was unemployed; in 1930, 8.7 percent; in 1931, 15.9 percent; and in 1932, 23.6 percent.[20] Unemployment was particularly acute during the first few depression years in the automobile, textile, and other durable-goods industries. Between March 1929 and August 1931, for example, the payroll of the Ford Motor Company dropped from 128,142 to 37,000 persons.[21] As joblessness increased, those who were still employed were compelled to accept reductions in actual wages. As a consequence, total wages within the industrial sector had fallen some 20 percent by June 1930, and the real weekly earnings of those who were employed in manufacturing and mining generally declined by 15 to 30 percent.[22] Moreover, in 1929 the work week for factory employees remained at about 50 hours, despite the massive amount of machinery that had been previously introduced and the increase in productivity and intensity of work.[23]

The response of unemployed workers involved millions of people and included sit-ins at relief stations to secure aid for unemployed families; demonstrations in front of city halls; occasional raids on food warehouses; hunger marches; and in thousands of instances, preventing marshals or police from evicting tenants who could not pay their rent. In addition, unemployed workers used such survival strategies as informal and formal cooperative movements, family and neighborhood networks of assistance, looting of supermarkets by individuals and groups, coal bootlegging, determined searches for work, and the innovative stretching of income. The more formal and political expressions of resistance activity by the unemployed, such as sit-ins, hunger marches, and direct resistance to evictions, were stimulated with the assistance of left-wing political organizations such as the Communist party, the Socialist party, the Musteites, and various Trotskyist groups.[24]

Leftist political groups played a major role in the organization of the unemployed during the early years of the depression. More likely than not, the agitation of leftist-organized resistance activity by the unemployed stimulated the passage of relief legislation during the Roosevelt administration. The Communist party, which during the 1920s had suffered great losses in membership mostly because of the repressive state actions, took the lead in organizing the already discontented unemployed working class. The Trade Union Unity League (TUUL) became the umbrella organization of the Communist party through which workers were organized into "revolutionary" unions at the point of production and efforts were made to organize the unemployed into groups that eventually became known as Unemployed Councils.[25] Through the Unemployed Councils, the Communist party organized marches and demonstrations throughout the United States to protest unemployment. On 11 February 1930, for example, the Communist party led a march of about 3,000 unemployed workers to Cleveland's city hall. Four days later, the Unemployed Council in Philadelphia led a demonstration of some 250 persons to city hall, who demanded an interview with the mayor. A week later, 1,200 unemployed workers marched upon the seat of municipal government in Chicago. In all three instances, police met the demonstrators with force and dispersed them. On 26 February 1930 a crowd of 3,000 persons was met by police with tear gas at Los Angeles's city hall, and in the following week at the city hall in New York City, police used brutal tactics to break up a demonstration by unemployed persons.[26]

Much of the activity of the Unemployed Councils centered on local demands for relief and unemployment insurance. However, in March 1930, the Communist party did organize demonstrations on a national scale for International Unemployment Day. The Unemployed Councils organized demonstrations in major cities throughout the United States; these involved more than a million people.[27] Confrontations with police broke out in Cleveland, where 10,000 people demonstrated, and in New York, where 35,000 people demonstrated and congregated at Union Square.[28] Despite police action, the Unemployed Councils continued to organize demonstrations at local relief stations and over the nonpayment of rent. For example, during the summer of 1930 the Unemployed Council organized 5,000 people in Chicago to march on the headquarters of lodging houses. The council demanded three meals a day, free medical attention, tobacco twice a week, and the right to hold council meetings in the lodging houses. When relief funds were reduced by 59 percent, the unemployed marched again, and the reduction was rescinded.[29]

The demonstrations organized by the Communist party in March were the first mass protests against the impact that the economic crisis had had on the working class.[30] After the demonstrations in March, the Unemployed Councils concentrated on local issues and organized many localized demonstrations in an effort to alleviate the burden of the unemployed. Frequent "rent riots" took place in Chicago and elsewhere, particularly in the black neighborhoods, where the Communist party was instrumental in incorporating black struggles within the larger workers' struggles. Demonstrations over rent were often followed by street meetings, and such tactics often culminated with police interventions in which beatings and arrests were common. Although many of the demonstrations were met with police attack, relief officials were forced to give out money for rent payments. In August 1931, for example, after a rent riot in which three policemen and many demonstrators were injured, evictions were temporarily suspended and some demonstrators received relief work.[31] In New York City between 1930 and 1931 the Unemployed Councils organized demonstrations in which groups of unemployed used physical force to prevent marshals from putting on the street the furniture of evicted people. Protest meetings took place on a regular basis. The police broke up one particular meeting in Union Square with a great amount of brutality. As a result of press coverage and adverse publicity, a second meeting, which involved an estimated 100,000 people, forced the mayor of New York to form a city-sponsored committee to collect funds to be distributed among the unemployed.[32]

On the national level the Communist party organized two hunger marches in Washington, D.C. The first march took place in December 1931; the second, in December 1932. The first march was met on the ramps of the Capitol by police armed with rifles and riot guns and backed up with concealed machine guns. The marchers demanded unemployment insurance but were denied admission to the floors of both the Senate and the House to plead their case. Governmental officials received a written petition yet gave no response. The marchers then congregated in front of the White House to plead their case but, again, with no results.[33] More than 3,000 people joined in the hunger march in December 1932. Herbert Benjamin, the head of the Unemployment Councils, was arrested by federal troops and police on the outskirts of Washington and was held for three days. Finally, the marchers were permitted to walk through the Capitol, accompanied by police. Once again, the marchers achieved no immediate results.[34]

The Communist party, through the Unemployed Councils, was instrumental in organizing the discontent of the unemployed and in registering the significance of the economic crisis to capitalists and state officials alike. Even more significant, the Communist party was able to link up the struggles of the unemployed with the struggles of employed workers. In Detroit the Communist party organized a regional march in March 1932 whose demands included jobs for the jobless, payment of 50 percent of wages to the unemployed, the seven-hour day, the end of speed-ups, rest periods, no discrimination against blacks, free medical care at Ford Hospital, and winter relief of $50 per family. Police attempted to break up the demonstration, but when the demonstrators refused to stop their march, police opened fire, killing four and wounding several others before the demonstration was dispersed. In response, the Communist party staged a funeral procession for the dead, which was attended by more than 30,000 people.[35]

The Socialist party also attempted to organize the unemployed. In May 1929 the National Executive Committee of the Socialist party urged local party branches to form "Emergency Conferences on Unemployment," not as mass pressure organizations of the unemployed, but rather as lobbying agencies for unemployment insurance, old-age pensions, and the abolition of child labor. Rarely did the Socialist party itself actively organize the unemployed; it concentrated instead on the electoral process. The League for Industrial Democracy, an offshoot of the Socialist party, organized the unemployed into more formal organizations, known as the People's Unemployment League. By mid 1932 the Chicago group organized more than 25,000 jobless into more than 60 locals. The Baltimore group had about 20 locals, which had between 7,000 and 12,000 members. The Socialist unemployed groups resembled the Unemployed Councils in acting as grievance representatives at relief stations, in fighting evictions, and in holding demonstrations and parades to urge higher appropriations for relief.[36] However, the Socialists never did organize the unemployed to the same extent as the Communists, partially due to internal dissension within the party, which was criticized for not taking a more active stance on the position of the working class during the economic crisis. A proposal to the New York local of the Socialist party summed up the difficulty in the following way:

> The Socialist Party has come to minimize the importance of the class struggle and the abolition of capitalism as the central issue in the fight for Socialism. Instead of stressing our fundamental position immediate reform measures have been emphasized. On this basis, it has not been difficult to attract to us elements who have not been clear about socialist principles. On the other hand, the working class to whom our fundamental appeal should be made has been woefully neglected.[37]

The third major leftist organization to attempt to organize the unemployed was the Musteites—followers of A. J. Muste, who began to organize Unemployed Leagues in 1932. The Conference on Progressive Labor Action, the formal organization of the Musteites, acted as an independent working-class center and was competitive with the American Federation of Labor, the Communist party, and the Socialist party in organizing workers and representing their interests. The Unemployed Leagues concentrated on organizing groups around self-help and attempted to push the unemployed toward political militancy. They were most prevalent in small rural industrial areas in Ohio and Pennsylvania. The Unemployed Leagues were quite successful in raising the demands of the unemployed on a local and regional level, but they never attained a national presence.[38] However, the political importance of the Musteites should not be underestimated.

It was not until the mid to late 1930s that the political significance of the Musteites became evident when they formed the American Workers party.

In addition to the activity of the unemployed, both spontaneous and that organized by leftist political organizations, there was some working-class resistance at the point of production during the early years of the depression. Few strikes were organized during that period compared to the twentieth century as a whole, however, and these strikes were basically defensive in nature—for example, resisting wage cuts and work speed-ups and stretch-outs; and a significant proportion of strikes had no union involvement.[39] In 1930 a total of 635 work stoppages were recorded; in 1931, 810; and in 1932, 841. The percentage of the strikes held to resist wage decreases rose from 14 in 1929 to 25.7 in 1930, 42.4 in 1931, and 50.6 in 1932.[40]

The most notable strikes of the first few years of the depression were those in the coal industry and in the northern textile industry.[41] Strikes to resist wage cuts erupted among textile workers in Massachusetts, New Jersey, and Pennsylvania. In 1931 the Communist party, through the Trade Union Unity League's National Textile Workers, conducted strikes in Lawrence, Massachusetts; Allentown, Pennsylvania; and Paterson, New Jersey. In February 1931, 10,000 workers at the American Woolen Mills in Lawrence struck against the speed-up and were able to force the company to rescind its earlier directives to increase the pace of work. In October and November 1931 a walkout of 23,000 workers completely closed the mills. There were also strikes against wage cuts in 1931 among silk workers in Allentown and at the silk mills in Paterson.[42]

Miners in Harlan County, Kentucky, struck as conditions in the coal industry grew worse. However, the United Mine Workers, which had suffered a severe loss of membership during the 1920s, was unable to sustain the strike, and violence between guards and miners left several dead. Similar actions were taken by miners in Arkansas, Ohio, Indiana, and West Virginia; and these met with similar violence on the part of employers. In April 1932, 150,000 miners in southern Illinois went on strike, and by summer, the coal-mining counties of southern Illinois had "become a battleground between armies of miners and deputies" as thousands of miners descended on the still-operating mines to shut them down.[43] The Trade Union Unity League's National Miners Union conducted coal strikes in Pennsylvania, Ohio, Kentucky, and West Virginia. In April 1931 more than 40,000 miners went on strike, and several mines were forced to close. The demands of the strikers were higher wages, the eight-hour day, and union recognition. Few of these demands were met, and violence was the rule rather than the exception. There were bloody injuries, as well as killings.[44]

The world economic crisis of the 1930s affected all classes in the United States. However, the working class suffered disproportionately from the crisis. The response of the Hoover administration to the plight of workers, both employed and unemployed, was less than satisfactory even to the most conservative elements of the working class. The Hoover administration made little, if any, attempt to aid the unemployed, other than forming the President's Committee on Unemployment, which merely investigated the conditions of the unemployed. Relief was, for the most part, left to state and local authorities.

Even with the mounting presence of leftist political organizing among the working class, the Hoover administration ignored proposals from leaders of the established organized-labor movement. John L. Lewis of the United Mine Workers and Sidney Hillman of the Amalgamated Clothing Workers both proposed some sort of economic-stabilization program which called for industrial planning and certain benefits for the workers. Even the conservative William Green of the AFL called for some sort of economic-planning measures that would improve conditions for workers.[45] However, the Hoover administration did little to please the proponents of such measures. The election of 1932 manifested the demands from both capitalists and workers for some sort of active governmental participation in the recovery effort from the depression.

The Political Scene

The State of the Left

When the economic crisis of the 1930s began to have its devastating impact on the working class, most left-wing political organizations were in a weakened state because of factional infighting and political repression during the 1920s. Yet it was the political organizations associated with left-wing politics that were most actively enmeshed in the struggles of the working class. These extraparliamentary struggles of the working class would clearly have an impact on the social and economic reforms associated with New Deal legislation. The degree to which these struggles affected state policy is still a matter of debate, but few would deny that working-class discontent increased as the depression wore on and that by 1932 even capitalists continued to be dissatisfied with the nonaction of the state administration. If political discontent continued to rise from both workers and capitalists, it was quite likely that the state would face a legitimation problem. As will be discussed later, the Roosevelt administration was aware of such discontent and acted accordingly to bring about changes that would have far-reaching effects for workers and capitalists alike. Whereas Democrats and Republicans were the social actors in the halls of Congress, Communists and Socialists acted to organize political activity more often than not outside of the electoral process. This left-wing political activity, although it has often been ignored in the recent literature on New Deal policies, nevertheless had an impact on U.S. politics during the 1930s both by offering an alternative to Democratic- or Republican-party politics and by struggling with and for workers for better working and living conditions. Too often an appreciation for political movements outside of the two-party system is lacking in examinations of the formation and the implementation of policy.

The Communist party was the most visible leftist political organization in working-class struggles during the first few years of the depression. During this period the Communist party presented itself as the revolutionary party of the working class, a disciplined advanced guard, and called for the "subordination of the individual to the line and to the activities of the Party and the revolutionary working class."[46] Although there were large membership drives in the years 1930 through 1932, the Communist party had problems in retaining its membership. For example, 5,125 new members were recruited in March 1930, but only 2,693, or 52 percent, became permanent members of the party.[47] The number of dues-paying members in December 1932 was 18,119, a gain of almost 8,500 since 1931. However, if the recruited ones had remained permanent members, the membership of the Communist party would have been 35,001 by the end of 1932.[48]

Immediately after the March 1930 International Unemployment Day, members of the capitalist class, state officials, and conservative labor-union leader William Green were made aware of the growing strength of the Communist party among the working class.[49] On 6 March, the day of the Communist demonstration at Union Square in New York City, Congressman Hamilton Fish, with the backing of the AFL, introduced a resolution into the House of Representatives to investigate Communist activity among the working class. The argument in support of the formation of the committee to investigate Communist activity was that communism was a threat to the internal security of the United States and that many of its leaders were aliens and should be deported. The House adopted the resolution, and before the year was out, Communist leaders were summoned before the committee. This committee would soon be known to millions of Americans as the infamous House Committee on Un-American Activities.[50]

Membership in the Socialist party, which suffered tremendously in the years following World War I, grew during the first few years of the depression—from 9,500 in 1929 to almost 17,000 in 1932.[51] Although its membership grew, the Socialist party became internally divided as the depression wore on. The Socialist party had a more reformist program than the Communist party had and was hesitant to engage its members in confrontation politics.[52] Internal divisions within the party between the so-called Old Guard and the new militants resulted in the Socialist party's assuming an essentially reformist line. It concentrated on research, education, and persuasion.[53] The Socialist party was not very visible within the working-class struggle, although it continued to get the largest electoral votes of any leftist political organization on a national scale. Because of the Socialists' preoccupation with electoral politics at the expense of working-class organizational activities, the party never regained the presence among the working class that it had enjoyed in the years before World War I. The Socialist party's Continental Congress on Economic Reconstruction in May 1933, which was designed to correspond to the First Continental Congress during the American Revolution, called for pressure to be brought on the state administration for unemployment and farm relief; but it was a dismal failure.[54]

In addition to the Communist and Socialist parties, a number of other smaller leftist groups were formed during the early years of the depression. The Conference on Progressive Labor Action (CPLA) was formed in May 1929 by Socialists, trade unionists, and labor educators as a propaganda and educational organization centered around opposition to both the conservative leadership of the AFL and the dual unionist approach of the Communist party. By 1931 the CPLA was clearly to the left of the Socialist party and had denounced the latter for its reformism and lack of a clear working-class orientation. The CPLA was broadly committed to form a mass labor party whose ultimate objective would be to establish a workers' republic. The CPLA saw itself as standing for action rather than theory. The move to the left within the CPLA during the early years of the economic crisis attracted many disenchanted members from the Socialist party. The CPLA dissolved in December 1933 and became the American Workers party, a Trotskyist group, only to merge a year later with the American Trotskyist Communist League of America to form the Workers party.[55]

The League for Independent Political Action emerged in 1929 as a left-liberal organization whose purpose was to discuss the means and the strategy for the creation of a new political party. The league was composed primarily of intellectuals and liberal journalists who had little ability to attract mass working-class support. Their disdain for the Communist party and socialism in general did little to generate much support for the league among the industrial working class. The league had disintegrated by the fall of 1933 because of the liberal Roosevelt policies that were being developed.[56] The league offered no real alternative to the Roosevelt coalition.

Although the Left was badly divided during the first few years of the depression, leftist political groups, particularly the Communist party, were gaining a strong presence within the working class—especially among the unemployed and the unorganized segment of the industrial working class. As the struggles of the unemployed and the unorganized heightened, leftist political groups, such as the Communist party and even the declining Socialist party, increased their membership. As Communist and Socialist involvement in the organization of the unemployed became more and more evident, capitalists and the Hoover administration, along with the conservative president of the AFL, William Green, became more and more fearful of an impending revolution. Green told the 1931 AFL convention, "I warn the people who are exploiting the workers that they can drive them only so far before they will turn on them and destroy them."[57] During the last few years of the Hoover administration, federal repression of leftists and militant industrial workers increased. Deportations for political reasons increased from 1 in 1929, to 18 in 1931, to 51 in 1932, and 74 in 1933. Beginning in 1931, the post office barred radical newspapers and periodicals from the mails. Many bills were introduced in Congress in 1931 to repress the growing strength of leftist political groups, but a more liberal-leaning Congress passed only one bill to deport alien Communists. Although the federal government set the tone of repression between 1929 and 1933, most of the repression was carried out on the local level. For example, the repression of free speech by local police increased during the first two years of the crisis so much that the American Civil Liberties Union stopped keeping a yearly account of free-speech prosecutions and interferences after 1930.[58] In spite of the increase in local forms of repression of radical activity, some local and state governments stressed reform over repression. The forces of repression were simply not strong enough to offset the growing resistance of industrial workers. Public sentiment was such that a growing number of governmental officials came to realize that repression of the Left would not help matters created by the crisis. Moreover, from the viewpoint of most Americans, it was the government, not the Left, that failed to solve the problems of the economic crisis.

Laissez-Faire versus State Intervention: The 1932 Presidential Election

The results of the 1932 presidential election indicated that the voters strongly rejected the manner in which the Hoover administration had attempted to offset the economic decline. By the time of the election, capitalists and workers alike were expressing discontent with the Hoover administration, which had done little to aid the increasing numbers of unemployed workers and had made little if any appeal to the most conservative elements of the trade-union movement. At the time of the election, no immediate relief from the crisis was in sight. The index of industrial production in the United States had declined by more than 54 percent from the peak in September 1929 to the trough in July 1932. Factory employment during the same interval had fallen by 64 percent. In other words, the wage bill of the factories included in the return was little over one-third of what it had been three years previously.[59]

The downturn in domestic business during the fall of 1929 was immediately followed by a sudden and prolonged drop in U.S. purchases from other countries. From a total of $4.4 billion in 1929, imports fell more than $1.3 billion in 1930 and an additional $1 billion in 1931. It was not until 1933 that a slow increase began. The physical volume of imports followed a course that closely paralleled the decline in industrial production, but the decline in total volume was accentuated by the exceptional weakness of prices for raw materials, which made up a large fraction of the aggregate.[60]

The decline in United States exports began earlier than the decline in imports and proceeded somewhat more gradually during the early years of the depression. Because of the larger totals involved, however, the absolute decline of $1.4 billion in 1930 was slightly greater than that in imports, as compared with $8.42 million in 1929. Further sharp declines in exports of $1.4 billion in 1931 and $0.8 billion in 1932 reduced the surplus to less than $0.3 billion in later years.[61]

Although the United States' crisis was especially acute at home, it also affected the crisis experienced on a world scale. The decline in purchases of foreign goods and services and the almost complete cessation in new investments abroad caused an extraordinarily rapid and severe shrinkage in the supply of dollars made available to foreign countries. The amount of dollars paid out or transferred dropped from a level of about $7.4 billion for the three years 1927 through 1929 to a mere $2.4 billion in 1932 and 1933, a reduction of 68 percent over a span of three years. The drastic decline in the world supply of dollars was one of the most severe disturbances to the world economy during the first few years of the depression; it directly reduced business activity abroad and produced foreign-exchange problems of tremendous dimensions.[62]

Initially, capitalists perceived the economic crisis as a normal downturn in the business cycle. The Hoover administration agreed with this reaction. Holding on to laissez-faire ideology, the Hoover administration declared that the depression could be overcome through voluntary measures adopted by leaders of the business, banking, labor, and agricultural communities. However, as the crisis deepened and no relief appeared to be in sight, various capitalists began to propose schemes for economic rationalization which called for some sort of governmental institutionalized assistance to the capitalist class. As mentioned earlier, in 1931 Gerard Swope of the General Electric Company (representing monopoly capital) proposed a plan that called for the self-regulation of industry through price fixing and profit control and that provided some minimal compensations for workers as well as an easing of the antitrust laws. In the same year, the Board of Directors of the Chamber of Commerce (representing primarily nonmonopoly capital) noted "the growing purpose on the part of business to eliminate unsound competitive practices by means of voluntary cooperation."[63] One year later, the members of the Chamber of Commerce, representing small- and medium-scale capital, endorsed a resolution suggesting that "anti-trust laws should be modified so as to make clear that the laws permit agreements increasing the possibilities of keeping production related to consumption."[64] The Chamber of Commerce supported stabilization through trade associations. The National Association of Manufacturers, representing small- and medium-scale capital in the more competitive industries, agreed.[65]

In addition to proposals for weakening the antitrust laws and for stabilizing production and consumption, there were proposals to increase the purchasing power of consumers, the working class in particular. Labor leaders such as John L. Lewis, Sidney Hillman, and even William Green proposed some sort of economic-stabilization program that called for industrial planning and the participation of organized labor in the planning process. However, the Hoover administration held to a laissez-faire stance. The 1932 presidential election took place in the context of a deepening economic crisis, with no attempt being made by the incumbent administration to respond either to representatives of capital or to representatives of labor. The election represented the general discontent and the overwhelming repudiation of state policies based on laissez-faire ideological premises.

The campaign and election of 1932 did not in and of itself represent major changes within either of the two parties. Although working-class struggles increased during the 1929–32 period, the Democratic platform made little effort to appeal to organized, unorganized, employed, or unemployed workers. The Republican party was in disarray, and with no alternative, it renominated Hoover as its presidential candidate. The Democratic party, the minority party at the outset of the depression, had more at stake with respect to whom it would nominate as the presidential candidate. The nomination of Franklin D. Roosevelt as the Democratic presidential candidate reflected a shift in control of the Democratic party and indicated an "activist" platform by proposing economic relief and some form of state intervention.[66]

The Roosevelt campaign was mild at best and made no direct appeal to the working class. Part of the reason that Roosevelt did not campaign on a consistent progressive platform was an attempt to hold the Democratic party together and to allow Hoover to defeat himself. By the time of the election it was really not clear what platform Roosevelt was running on and what his position was on various issues as he attempted to appeal not only to northern conservatives and liberal Democrats but also to the southern Democratic bloc. In short, Roosevelt was careful not to alienate either rightist or leftist elements within his party. When talking to business leaders, he stressed balancing the budget and saving the free-enterprise system. When speaking to workers and newly enfranchised immigrants, he stressed the "forgotten man and the need for a redistribution of wealth."[67]

The 1932 election, which gave Roosevelt a clear victory and the Democrats a majority in both the House and the Senate, reflected a repudiation of Republican-party politics during the crisis period rather than a clear-cut support for the Democratic platform. Although a significant number of Republican senators and congressmen aligned themselves with a more reformist position, conservative Republicans firmly controlled the Republican party during the early years of the depression. The Democratic party, on the other hand, was able to achieve majority status by incorporating the interests and needs of a new electorate that had previously been outside of the national system of political bargaining. Urban ethnics, urban workers, and racial minorities appear to have formed the necessary voting bloc in electing not only a Democratic president in 1932 but also liberal Democrats to the House and the Senate.[68] This new electoral base of the Democratic party, along with heightened class tensions, forced the Democratic administration to fulfill many of its promises of active reform. The overwhelmingly liberal-Democratic Congress made the passage of the initial New Deal legislation quite harmonious.[69]

The election of a Democratic president and Congress in 1932 provided the context in which significant reforms could be enacted during the depths of the economic crisis. The majority status of the Democratic party, made possible by the incorporation of a new party base made up of primarily urban working-class ethnics, provided for the leftward movement of the party after 1932. Although Roosevelt and the Democratic party never developed a consistent accumulation strategy with a clear ideological underpinning, a vote for Roosevelt and the Democrats meant a repudiation of laissez faire. Workers were not alone in calling for some state-sponsored programs to aid in economic recovery. Capitalists representing monopoly capital, medium-scale capital, and nonmonopoly capital had also stressed some form of state-sponsored and -supported programs of economic recovery. To both labor and capital, Roosevelt and the Democratic party represented action. Whereas workers perceived the election of Roosevelt as an important step in achieving a better standard of living and economic security, important elements of the capitalist class perceived Roosevelt's election as an important step toward economic recovery and renewed accumulation. The reformist wing of the capitalist class achieved its mandate to put forth policies for economic recovery and stabilization with the Roosevelt election.[70] The changing relationships between state, party, and class provided for far-reaching state-sponsored reform programs during Roosevelt's first term in office.

CHAPTER FOUR

The National Industrial Recovery Act as a State Solution to the Crisis

My impression is that the country wants and would gladly support a rather daring program.

—*A. A. Berle, Jr.*

Many important problems face the nation. Production must be balanced with consumption both in industry and agriculture so that fair prices may be obtained. The extraordinarily low prices of agricultural commodities are affecting not only the farmers but also the workman in the city who is out of a job because the farmer has no income with which to buy goods. Disastrous wage cutting, as the result of ruthless competition, is likewise curtailing the purchasing power of the nation and adding to unemployment. Remedies for these troubles face your administration.

—*Henry I. Harriman and William Green*

RECOVERY PROPOSALS AND THE ROOSEVELT ADMINISTRATION

The Roosevelt administration's New Deal policies were both a culmination of previous recovery proposals and a response to the ongoing class struggle.[1] Our particular concern is the manner in which the balance of class forces during the depression years shaped the formulation and implementation, and hence the consequences, of various state policies. In general terms, policy formulation involved a process of placating competing groups—between fractions of capital and between capital and labor—in the search for the most effective policies to ensure favorable conditions for economic recovery and the further accumulation of capital. Economic and social policies arising out of branches and agencies of the state apparatus sought to coordinate business information, subsidize backward but politically important sectors such as agriculture, retard social disintegration through social-welfare programs, control the rate of technological change, guarantee both fiscal flexibility and stability, and assure the cooperation of labor with capital. The entire New Deal program, although it was drafted and designed by a variety of state managers, officials, and legislators, represented the contradictions of class relations in American society and the attempt of the state administration to resolve those contradictions and conflicts in order to provide conditions for the uninterrupted accumulation of capital. Whereas the balance of class forces conditioned the formulation of New Deal policies, these policies in turn had an impact on the balance of class forces.

Prior to Roosevelt's election, the notable Brain Trust (Adolf A. Berle, Jr., Raymond Moley, and Rexford G. Tugwell) suggested a variety of economic measures in an attempt not only to win the presidential election but also to provide an accumulation strategy for economic recovery. These proposals for recovery clearly indicated that an assessment of the balance of class forces shaped the proposals and that Roosevelt's top advisors recognized the need for a new strategy of capital accumulation. This new strategy for accumulation was unlikely to arise out of the capitalist class itself; the state administration would have to assume the lead in the restructuring process. Yet whereas the balance of class forces might have indeed shaped recovery proposals, the policies that were eventually implemented had unintended consequences. These unintended consequences arose out of the very nature of class relations during Roosevelt's first term in office.

In May 1932, Berle and Louis Faulkner of the Security Research Department at the Bank of New York and Trust Company jointly prepared a memorandum on the crisis and on possible avenues of recovery.[2] The memorandum was later discussed with Roosevelt and four other top advisors. The memorandum was extremely important in the development of the presidential campaign as well as the entire tone of the New Deal.[3] The memorandum contained three parts: an analysis of the major causes of the depression (which was argued to be essentially underconsumption), recommendations for emergency measures, and long-range proposals for economic restructuring. The section on emergency measures centered on an extension of the Reconstruction Finance Corporation which provided loans to revitalize production and add some security to employment.

The third section of the memorandum, concerning long-range proposals, provided the outlines for a new accumulation strategy. The memorandum recognized the fact that the industrial economy was becoming increasingly concentrated and that this tendency, if unchecked by economic intervention on the part of the state, could lead to "increasing intensity of depression," thus causing "a wholesale dislocation amounting to revolution in fact, if not in name." The memorandum also argued that industrial wealth and income had become more concentrated during the depression, with "not more than two thousand" men controlling the whole of American industry. Berle and Faulkner argued that "the handful of dominant individuals do not agree on a policy; assume little responsibilities to their community, to their customers or to their labor; have no cohesion; fight among themselves for supremacy within their industry. Industries fight against each other." With this understanding of the changing nature of industrial development, the Berle-Faulkner memorandum stated that the antitrust legislation that was designed to curb monopoly growth was not and could not be implemented. The memorandum suggested that the appropriate method of handling this was to amend the antitrust laws so as to allow consolidations and even the creation of monopolies at will; however, when in any industry carrying on interstate commerce there occurred a concentration of 50 percent by two corporations, the monopoly corporations would be subject to federal regulation. The federal regulation would include required uniform prices, some control over security issues, and further consolidation within the industrial branch. The long-range policy suggestions included old-age, sickness, and unemployment insurance. Berle and Faulkner linked the necessity of these social-welfare programs with the tendency towards the concentration and centralization of capital, arguing:

> Although apparently differentiated from problems of concentration, insurance against old age, unemployment and sickness really becomes necessary as a result of concentration. The theory that such insurance is unnecessary and unwise is based on the premise that individual action at liberty is the best safeguard of the individual. Where businesses are largely small and competitive, this may be true. In concentrated industry, the individual has no real liberty of action; he is at the mercy of a uniform system with which he cannot possibly cope.

The memorandum stated that corporate profits should be available to cover unemployment insurance but that industrial capital did not recognize the obligation. Moreover, excess capital that might have been available in the past was locked up in plant investments. Berle and Faulkner argued:

> It is imperative that this situation be not permitted to occur. . . . The answer appears to be in government unemployment, old age and sickness insurance; set up as a charge on earnings of industry, and arranged with sufficient flexibility so that where a corporation provides its own insurance in these regards, within standards laid down by the government, such insurance could be recognized as satisfying the obligation of the company.

This final section of the Berle-Faulkner memorandum regarding industrial concentration clearly indicated that the dominance of monopoly capital within the accumulation process was most definitely recognized by potential state managers and that there was a need to adjust state policy and invoke a new accumulation strategy—a strategy that would alter the trajectory of capitalist development in the United States.

In July 1932 Moley and Tugwell prepared a memorandum for Roosevelt in which they outlined the policy recommendations of the Brain Trust.[4] With respect to industrial recovery, the memorandum included a discussion of the concept of an economic council that would be attached to the executive branch and would help to formulate general economic policies. It also stated that Henry Harriman, president of the Chamber of Commerce, was extremely interested in the formation of such a council and that the national Chamber of Commerce supported the proposal. The memorandum also contained the suggestion that the Chamber of Commerce be consulted prior to a separate preparation of a memorandum on the economic-council idea because of the Chamber's importance with respect to "business opinion." Moley and Tugwell argued that the concept of an economic council was "perhaps the most important single item in the general scheme for reconstruction of economic activity." This economic council could provide the mechanism for arriving at compromises between monopoly and nonmonopoly capital.

By August 1932 it had become quite clear that the strategy of the Roosevelt election campaign was going to center on economic-reconstruction measures that would focus on some sort of industrial-stabilization program. In a revealing memorandum to Roosevelt, Berle outlined the significance behind economic stabilization: it included a program of legislation under which the government could deal with monopoly growth in industry, and it implied a revision of the antitrust laws. He suggested some kind of government machinery along the lines of an economic cabinet that would serve to collect information and provide a continuous economic audit as well as a coordination of the various relief measures, such as old-age pensions and sickness and unemployment insurance. Because of increases in the concentration and centralization of capital within the accumulation process, Berle argued that the state apparatus would have to initiate the policy suggestions that are outlined above in order that the state apparatus could aid in "regulating and unifying" the capitalist class. Berle further argued: "Were the few thousand men running things a coordinated group, you would at least have a government of sorts. Actually, they are in the state of the political feudal barons in France before a centralized French government unified them." If the administration did not adopt the necessary policies that would seek to organize the capitalist class, he argued, "either the handful of people who run the economic system now will get together making an economic government which far outweighs in importance the federal government; or in their struggles they will tear the system to pieces. Neither alternative is sound national policy."[5]

After Roosevelt's election in November, Berle proposed that a program of legislation be presented via Moley, at a special session of Congress if necessary.[6] Berle stated that the economic situation might change for the worse and that therefore his suggested policies would have to be shifted according to existing economic conditions. He did state quite strongly, however, the urgency of the proposed legislation. Berle maintained that by 4 March 1933 "we may have anything on our hands from a recovery to a revolution. The chance is about even either way. My impression is that the country wants and would gladly support a rather daring program." Berle proposed as fundamental legislation: (1) a farm-relief act that would include some sort of domestic allotment plan or some other plan designed to increase the purchasing power of the farmer—he argued that this was absolutely essential; (2) legislation for industrial stabilization, which would include limited permission to industries to get together, under suitable supervision, on stabilization plans, provided they would include some guarantee of greater employment; (3) a relief act, which might be coupled with an unemployment-insurance program; and (4) a policy that would address the issue of currency, debt, tariff, taxation, and a balancing of the budget.

Some of the proposals of the Brain Trust were eventually incorporated into New Deal policies. Economic-recovery proposals were geared to the specific interests of monopoly capital, reflecting the general changes occurring within the accumulation process. Yet the concrete policies of the Roosevelt administration were a response to the immediate conflicts of the time. What is apparent from the earlier discussions of recovery proposals is that a recovery and relief policy were imminent in order for economic activity to resume, albeit on a different scale. What was never discussed in these earlier plans, however, were provisions for labor, although the administration had some concern about unemployment. This concern arose out of the prevailing conventional wisdom that a key to economic recovery was to increase purchasing power. The role of trade unions and organized industrial labor was never an issue that either Roosevelt or his advisors took to be a pressing matter. The early recovery proposals clearly implied that fundamental changes were occurring in basic industry and mass-production industry. The industrial sector was developing in such a fashion as to require some form of state aid in regulating competition. Whereas these proposals reflected the changing character of competition between firms, they paid little attention to the changes in the relations of production within firms.

What is evident from the personal papers of Roosevelt's advisors, as well as from governmental documents of the period, is that the entire New Deal program was not clearly thought out by anyone, least of all by Roosevelt himself. This is not to deny that there were some sorts of industrial stabilization and reemployment programs on the agenda of the new administration. Tugwell sums up policy making in the higher echelons of the New Deal administration in his diaries as follows:

> I can't go into the differences of opinion involved in this [farm legislation] although they are very strong and general. But it all came about, again, because FDR does not realize what the issues are and is careless in his commitments. . . . He tells several of us to do the same things, and then forgets. This is all right when it involves study and reporting to him, but when it involves handling a political situation the results are apt to be ludicrous. This is a case in point. The agreed strategy on the farm bill has been to have the farm leaders adopt it and promote it in Congress; and on the credit adjustment an effort was to be similar. FDR told HM and myself separately to see this through. Luckily we discovered in time that we had been given the same instructions and worked together on the first trip to Washington and we got the farm leaders together on the domestic allotment plan and shaped the bill now before the house.[7]

This confusion within the executive branch continued even during the crucial period of the drafting of the NIRA, which was to be the major recovery program of the Roosevelt administration. Berle, who had previously been instrumental in formulating recovery proposals, wrote Moley in April 1933 to inquire if the Black Thirty Hour bill, which was currently before the Congress, was an administration-sponsored bill. It appears that although Berle was traveling around the country building support for an administration-sponsored recovery plan, he had no idea what was happening on Capitol Hill.[8] Although state managers might have indeed outlined a variety of programs for economic recovery, the coordination of efforts to formulate and implement a new accumulation strategy was clearly lacking within the ensemble of state institutions. These chaotic and often contradictory institutional relationships merely mirrored conflictual and contradictory class relationships, especially the lack of a capitalist consensus on a new accumulation strategy.

When Roosevelt took office in March 1933, many recovery plans had been proposed, all of which included some form of industrial stabilization. Within five days of the president's inauguration, the so-called Hundred Days began. Within three months, major economic policy was formulated. Serious consideration of a program or policy for industrial recovery did not occur until April, for reasons that I shall discuss more fully below. As noted previously, business organizations such as the Chamber of Commerce and the National Association of Manufacturers supported a revision of the antitrust laws.[9] State administrators called for governmental standards on minimum wages, maximum hours, and unemployment insurance. This appears to have been motivated by the effort to increase the purchasing power of consumers.[10] The culmination of these and other recovery proposals into what became known as the National Industrial Recovery Act occurred when the Black Thirty Hour bill provided the stimulus for such a recovery measure.

Immediate Stimulus to the NIRA: The Black Thirty Hour Bill

During its first month, the Roosevelt administration was preoccupied with policies relating to banking, agriculture, and relief, and it did little in attempting to develop an industrial-stabilization program. An attempt to develop a legislative proposal embodying some form of industrial-stabilization scheme came only after the passage by the Senate of the Black Thirty Hour bill on 6 April 1933. Moreover, Black's bill was instrumental in moving the Roosevelt administration to a serious consideration of a national industrial-recovery measure that would include some concessions to organized labor. In November 1932 the AFL convention in Cincinnati called for a five-day work week and a six-hour day in order to increase employment and purchasing power.[11] In December 1932 Senator Hugo L. Black of Alabama introduced a bill into Congress that incorporated the demands of the AFL. Black's Thirty Hour bill called for a prohibition on the interstate shipment of goods produced by labor that was working more than six hours a day and five days a week. Black claimed that his proposal would create six million jobs.[12] Charles Roos quotes Black as having said: "Labor has been underpaid and capital overpaid. This is one of the chief contributing causes of the present depression. We need a return of purchasing power. You cannot starve men in industry and depend upon them to purchase."[13]

Black's Thirty Hour bill, according to Ellis W. Hawley, "reflected the popular notion that available work should be shared; it enjoyed the support of organized labor; and in an atmosphere of the time, it seemed likely to win the approval of the House as well as the Senate."[14] However, Roosevelt was opposed to the bill; he believed that it was too rigid, that it was perhaps unconstitutional, and that it would lead to an actual drop in purchasing power because of the lack of minimum-wage provisions.[15] The best strategy for organizing opposition to Black's Thirty Hour bill was seen to consist of presenting a better proposal for stimulating both recovery and employment. Clearly, the proposed measure would have to include some concessions to organized labor. Not only did the Black bill incorporate the demands of the AFL, but William Green, president of the AFL, suggested that the Black bill "struck at the roots of the problem—technological unemployment"—and went on to intimate that he would call a general strike in support of the thirty-hour week.[16]

After the passage of the Black bill in the Senate on 6 April, Secretary of Labor Frances Perkins, at Roosevelt's request, proposed a number of amendments to the House Labor Committee in an effort to develop a workable substitute to the bill as it passed the Senate. Perkins's proposals included the establishment of minimum-wage levels based upon the recommendations of special industrial boards—agencies upon which labor, management, and the government would each have representatives. A similar board, she suggested, might grant limited exemptions from the requirement of a thirty-hour week and, in certain circumstances, might empower the secretary of labor to limit the hours of operation of any unit in industry when because of, for example, continuous operation, it was securing a disproportionate share of the market and was threatening to displace other industrial units.[17]

Perkins's proposed amendments to the Black bill produced protests from all fractions of the capitalist class and from organized labor. In general, capitalists argued that the proposed amendments were much too rigid and that if ever put into operation, they would most likely dislocate industry, increase production costs, and aggravate unemployment. Moreover, capitalists were opposed to the intimation that the secretary of labor would have the power to dictate wages to industry instead of relying upon the judgment of "experienced and responsible management." Harriman of the Chamber of Commerce argued that constructive wage-and-hour legislation should be based upon the principles of "industrial self-government" that had been recommended by such organizations as the Chamber of Commerce and the National Association of Manufacturers. These capitalists argued that the antitrust laws should be revised so as to allow capitalists to enter into voluntary trade-association agreements covering such things as hours, wages, and unfair competition. Such agreements should then be approved by an appropriate governmental agency; and once approved, they should be enforced upon "irresponsible" capitalists.[18] Organized labor, through its spokesperson William Green, also opposed the Perkins amendments, arguing that the amendments, as stated, would vest in industrial boards the power to stipulate minimum wages, which would eventually become the maximum wage.[19]

At the same time that Roosevelt requested Perkins to develop amendments to the Black bill, he also requested Moley, a member of his Brain Trust, to undertake a serious investigation of the recovery proposals emanating from the business community and within the ranks of the state administration. Roosevelt directed Moley to develop a program for industrial mobilization that would appease both capitalists and workers and therefore would serve as a substitute to the Black bill. Eventually this worked. Once hearings had opened before the House Labor Committee, there was much discussion over the opposition of both organized labor and business organizations such as the NAM and the Chamber of Commerce. The Black bill was sidetracked in the House and was buried in the fervor of New Deal legislative proposals.

During the last weeks of April and the first weeks of May, presidential appointees and advisors, senators, and business groups, mobilized behind the Department of Commerce, worked on separate drafts of a recovery measure. Out of the confusing and complex process of drafting, a single recovery measure emerged.[20] Although the precise manner in which the final draft evolved is somewhat unclear, it is evident why the measure included provisions for a temporary relaxation of the antitrust laws, provisions for governmental support for trade associations, and provisions granting industrial labor the right to organize and bargain collectively. Leaders of industrial and trade associations and representatives of organized labor were all successful in representing their particular interests to key members who were involved in the drafting process, such as Senator Robert F. Wagner and John Dickinson, assistant secretary of commerce. What emerged out of the chaotic process was a recovery measure that reflected the balance of class forces of the time.

By early May there were two major drafts of a recovery measure. The first measure, sponsored by Senator Wagner, combined a program of public works and governmental loans with a plan for industrial self-government through trade associations. The second version, proposed by Gen. Hugh S. Johnson, who had had experience with the War Industries Board, laid more stress on the federal licensing of business which emphasized the prospects for national economic planning.[21] Henry Harriman wrote Roosevelt expressing his genuine interest in the industrial bill that was in preparation and stated that he preferred Wagner's version of the bill "which makes greater use of trade associations; but I do feel that the sanctions of General Johnson's should be added."[22] Harriman conceded that the sanctions might not be held constitutional after the "emergency is over" and continued to suggest that major aspects of the measure be made permanent. Harriman reasoned that

> the psychology of the country is now ready for self-regulation of industry with government approval of agreements reached either within or without trade conferences. When prosperity has returned, selfishness or self-interest, whichever you prefer to call it, may have again asserted itself to such a degree that a sound law cannot be passed, hence my great desire that the measure be a permanent one but with the drastic sanctions made temporary.

On 10 May, Roosevelt called the principal drafters of both the Wagner proposal and the Johnson proposal to the White House and appointed a new committee, consisting of Wagner; Johnson; Donald R. Richberg, a labor lawyer for the railroad unions who worked on the Johnson proposal; Dickinson, Frances Perkins; and Lewis Douglas, director of the Bureau of the Budget, to come up with a single satisfactory measure that could be presented to Congress. The NAM demanded that there be more business representation on the new drafting committee, and with a threat of NAM opposition to the recovery measure, Roosevelt appointed a business advisory committee consisting of representatives from the Chamber of Commerce and the NAM as well as other business leaders who represented the interests of large-scale corporate capital, such as Lammot Du Pont, to confer with the new drafting committee. By 13 May the drafters had reached a compromise, and the proposed recovery measure was satisfactory, in its essentials, to the business advisory committee. The final version contained something for nearly all of its major drafters. The authority to formulate codes of fair competition satisfied those who expressed the need for some sort of industrial self-planning.[23] In March 1933 Robert Lund, president of the NAM, stressed the need for "constructive experiment and concurrent investigation to check" the trend towards underconsumption. Lund argued: "Individual action cannot arrest the progressive accentuation of these conditions. Its correction requires cooperative action among and within industries, stimulated but guarded by the Government."[24] Section 7a, with its promise of collective bargaining and minimum labor standards, made the measure attractive to those who were pushing for the interests of organized labor and trade unions. The provisions for federal licensing gave some hope to those who stressed the need for national economic planning.

The recovery measure, soon to be known as the National Industrial Recovery Act (NIRA), received the endorsement of both capitalists and organized industrial labor before the final draft went before Congress. Hillman, representing organized labor in the garment industry, and Lewis, representing organized labor in the coal industry, supported business proposals for the suspension of the antitrust laws and argued that industrial codes also protected labor in that they offered "high-wage businessmen badly needed protection from operators who connived to under-sell them by exploiting their workers."[25] The AFL viewed the NIRA as a big step forward in industrial economic planning, rationalization, and stabilization. The position of the capitalist class on the NIRA was made equally clear. Hugh Johnson, soon to be head of the National Recovery Administration, spoke with leading industrial capitalists who had come to Washington during the weeks of the final drafting of the NIRA; they discussed all phases of the recovery measure, including section 7a, which presumably allowed industrial labor to organize. In general, industrial capitalists, especially those associated with the NAM, were suspicious of section 7a. However, the wording of the stipulation in regard to union recognition was left rather ambiguous, and capitalists were assured by Johnson that section 7a would not threaten the continuation of the open shop. On the whole, all fractions of capital were willing to accept section 7a in exchange for the passage of the entire bill—especially those aspects which imposed price controls.[26]

When the final draft of the NIRA was presented to Congress on 17 May, the proposal appeared to have something for both capitalists and organized labor. Large-scale capitalists received governmental authorization to draft code agreements that would be exempt from antitrust laws, and small-scale capitalists received governmental licensing of business practices. Organized labor received section 7a, which presumably guaranteed the right to organize and bargain collectively and stipulated that the industrial codes of fair competition should set minimum wages and maximum hours. Roosevelt recommended immediate action on the proposed recovery legislation and said that Congress should provide the necessary machinery for "a great cooperative movement throughout all industry in order to obtain wide reemployment, to shorten the working week, to pay decent wages for the shorter week and to prevent unfair competition and disastrous overproduction."[27]

Legislating the National Industrial Recovery Act

Nonmonopoly capital made a concerted effort to influence the formulation of the National Industrial Recovery Act through business associations such as the Chamber of Commerce and the National Association of Manufacturers. Monopoly capital, however, was represented through individuals and state administrators whose policy proposals clearly reflected the particular interests of monopoly capital. Although both monopoly and nonmonopoly capital endorsed the National Industrial Recovery Act prior to its introduction to Congress, the endorsement was not without reservations. Systematically, all fractions of the capitalist class opposed section 7a. However, since the labor provisions were worded ambiguously, capitalists did not oppose the entire recovery measure on the basis of their dissatisfaction with section 7a. The inclusion of section 7a was the result of the administration's desire to sidetrack the Black Thirty Hour bill, which was before Congress at the same time that the NIRA was proposed as the administration's key recovery plan. Black's bill had been stimulated both by the unemployed struggles of the early depression years and by the 1932 call from the AFL convention in Cincinnati for a five-day workweek and a six-hour workday. Moreover, the Black bill incorporated the popular notion that an increase in purchasing power was a key to economic recovery.

Section 7a had never been discussed in early recovery plans proposed by the Roosevelt administration or by individuals representing capital or labor. Its inclusion reflected the influence of demands by employed and unemployed labor (and potential labor struggles) among those state administrators who eventually were responsible for passing the NIRA (e.g., Senator Wagner). The proposals of the upper echelons of the state personnel (Roosevelt's advisors) reflected the changing balance of forces within the capitalist class. These proposals recognized that the nature of the accumulation process had changed since the turn of the century. Firms had grown in size and scale, markets had become national in scope, and the alteration in the industrial sector was not self-regulating. In this changing economic climate and coupled with severe economic depression, state activity would have to be altered in order to aid in providing conditions for profitable capital accumulation. However, these proposals could only successfully be implemented if nonmonopoly capital supported such measures. The debate over the NIRA that took place in the Senate manifests more clearly the conflicts between the interests of monopoly and nonmonopoly class fractions.

Capitalist hesitation regarding full-fledged support of the NIRA did take place prior to congressional discussion of the recovery measure. Capitalists of all persuasions were united in maintaining their class position of domination. All feared trade unions as potential usurpers of power, whether at the level of the shop floor or the level of the state. Small-scale capitalists, in both monopolized and more competitive branches of industry, feared that the NIRA, if implemented, would favor monopoly capital over nonmonopoly capital. This fear arose from the logic that a weakening of antitrust revisions would provide a more favorable climate for monopoly growth, and large-scale firms would be financially able to bargain with unions, whereas small-scale firms would constantly have to lower the cost of labor in order to remain competitive in the marketplace. Nonmonopoly capital feared that collective-bargaining arrangements would lead to bankruptcy.

Most of the opposition to the NIRA came from antitrusters and small-scale capitalists who stressed the evils of monopoly and who were reluctant to admit the dominance of monopoly capital within the accumulation process. A great deal of congressional debate centered around the efforts of administration spokespersons to convince such opponents that the measure would strengthen the competitive system rather than destroy it. For example, Wagner argued that the proposed bill, by providing a method of rationalizing small business, would remove the incentive for further mergers and consolidations and that the real intention of the measure was not to abolish competition but to "purify and strengthen it," albeit on a new level.[28]

The proposed recovery measure attracted some debate over both section 7a and the implications of the measure for monopoly growth, although the House passed the bill with few changes after a bit more than a week of hearings. However, a significant amendment was included in the House bill at the insistence of William Green, speaking on behalf of the AFL. Green's amendment essentially strengthened section 7a by modifying the language of the clause, which made explicit the protection of workers from coercion by antiunion employers, and through other changes in phraseology that specifically exempted workers from having to join a company union as a condition of employment. The adoption of the amendments by the House was a signal to organized labor that the state administration was committed to give "labor a fair share," and Green stated that if the necessary amendments were made, he could guarantee that the full support of labor would be placed behind the NIRA.[29] Persons who opposed the NIRA on the grounds that the act would hasten monopoly growth were easily ignored in the overwhelmingly Democratic House. Democratic leaders supported the bill, and of the 311 House Democrats, 131 were newly elected from traditionally Republican districts and followed the Democratic leadership in voting.[30] On 26 May the House passed the measure by the overwhelming vote of 325 to 76.[31]

The NIRA ran into greater difficulties in the Senate, where there were efforts to eliminate the licensing provisions, to strip section 7a from having any far-reaching protection for workers, and to add a manufacturers' sales tax. All of these efforts were defeated, although amendments were adopted by the Senate to limit the duration of licensing powers to one year, to authorize the establishment of import controls, and to revamp the new taxes that were to help finance the public-works program.[32] Nonmonopoly capital's fear of growing monopolization was manifested in amendments proposed by Senator William E. Borah which would provide that no code should permit combinations in restraint of trade, price fixing, or other monopolistic practices. After much opposition from monopoly capital to the amendment, the Senate removed the prohibition on price fixing but kept the prohibition on "monopolies" or "monopolistic practices."

Letters from both nonmonopoly and monopoly capital were sent to the Senate Finance Committee during the Senate hearings on the NIRA. Nonmonopoly capital expressed concern that a weakening of the antitrust laws would promote monopoly growth. Both monopoly and nonmonopoly capital were concerned with the implication of 7a for union recognition and union organization. Telegrams came into the Senate Finance Committee expressing opposition to Borah's amendment, and some letters suggested that if Borah's amendment were passed, the NIRA would become nothing more than a labor measure. Monopoly capital indicated a desire to be exempt from the antitrust laws and argued that price and production controls were necessary for economic recovery. However, there were also letters and telegrams from small- and medium-scale capitalists which stressed that the measure was anti-small-business and promonopoly, because small manufacturers could not command the same price as large manufacturers. For example, a group of small rubber manufacturers wrote: "We have examples of the giant tire companies already showing their attitude on formation of code by employing a corporation lawyer who is chief counsel for one of the giant tire companies to write the code and then become policeman to enforce same. . . . We beg of you to use all of your influence to defeat the bill in its entirety. Otherwise it will be the end of independent manufacturers."[33] Despite protests such as this from nonmonopoly capital, the NIRA passed and provided for codes of fair competition and weakened antitrust laws.

The capitalist class's position on section 7a was much more unified than was its position on the issue of monopoly. Small-scale businessmen sent letters to the Senate Finance Committee suggesting that section 7a be dropped from the industrial-recovery bill. Small-scale capitalists argued that the labor provisions should be amended "to put a proper restraint on labor unions so as to guard against their taking action detrimental and unfair to manufacturers." Other small- and medium-scale capitalists objected to the labor provisions of the NIRA on the basis that it was impossible to operate a plant with fourteen or fifteen separate unionized crafts and that many individual firms would be forced to close. Other capitalists agreed that "section 7a is un-American and is a serious menace to progress of our industry." Some even went so far as to argue that "non-union employees have fared better at all times than union employees of competitors and we feel it is in their interest, as well as the company's that they should remain non-union." Campbell Soup Company argued that section 7a should be eliminated altogether: "It is therefore our contention that section 7a providing for the so-called 'collective bargaining and organization' conceded power to and will result in benefits only for organized labor leaders. We feel that this measure will be nothing better than a burden to industry and the consumer public in their struggles to regain prosperity and will result in no real benefits to the means of employees." Local Chambers of Commerce suggested either that section 7a be eliminated entirely or that it be revised in such forms as "to have as its basis a rule giving equal freedom to both employers and employees in establishing or continuing their employment relations." Industrial financiers suggested that section 7a be deleted from the proposed piece of legislation.[34]

The NAM took the lead among capitalist organizations in opposing section 7a. James Emery, representing the NAM in testimony before the Senate Finance Committee, objected that as drafted, the recovery measure left it to the discretion of the administrator of the National Recovery Administration (NRA) to transform the entire measure into exclusively federal control of employment relations. Emery maintained that at least three times as many employers operated under employee-representation plans (company unions) as dealt with a trade union. Thus it would be unwise to adopt a program that created the impression of seeming to "disrupt a satisfactory existing relation" at a time when it was most important that "good will and understanding" should prevail in employment relations. Emery also argued that the wording of the act implied that labor was granted certain rights under the NIRA but that employers' rights were not equally defined.[35] The objections of the NAM and other capitalists who testified at the Senate hearings to section 7a were not strong enough to suggest that the entire bill would be defeated if 7a remained within the recovery measure. However, it was quite clear that any attempt at the enforcement of section 7a would entail bitter struggle.

Capitalists' objections to section 7a centered on the strong desire for maintenance of the open shop. What capitalists feared most was the implementation of government-mandated trade unions. Capitalists feared that the "happy relationship which has existed between employer and employee in this country the past 10 years" would be endangered by any wording in the labor provisions that would imply an end to the open shop.[36] However, in spite of the attack on section 7a made by representatives of the capitalist class, specifically those representing mass-production heavy industry, section 7a remained intact as amended in the House hearings. It would appear that at a bare minimum, the labor provisions of the NIRA protected workers from coercion to join company unions, and it gave them the right to establish and join independent trade unions of their choosing.

The capitalists' opposition to section 7a in congressional hearings was not convincing enough to persuade an overwhelmingly urban liberal Democratic Congress. As Kenneth Finegold and Theda Skocpol have correctly pointed out, congressional Democrats were eager to consolidate their electoral majorities by supporting and enacting prolabor legislation. With the urban industrial working class becoming a major electoral bloc for urban Democrats, it is not surprising that pressures from industrial workers, both employed and unemployed, played a major role not only in moving congressional Democrats to favor prolabor legislation but also in moving the Democratic party itself left of center in the political arena.[37]

The Senate passed the NIRA, and Roosevelt signed the measure making the National Industrial Recovery Act law on 16 June 1933. The NIRA, as debated and finally passed, contained three titles—two of which dealt with public-works projects and the taxes that would finance them. Our immediate concern here is with title 1, which was concerned with the organization of industry. Under title 1, a national emergency was declared, which justified a partial suspension of the antitrust laws for a period of two years. The general purposes of the act, as stated in the first section, were the promotion of cooperative action among trade groups, the elimination of unfair competitive practices, the expansion of production, the expansion of consumption by increasing purchasing power, the reduction in unemployment, and the conservation of national resources. Subsequent sections of title 1 established rules for the formulation of industrial codes to implement the general purposes stated in section 1. The executive branch had the authority to accept codes for fair competition from trade or industrial associations or groups and to impose a code if no agreement could be reached within any given branch of industry. The executive branch also had the responsibility of ensuring that the codes were not designed to promote monopoly. Section 7a, which applied to industrial labor, stated that employees had the right to organize and bargain collectively through representatives of their own choosing and that employers were required to comply with the provisions for maximum hours of labor, minimum rates of pay, and other working conditions approved by the executive branch. Title 1 of the NIRA limited its application for a period of two years and designated the executive branch to create appropriate administrative agencies for the implementation of the provisions of title 1.[38]

The final version of the NIRA as passed by Congress and signed by Roosevelt was ambiguously worded; it allowed different groups, fractions of capital, and organized labor to read what they wanted to into the recovery measure. Labor thought it had received the signal for mass organizing and collective bargaining with governmental protection. Capitalists generally thought they had received much-desired price and production controls. Monopoly capital received a lifting of the antitrust laws. Smaller and more competitive capitalists thought they had received protection from monopolies and that they could now save themselves from the more disastrous consequences of monopoly growth. One interesting question regarding the NIRA is why, after such capitalist opposition to section 7a in the Senate hearings, section 7a was left intact as it passed the House. Organized labor did not present an overt threat to the "satisfactory" relationship between labor and capital prior to the proposal of the NIRA. However, once the labor provisions were amended in the House, it would be difficult for the Senate to dismiss what labor had already been granted. State administrators feared that the Black bill would be revived if the NIRA did not include section 7a, and they believed that capitalists would accept the act even with that section included. The opposition to section 7a in the Senate never really gave the impression that capitalists would oppose the entire act on the basis of section 7a. On the part of Roosevelt's staff there appeared to be a growing awareness of the increasing presence of the Communist Left among the working class (i.e., among the unemployed as well as employed). Concessions made to the anti-Communist AFL would be seen as one way of co-opting the impending class struggle (by strengthening the AFL and undermining the Communists) and of preventing a direct challenge of capitalist social relations of production and also, perhaps, capitalist rule at the level of the state itself.[39] Moreover, the mere inclusion of section 7a in the final version of the NIRA did not necessarily imply that the interpretation and implementation of section 7a would be uniform within various branches of industry.

Hawley has convincingly shown that the NIRA was a contradiction in terms. One clause of the NIRA exempted the proposed codes from the antitrust laws, and another clause provided that no code should be so applied to "permit monopolies or monopolistic practices, or to eliminate, oppress, or discriminate against small enterprise."[40] The contradictions within the NIRA and the ambiguity over section 7a were glossed over in the congressional debates and were passed on to the executive branch through the establishment of the National Recovery Administration to supervise the preparation of codes of fair competition and to enforce their observance. During the two years the NIRA was in operation, capitalists debated among themselves about the content of trade-practice provisions, their contribution to collusive agreements, their effects on small and more competitive firms, and the extent to which they promoted the growth of monopoly. Both capitalists and leaders of organized labor also debated the interpretation of section 7a. The interpretation of section 7a was eventually determined through the class struggle between industrial wage labor and capital. The debate between capitalists over the "monopoly" issue was temporarily resolved by the determination that the act was unconstitutional.

The National Recovery Administration and the Codes of Fair Competition

The National Recovery Administration (NRA) was the state agency created to supervise the preparation of codes of fair competition and to enforce their observance. Codes supposedly were to be drafted with the participation of capitalists, workers, and "consumers." The Industrial Advisory Board, composed of business leaders who rotated in office and served in Washington for limited periods, advised on all matters of industrial policy. The Consumers' Advisory Board was established to represent the interest and viewpoints of consumers and to advise on how provisions of codes affected prices to consumers and standards of quality. The Labor Advisory Board, made up of organized labor leaders and a few individuals who were supposedly sympathetic with the needs of organized labor, advised on labor questions—especially hours, wages, and working conditions.[41] The NRA, modeled in many ways after the War Industries Board during World War I, was essentially designed to aid in the rationalization and coordination of industrial production.

The NRA supervised the preparation of codes of fair competition by transferring to each branch of industry the responsibility of bringing about general prosperity via self-consolidation. Hawley has convincingly shown that the former trade-association regulations, which could not be applied in the 1920s, now became the NRA codes.[42] The major firms (monopoly capital) within each branch of industry were able to define the codes that were to emerge—much to the disadvantage of smaller nonmonopoly firms. Each branch of industry was allowed to define its own price and production controls with few if any restrictions. Every branch of industry did this in accordance with the distribution of the political power that was possessed by each fraction of capital within its branch.[43] To some extent, monopoly capital was strengthened at the expense of nonmonopoly capital, but this only speeded up a process that was going on quite apart from NRA codes.[44] The NRA was dominated by monopoly capital; it was made impermeable to all but monopoly interests. Hawley argues that the NRA codes were "designed by specific economic groups to balance [their] production with consumption [of their products] regardless of the dislocations produced elsewhere in the economy."[45]

The codes were supposed to be drafted with the participation of both labor and capital. Nevertheless, the labor provisions in the codes appeared to be designed to give concessions to labor only insofar as such concessions provided mechanisms that would help to control labor and minimize strikes. These mechanisms were manifested in the mediation functions of the Labor Advisory Board and in the labor provisions of the various industrial codes. However, the mediation mechanisms proved to be ineffectual. The NRA unsuccessfully sought peaceful settlements for tensions between capital and labor which were compatible with the further development of capitalism in the United States.[46] The various boards and committees that were established under the NRA provided mechanical means to reduce the area of potential conflict for "mitigating the violence of disputes which do break out from time to time."[47] Organized labor was formally recognized under the NRA codes in the attempt to incorporate organized labor into a system of monopoly capitalism and to institutionalize labor's subordination to capital within the political bargaining process.[48]

Initially, business leaders expressed the desire to suspend the antitrust laws and to institute codes of fair competition which would provide production and price controls. The regulation of price and production was thought to be a safeguard for small- and medium-scale capitalists against the increased concentration and centralization of capital and to provide protection for their individual competitiveness in the market. Nonmonopoly capital looked to the state administration for temporary protection against being driven out of the market and forcibly being "bought out" by the larger monopoly firms. However, the actual code-drafting process did not coincide with the desires of smaller capitalists. The codes were supposed to include price and production controls that would enable small- and medium-scale capitalists to remain competitive in the market, but the actual codes for numerous branches of industry entailed price and production quotas that were unprofitable for nonmonopoly capital. Moreover, the high price controls in some codes reflected the price that consumers paid, not the cost of production. Higher prices for commodities were rationalized as a method of maintaining higher cost of production for small businessmen.[49]

Labor representation on the code authorities was minimal. Wage and hour provisions were plagued with loopholes and exceptions. The mandatory labor provisions provided by section 7a of the NIRA were rarely included in the code provisions, and many codes were the result of debate between capitalists and state officials who represented capital although under the veneer of being "social servants." The proper interpretation of section 7a was debated throughout the code-making process and, indeed, throughout the life of the NIRA itself. NRA administrators saw their job to be the impartial enforcement of section 7a. The NRA maintained that it was not within its purpose to organize either labor or management and that while it recognized the right of labor to bargain collectively, it would not deprive them of the right to bargain individually—it would not oppose company unionism. The NRA itself did not provide the machinery to implement section 7a. In response to the wave of strikes in late 1933 it developed the National Labor Board, which was supposed to enforce section 7a and to settle labor disputes. However, the exact nature of the authority of the National Labor Board was never made explicit; this left the board ineffectual both in aiding labor through the implementation of section 7a and in settling labor disputes.[50] Hugh Johnson, the administrator of the NRA, argued: "I do not believe that there is any constitutional guarantee of freedom to exploit labor anymore than there is a constitutional guarantee to run a newspaper in a fire trap."[51] There was little evidence of a marked support for labor, in particular organized industrial labor, in the administration and implementation of the codes of fair competition.

Six months after the official enactment of the NIRA, many groups began publicly to criticize the NRA codes. Women complained about higher prices, large-scale capitalists complained about regulation, small- and medium-scale capitalists complained about monopoly growth, and organized labor complained about the inadequacy of section 7a.[52] Both the Chamber of Commerce and the NAM attacked the NRA for serving as an instrument of large corporations.[53] Although the leadership of these two prominent organizations of capitalists had supported the NRA prior to its implementation, local groups clearly deviated from the position of their leadership. Most small- and medium-sized capitalists were quite aware of the major role that the larger firms played within each branch of industry in the drafting of the various codes. Even Roosevelt was aware of the leadership of monopoly capital when he wrote Hugh Johnson in July 1933: "How about getting a list of the big companies who will sign up the voluntary agreements and release it for Wednesday morning papers and follow each day with a number of big companies? I think the little fellows will follow the leaders."[54]

Union representatives argued that the NRA was producing more company unions and that it was stimulating monopolistic price fixing because large corporations were dominating the code authorities and were using their power to stifle competition and to cut back production. Organized labor further attacked the NRA for its failure to make union recognition a major part of its program. This attack came after a policy declaration by the NRA, which refused to agree that a union which had majority support had the right to bargain for all workers in a particular plant. The NRA supported the principle by which the rights of representation would be given to a majority of workers, including those in company unions.[55]

By the fall of 1933, policy debates had developed within the NRA boards over two main issues: (1) that the codes and implementation of the NIRA were stifling competition, fixing prices and production levels, and actually retarding recovery and (2) that the implementation of the NIRA and the policy of the NRA were causing structural changes in the direction of monopoly, giving the more "powerful" firms of certain branches of industry the opportunity to crush smaller firms.[56] The accusations of monopoly growth were only partially valid for those highly competitive sectors of industry in which monopoly capital had no large share of the market. The NIRA and NRA policies were constructed to appeal to a variety of conflicting groups in an effort to organize the capitalist class at the same time that minimal concessions were being made to significant portions of the working class. Monopoly capital and portions of nonmonopoly capital initially perceived the recovery measure as a way of rationalizing economic activity, reducing competition, and ensuring profits. Economic planners, specifically Roosevelt's economic advisors, initially perceived the recovery measure as a way of reorganizing economic institutions so as to create a mass consumption market, which they thought was essential for economic recovery. Nonmonopoly capital—small-scale capitalists and agents of the petite bourgeoisie—initially perceived the recovery measure as a way of strengthening the competitive system and helping small enterprise through the formulation of rules to keep competition from evolving into monopoly. Finally, leaders of organized labor initially perceived the NIRA as a means of strengthening the trade-union movement and eliminating sweatshops.[57]

The implementation of the NIRA and NRA policy directives had consequences that were not anticipated either by fractions of the capitalist class or by organized-labor leaders. Ironically, contrary to its design, the NIRA and the NRA's implementation of the act actually worked to disorganize the capitalist class and to organize the working class. The issue of monopoly growth and national planning intensified the conflicts within the capitalist class, and the debate over the interpretation of section 7a tended to heighten the struggle between wage labor and capital. Paul Conkin has suggested:

> As codes were scrutinized, as the NRA was endlessly and critically investigated, more and more business men became disillusioned with the NRA.

> After an ailing NRA was declared unconstitutional in 1935, many business men gladly went back to clandestine collusion, happy to be rid of legal cooperation under the glare of unfavorable publicity and with an ever present threat of unhelpful government interference.[58]

The NRA codes and the consequences of the implementation of the NIRA were being debated within Congress and within the NRA itself at the same time that alternative recovery measures and a heightened class struggle between wage labor and capital were emerging outside of the legislative process. The Chamber of Commerce and the NAM created special committees to study the implications of the NIRA; within a year after the official enactment of the NIRA, they proposed a new form of recovery measure. The NAM argued against the centralization of the state apparatus and against the governmental regulation of all business activity. The NAM also argued that the federal government should not exercise its authority over the local relationship between workers and capitalists. It believed that it was justifiable for the government to control the conditions of labor and the relationship between employers and employees for firms involved in interstate commerce (i.e., the larger, more monopolized firms), but the government should not interfere with the relationship between employer and employees of small firms involved in intrastate trade. For the NAM, intrastate trade was a local matter, outside of the purview of federal regulation. The NAM was also quite forceful in objecting to labor unions and argued that any recovery measure should "protect men in their right to work." Consequently, the NAM was adamant in its opposition to any form of federal unemployment insurance or social security.[59] A Chamber of Commerce committee, established to review the implications of the NIRA, issued a special report which suggested that the law should not be reenacted or extended but that some new form of legislation should be established which would uphold the principles of the NIRA—namely, provide some safeguard to nonmonopoly capital. The Chamber of Commerce agreed with the NAM's position that any new form of codes of fair competition and regulation of economic activity should be limited to those engaged in or affecting competition in interstate commerce. The Chamber of Commerce also argued that any new recovery measure should revise the labor clause so as not to imply that company unions were illegal or to threaten the open shop.[60]

The disenchantment with the NIRA from the members of both the NAM and the Chamber of Commerce deviated somewhat from the leadership of the respective organizations. President Lund of the NAM was always explicit about his concern with the possibility of labor difficulties for nonmonopoly capital. Lund argued as early as November 1933 that it was "unnecessary and extremely unfortunate that the labor clause was written into the Recovery Act." He further argued that "there is nothing sadder or more pathetic than the plight of these small business men, which have given their unstinted cooperation to the Recovery program and yet are being destroyed by it." In spite of these seemingly devastating critiques, Lund wholeheartedly favored supporting the NIRA.[61] More striking than Lund's position with respect to rank-and-file members of the NAM was the position of Harriman, president of the Chamber of Commerce, with respect to the local Chambers. Harriman assured Roosevelt in September 1934, after the Chamber of Commerce had recommended that the NIRA not be extended or reenacted, that the criticisms of the Chamber of Commerce were in fact constructive and that it still very much supported the principles of the NIRA. However, he stressed the need to amend the labor provisions and to ensure that the new recovery measure should not apply to firms involved in intrastate commerce. Harriman further assured Roosevelt that he "recognized the great value of cooperation between government and business, and cooperation between labor and business, in the settlement of our industrial problems."[62] Thus, the leadership of both the NAM and the Chamber of Commerce argued that state regulation was fine to a point but that it would not be allowed either to alter the position of labor vis-à-vis capital or to favor monopoly capital over nonmonopoly capital.

There were as many differences of positions among the leadership of organized labor and other spokespersons of the working class as there were among business leaders. Leaders of organized labor strongly supported the NIRA at its inception and became disenchanted with the recovery measure only after it had become clear that section 7a was not being implemented as anticipated. Representatives of the rank-and-file working class and leftist political organs of the working class expressed their dissatisfaction with the recovery measure in quite another form. In contradistinction to the position of organized-labor leaders, leftist political groups with a working-class base had from the very first perceived the NIRA as a tool of the capitalist class. Organized-labor leaders sought to carry out the class struggle on the economic level (i.e., to gain better conditions of work for portions of the working class within the existing capitalist order), while leftist political groups sought to carry on the class struggle at the political level (i.e., by calling into question the nature of exploitation and the rule of the capitalist class).

The Communist party criticized the NIRA for speeding up the process of concentration and centralization of capital and, hence, strengthening monopoly capitalism and intensifying the contradictions of capitalist development within the United States. The Communist party also criticized the labor provisions of the NIRA, calling the NIRA a "large-scale effort at indirect militarization of labor. . . . In industries the effort is to establish a semi-military regime under government fixed wages, compulsory arbitration of all disputes with the government as arbiter, abolition of the right to strike and of independent organizations of workers." The Communist party argued that the labor section of the NIRA was the clearest tendency toward American fascism and was, for the working class, an industrial slavery act. In April 1934 the Communist party was still firm in its opposition, stating that the aim of the NIRA was to "bridge over the most difficult situation for the capitalists, and to launch a new attack upon workers with the help of their leaders, to keep the workers from general resistance, to begin to restore the profits of finance capital."[63]

Criticism of the NIRA took a different form within the Trotskyist Left. Trotskyist groups joined together in late 1933 to form the American Workers party (AWP), a revolutionary political party that perceived the recovery measures of the Roosevelt administration as inadequate with respect to the conditions of the working class. The American Workers party proposed to devote special attention to the conditions of black people as well as the politicization of technicians. The AWP maintained that racial prejudice had artificially created a division within the working class and that black workers and white workers should unite to overthrow the common enemy of capitalism. The AWP focused on the organization of technicians who could be utilized to plan and establish a new order in which the "masses" could achieve "abundance and leisure if they will."[64]

Although the Communist and Socialist Left expressed opposition to the NIRA and the trajectory of capitalist recovery plans, this opposition had little significance in terms of altering the position of legislators on state policy. It did, however, have an indirect impact since these leftist political groups were engaged in organizing campaigns among the working class and as such were furnishing additional fuel to working-class discontent with the implementation of the NIRA. However, the position of the political Left was not always publicly revealed throughout the remaining years of the depression. In particular, the Communist party changed its line after 1935 and supported the policies of the Roosevelt administration. In many ways, after the demise of the NIRA, the Communist party was put in a defensive position, reacting to policies instead of formulating an alternative to the New Deal program. As such, Communist and Socialist opposition to the New Deal program was lukewarm at best.

The Demise of the NIRA

The entire concept of capitalist planning to overcome the economic crisis and to stimulate economic recovery was under attack from almost all groups representing capitalists, workers, and consumers. One deviation from this general tendency was a group called the Continental Committee on Technocracy. Its members circulated petitions in early 1934 for "Technocracy" as a practical planned economy to solve the economic problems facing the American people and essentially called for a planned system of production and distribution, while maintaining the character and nature of capitalist social relations of production and capitalist development in general.[65] The National Resources Planning Board also advocated, and continued to advocate even after the expiration of the NIRA, the need for some form of national economic planning.[66]

One year after the implementation of the NIRA, capitalists became very much divided over the monopoly issue but very much unified over the fact that the labor provisions were much too "liberal" and that labor-union leaders were "taking advantage" of influential governmental officials to the detriment of individual capitalists. It is clear that the labor provisions of the NIRA rejuvenated labor militancy; there were more strikes and a greater rise in labor militancy during the first year after the enactment of the NIRA than during any previous year. Complaints that the NRA codes were reenforcing the growth of monopolies increased the longer the NIRA remained in force. Moreover, small-scale capitalists argued that the depression was continuing despite the NRA's efforts to increase production and reduce unemployment. Even Berle conceded, as early as July 1934, that the code authorities were largely composed of and dominated by the major firms within each branch of industry because the principal directive was toward employers of labor and because such firms frequently employed more labor than all of the smaller firms put together. Berle also conceded that the larger firms within each industry apparently were using the information collected by the code authorities in an effort to eliminate their smaller competitors.[67]

The massive amount of complaints by small-scale nonmonopoly capital about the growth of monopoly as a result of the manner of implementing the NRA codes of fair competition forced the administration to establish a review board to investigate the matter less than a year after the establishment of the NRA. There were conflicting reports about the extent to which the NRA codes had fostered monopoly growth. Conflicts within the Review Board reinforced nonmonopoly capital's attack on the NRA as an "instrument" of monopoly. In May 1934, two members of the Review Board stated that the tendency of the NRA codes was toward monopoly and the elimination of the owners of small businesses. These two members of the Recovery Review Board, who subsequently resigned, further charged the state administration with concealing the true facts of monopoly growth from the "public."[68]

In January 1935 state administrators began to discuss the desirability of extending the NIRA and retaining the NRA as a state agency. At the same time, the NRA itself was torn by conflict. Small-scale capitalists continued to express their disillusionment with the NIRA through their representatives within the state administration.[69] In spite of the conflicts expressed during the price hearings of the NRA, Roosevelt recommended in February that Congress extend the NIRA and the NRA in a modified form for another two years. The modifications were to include an extension of the labor provisions and were to restrict price and production controls to those that were needed in order to protect small-scale capitalists, check monopolistic practices, prevent destructive competition, and conserve national resources.

Roosevelt's recommendations were debated at length in the Senate, where there was strong sentiment not to reenact the recovery measure in any form. The

Senate amended Roosevelt's proposal significantly by exempting businesses involved in intrastate commerce, barring all price fixing except for the mineral-resources industry, and extending the NIRA only until April 1936. Debate in the House contradicted the sentiments of the Senate. It appeared in May that there was a growing likelihood of a deadlock between the House and the Senate which could block any action at all. Compromises were suggested, but the dilemma over what to do with the NIRA and the NRA was eventually resolved, not within the executive or the legislative branch, but within the judiciary branch of the state apparatus. On 27 May 1935, in a unanimous decision, the Supreme Court ruled that the entire system of the NRA codes of fair competition, with all their appendages, was unconstitutional.[70] The combined opposition of both capitalists and workers eventuated in the Roosevelt administration's acceptance of the death of the NIRA. No attempt was made to revive it.

The case that eventually caused the end of the NIRA began in June 1934, when a member of the Justice Department investigated a Brooklyn poultry corporation for alleged violations of the live-poultry code. The Schecter Poultry Corporation, composed of four brothers, was found guilty in district court in October on nineteen counts, which included the disregarding of wage-and-hour regulations, the filing of false reports, and the selling of unfit and uninspected poultry. The Schecter brothers appealed, and the administration decided to make the case a test case for the constitutionality of the NRA codes. The case was brought before the Supreme Court, at which time the Schecter brothers based their argument on three points: (1) the code system amounted to an unconstitutional delegation of legislative power, (2) their business was outside the scope of the commerce power, and (3) they were being deprived of liberty and property without due process of law. The Court decided in favor of the Schecter brothers, ruling that the code authorities thus conferred were an unconstitutional delegation of legislative powers.[71] This ended, at least temporarily, the debate over, and the lives of, the National Recovery Administration and the National Industrial Recovery Act.

Contradictions of State Policy

The National Industrial Recovery Act was the main focus of the Roosevelt administration's initial response to the economic crisis. The formulation of the NIRA was the culmination of a strategy to bolster capital accumulation and to unify and organize the capitalist class in a time of severe economic crisis. The capitalist class was divided over the best avenue for economic recovery. The Roosevelt administration attempted to unify the capitalist class by appealing to the proposals of nonmonopoly capital while instituting policies that actually served to strengthen monopoly growth through a new accumulation strategy. The NIRA, as first conceptualized, was acceptable to monopoly and nonmonopoly capital.

All fractions of capital sought some form of economic stabilization and rationalization during the early years of the crisis, although no agreement was reached on a specific policy. The suspension of the antitrust laws that was incorporated into the codes of fair competition was supported by the leadership of nonmonopoly capital through such organizational forms as the Chamber of Commerce and the National Association of Manufacturers. Clearly, monopoly-capital interests were represented with the suspension of antitrust laws since now the concentration and centralization of capital could be accomplished without legal sanctions. Business organizations that represented nonmonopoly capital perceived the suspension as a means to control production in order that smaller firms might not suffer with the narrowing of the competitive market.

The labor provisions of the NIRA were not part of earlier recovery measures proposed to the executive branch. Both state administrators and capitalists recognized the need to increase purchasing power among workers because it was believed that underconsumption had been a major cause of the depression. Robert Lund of the NAM summed up this position quite clearly in March 1933:

> The long continued shortage of consumption following an unprecedented expansion of productive and distributive capacity disrupted the orderly functioning of our competitive processes. Competition of overexpanded producers to obtain some share of the shrunken demand has resulted in a panic of distressed selling. Each producer, forced by the pressure of his needs, has, in many major industries, been disposing of goods without regard to real cost and thus spiralling downwards toward progressively lower levels. This has led to under-wages and diminished purchasing power and threatens to become worse.[72]

The desire for an increase in mass purchasing power, however, did not entail granting industrial labor the right to organize and bargain collectively. This aspect of the labor provision was incorporated primarily in order to sidetrack the Black Thirty Hour bill which was supported by organized labor and prolabor legislators but was opposed by the administration. Hence, section 7a of the NIRA was a concession made to the leaders of organized labor and those in the administration who favored prolabor legislation. Moreover, this concession was made only after the support of organized labor for the Black Thirty Hour bill had been made clear. Once Black's bill had passed the House, a satisfactory substitute that gave something to organized labor was on the agenda in order to prevent any class unified action on the part of the industrial working class.[73]

The formulation of the NIRA reveals the process by which the state administration attempted to overcome obstacles to capital accumulation and simultaneously respond to class conflict and class contradictions. However, the state apparatus is not outside of basic class contradictions, and state policy mirrors the larger antagonisms and contradictions of class society. The NIRA, in its legislation and implementation, reflected the basic conflicts within the industrial capitalist class. Ironically, the attempt of the state administration to overcome obstacles to accumulation by concentrating on a new accumulation strategy that would alleviate antitrust provisions, regulate production, and control prices actually served to disorganize the industrial capitalist class by making fractional conflicts more evident. These conflicts were primarily over perceptions of monopoly growth and regulated competition. The fact that large-scale corporate capital profited during the NRA period and that small-scale capital experienced losses is a key indication that the NIRA had little impact in altering the trajectory of profitable accumulation for large-scale corporate capital and of economic difficulties for smaller-sized firms.[74] The NRA was a highly centralized state agency that corresponded more closely to the desired ends of monopoly capital than to the rules of nonmonopoly capital. It is not unexpected that the code authorities, whose strategy it was to revive profitable accumulation, would further the interests of monopoly capital during a time when monopoly capital was dominant within the process of accumulation, particularly with respect to the industrial sector. Nevertheless, the state does not simply mirror the dominant fractional interest of capital. Nonmonopoly capital's persistent opposition to the NIRA made it rather easy to dismiss the entire code system once the Supreme Court had ruled the codes unconstitutional. Monopoly capital, while clearly enjoying economic dominance, had yet to secure political hegemony by the mid 1930s. Yet the political and economic power of monopoly capital did not wane with the code authorities.

The entire development of the NIRA involved a contradictory process in which no one within the state administration knew the policy objectives of other branches or agencies. Block's notion of the autonomy of state managers in designing economic policy that transcends narrow fractional interests oversimplifies the fact that class conflict provides limits to what state managers can actually accomplish. For example, even though Berle seemed to be quite aware of the economic and political climate and though his policy recommendations prior to the formation of the NIRA transcended narrow interests, his proposals were limited, not because of "business confidence," but because of the fractional conflicts of the capitalist class. The conflict that arose during the NIRA period clarified conflicting views of monopoly growth and exacerbated divisions within the capitalist class, although this did not occur according to a preconceived plan. Rather, the ad hoc fashion in which the NIRA evolved and was subsequently administered provides evidence for the perception of the capitalist state apparatus as a structure having its own internal contradictions that reflect contradictions and conflicts between classes. The fact that the NIRA ultimately protected and even encouraged monopoly growth does not necessarily imply that monopoly capital's interest was shared by state administrators. The uncoordinated efforts of the state administration in enforcing codes of fair competition simply reflected the expectation that the more powerful firms within the accumulation process would, more likely than not, also dominate the code authorities to the former's advantage. Skocpol's analysis of the administrative weakness of the NRA is quite instructive, yet it underestimates the degree of class conflict that was embedded within the agency itself. Skocpol misses a very crucial point when she argues that the capitalist class was highly organized by 1932.[75] Had this been the case, the administrative weakness of the code authorities might provide a useful explanation for the fate of the NIRA. But indeed, as acknowledged by Roosevelt's top advisors, the industrial capitalist class was highly disorganized in regard to providing a program for economic recovery. It appears that a better explanation for the fate of the NIRA and the NRA is that the fractional conflicts of industrial capital prevented any administrative cohesiveness.

Yet the argument about administrative weaknesses and state capacity to implement certain economic policies is not without merit. The experience of the NIRA and the NRA code authorities foreshadowed the trend for the executive branch of the state apparatus to organize and reorganize departments and decision-making centers that would eventually circumvent conflicting interests. In many ways, the experience of the NIRA reflected the growing urgency for the reorganization and centralization of decision-making groups in such a fashion so as to provide for the smooth implementation of coherent policy directives. The alterations inside the industrial sector which involved changes in relationships between firms as well as within firms required a more coordinated effort on the part of state activity. As firms became more national in scope and as the class struggle between wage labor and capital became national in scope, the state was called on to assure conditions both for profitable accumulation and for social peace and harmony. This greater state involvement in economic and social relationships proved to benefit monopoly capital. However, the implementation of policies that favored large-scale corporate capital over nonmonopoly capital was not accomplished in a conscious or preconceived manner; instead, it evolved as a response to the immediate conflicts and conjunctural conditions.

Although industrial capitalists were divided over the impact of the codes on monopoly growth, capitalists were unified in their opposition to the labor clause. Section 7a was a concession to organized-labor leaders and was stimulated by the Black bill. Section 7a, with its implication of guaranteeing the right of labor to organize and join unions of its own choosing, actually heightened class contradictions and served to intensify the class struggle between industrial wage labor and capital.

In essence, the NIRA was the state administration's attempt to offset economic decline, overcome obstacles to the accumulation process, and unify the capitalist class while simultaneously making concessions to organized-labor leaders to offset the potential of independent working-class political organization. Intracapitalist conflict intensified over the monopoly issue and temporarily halted major structural transformations within the administrative apparatus of the state in the late 1930s. The rejuvenation of labor militancy organized the industrial working class and necessitated alterations, with respect both to relations between organized industrial labor and the political bargaining process and to social relations within the firm. The case of the NIRA makes clear that the policy-making process is one of contradictions and that it reflects a changing or stabilizing balance of forces within economic-class relations. Because the state apparatus continued to reflect the balance of class forces throughout the decade of the 1930s, state policies provided the structural conditions by which struggles and conflicts were waged. The subsequent character of the class struggle, as determined by and reflected through state policies, reconstructed the objective limits for the uninterrupted accumulation of capital.

CHAPTER FIVE

The Monopoly Debate and Intracapitalist Conflict

> In an age of plenty, like the present stage of American industry, abundant production creates intense struggle for markets. . . . The NRA has given the sanction of government to self-governing combinations in the different industries. Inevitably this means control by the largest producers. Not only is there conflict between large and small business in the same industry, but similar conflicts arise as between different industries.
>
> —*Clarence Darrow and W. O. Thompson*

> Thus the NIRA clearly reflects its class character as an attempt of the capitalist to find "a way out of the crisis" by passing the burdens on to the shoulders of the masses of workers and farmers. The NRA reflects the inability of so-called "enlightened capitalism" to operate a "planned economy" to improve the living standards of the masses.
>
> —*W. O. Thompson*

The National Industrial Recovery Act was part of the state's attempt to formulate a new accumulation strategy.[1] On the one hand, the labor provisions of the NIRA were an attempt to short-circuit independent working-class political mobilization by channeling working-class discontent within limits compatible with profitable accumulation. On the other hand, the formulation of the various industrial codes was an attempt to organize an otherwise divided industrial capitalist class around an industrial policy that would ensure renewed accumulation. However, the NIRA succeeded neither in politically organizing the capitalist class nor in containing the struggles of the industrial working class. With respect to industrial capital, the NIRA, with its codes of fair competition and a suspension of the antitrust laws, led to the immediate benefit of large-scale corporate capital, while few benefits accrued to small- and medium-scale capital. By aiding monopoly capital and by not having the equivalent impact on nonmonopoly capital, the implementation of the NIRA served to intensify conflicts between monopoly and nonmonopoly capital on the political terrain.

Intracapitalist conflict developed over the "monopoly issue," and it took place in the halls of Congress. Theoretically speaking, although monopoly capital was clearly dominant within the accumulation process, it had yet to assume a dominance within the political sphere. The political alliance of capital was in disarray during the depression. In many ways, the attempt of the state administration to organize the capitalist class behind a new accumulation strategy required that monopoly capital assume a dominant position within the political alliance of capital. Prior to the economic crisis of the 1930s, both monopoly and nonmonopoly capital shared in political domination, although monopoly capital was gaining dominant status, as witnessed through the NIRA experience. However, the process of monopoly capital's assuming a dominant political position did not entail a simple seizure of state power by which the state and monopoly capital became one and the same. Rather, the new accumulation strategy that was proposed by the Roosevelt administration—a strategy that involved rationalizing industrial resources—favored large-scale capital. In many ways, the accumulation strategy of the Roosevelt administration, if it were to succeed, meant organizing large-scale capital into a dominant fraction of capital on the political terrain. The manner in which monopoly capital was organized into the dominant political fraction involved a process of intrastate conflict.[2] Supreme Court decisions in 1935, which ruled that the NIRA codes of fair competition were unconstitutional, and the investigation of monopoly growth by the Temporary National Economic Committee (TNEC) placed political checks on the rhythm of the process of concentration and centralization of capital. State policies that appear to favor nonmonopoly capital might indeed be a necessary component for the continual accumulation of monopoly capital. Such "political checks" may have a positive effect on the balance of class forces in that the growth and expansion of monopoly capital may not have as negative effects for nonmonopoly capital as they would have without such checks, and the balance of class forces continue to be reflected within the policy-making process.[3]

The National Industrial Recovery Act, the cornerstone of the New Deal program of economic recovery, was an attempt by the state administration to implement the most effective form of economic recovery. The NIRA, as first formulated, was welcomed by all fractions of the capitalist class as well as by leaders of organized labor. However, as the NIRA was implemented, nonmonopoly capital objected to the dominance of monopoly capital in the implementation process, while labor objected to the lack of implementation of the labor provisions. The TNEC investigations demonstrated that the growth of monopoly capital implied changes in the basic assumptions regarding the competitive nature of capitalist development in the United States.

The TNEC investigation, as well as the report of the National Recovery Review Board before it, bore evidence to the charges made by nonmonopoly capital with respect to the growth of monopoly capital. The findings of the Bureau of Internal Revenue revealed a higher degree of monopoly growth for 1935, the year the NIRA was declared unconstitutional. Of all corporations that reported to the bureau, 0.1 percent owned 52.0 percent of all assets. Moreover, 0.1 percent of all corporations earned 50.0 percent of their combined net income. Less than 4 percent of all manufacturing corporations that reported earned 84 percent of all net profits.[4] If the NIRA did not foster monopoly growth, it surely did not curtail the growth of monopoly capital. This documentation of monopoly growth caused members of the state administration to become quite aware of the need to regulate monopoly capital.[5] Members of the state administration sought to achieve a more unified relationship between the dominance of monopoly capital in the accumulation process and the general recovery program—including changes within the political arena.

Capital's Response to the NIRA

The NIRA initially appeared to provide benefits to all fractions of the industrial-capitalist class. Large-scale capitalists were granted a suspension of the antitrust laws, which provided the opportunity for expansion on an increased scale. Smaller-scale capitalists received price and production controls and supposedly some form of protection from unfair competitive practices of monopoly firms, which allowed them to be in a more "competitive" position within the industrial market. Capitalists were hesitant about the labor provisions of the NIRA at the time of its passage into law, but then they generally welcomed some form of state-initiated attempts at economic stabilization. However, the establishment of the NIRA and the actual implementation of the codes of fair competition left much to be desired from the frame of reference of capitalists, regardless of the size of the firm or the profitability of its enterprise. Nonmonopoly capital's disenchantment with the NIRA was centered on the accusation that the NRA and the manner of implementation of the NIRA fostered the growth of monopoly capital to the disadvantage of nonmonopoly capital. Although the implementation of the codes of fair competition was clearly in the immediate interest of monopoly capital, monopoly capitalists, "once they tasted the sweet immunity from the anti-trust acts, were irked by the growing tendency of the NRA to return to economic and legal orthodoxy, disallowing tactics that went beyond fair competition and were inimical to all competition."[6] When economic recovery for large-scale capital appeared to be under way, these same capitalists became more wary of governmental intervention.

Small-scale capitalists complained about monopoly growth during the entire period of the NIRA. These complaints began as early as six months after the official enactment of the law and continued throughout its existence. These complaints largely centered on the abuse of governmental sanctions for monopoly capital, the generalized growth of monopoly firms, and the decline of the small entrepreneur. During the final few months of the NIRA, complaints regarding the degree of monopoly growth and the degree to which the codes of fair competition placed burdens on small-scale capital were as forceful as ever. A letter from Congressman Henry C. Luckey to FDR in early 1935, stating the criticisms of the NIRA that were being expressed by Luckey's constituents in Nebraska concerning the possibility of an extension of the NIRA, exemplifies the general position of small-scale capitalists over the evaluation of the NIRA codes of fair competition:

> The multiple restrictions placed on the small business man have resulted in an unfair and unnecessary discrimination against him to the advantage of a rapidly growing, monopolistic group of big business concerns. The small business man has little time to familiarize himself with the complicated rules and regulations which change frequently, and only too often as a result of these rules, finds himself compelled to close his business rather than carry on the unequal struggle.[7]

In March 1934, less than one year after the official enactment of the NIRA, Roosevelt created the National Recovery Review Board, under the chairmanship of Clarence S. Darrow. The purpose of the Review Board was to ascertain and report to FDR whether any code or codes of fair competition were designed to promote monopolies or to discriminate against small business or whether they permitted monopolies or monopolistic practices. The Review Board was also supposed to recommend to FDR any changes in the approved codes which would rectify or eliminate the possibility of the growth of monopolies that were perceived to be detrimental to small-scale capitalists. Members of the Review Board heard complaints concerning twelve approved codes during the first five weeks of the board's existence. These complaints came from smaller-sized capitalists within each industrial branch covered by the codes. The bulk of the complaints centered on the difficulties being experienced by small-scale capitalists. The major complaint was that "small independent business men were largely ignored, both in the writing of the codes and in filling the various committees set up to enforce the codes."[8] Small-scale capitalists documented that large-scale capitalists had supervised the writing of the codes and that they then had also administered and enforced the codes of fair competition. The National Recovery Review Board suggested, after the five weeks of preliminary investigation, that further investigation be undertaken into the issue of the impact that the NIRA was having on monopoly growth.

The report of the National Recovery Review Board reinforced the charges made by small-scale capitalists that the NRA was a state agency that ruled in the interest of monopoly capital. Darrow's report found a trend toward monopoly and oppression of small business in almost all of the eight codes that it covered. The report singled out the steel and motion-picture industries, in which monopoly and monopolistic practices were extreme—to the complete detriment of smaller-scale enterprises. The report stated that only the cleaning-and-dyeing code was free of monopoly, and this code was not even being enforced by the code authorities. The report recommended that most price and production controls be eliminated and that major changes be made in the composition of the code authorities.[9]

There was not total agreement on the final report of the board. On 3 May, Darrow and his partner William O. Thompson forwarded to Roosevelt a special supplementary report of the National Recovery Review Board. Darrow and Thompson's supplementary report was more strongly worded than the final report. It sharply criticized the NIRA, along with the NRA and code authorities, for fostering monopolistic practices and for providing the mechanisms that would eliminate small business concerns entirely from the industrial sector. Thompson and Darrow also criticized the implementation of the NIRA, arguing that

> the dangers of monopoly which are inherent in the National Industrial Recovery Act cannot even be revealed to the people of the United States, if factfinding and enforcement are thus controlled by industrial combinations. To permit the National Recovery Administration to carry these obligations is to expect violators of law to sit in judgment upon and condemn themselves.[10]

After discussing the problems in regard to capital accumulation in an epoch in which monopoly capital was dominant within the accumulation process, Darrow and Thompson argued that it was not possible to "go back to unregulated competition" in a situation "where technological advance had produced a surplus so that unregulated competition demoralizes both wages and prices and brings on recurrent and increasingly severe industrial depression." Darrow and Thompson, in essence, argued that given the situation within the capital-accumulation process, the only way to guarantee a high standard of living and to avoid future depressions was through the socialized ownership and control of industrial production. They suggested that there were only two possible positions for state administrators to take with regard to monopoly growth. One was the regulation of monopolies by state activity, the general tendency of the policy directive of the NRA. According to Darrow and Thompson, this would mean the elimination of small business in the long run. The other choice, they argued, was a planned economy, with the socialization of the means of production. Planned economy did not mean the sanction of government to sustain profits. Darrow and Thompson were advocating a nascent form of socialism. Their final conclusions were: "The NRA is at a present stage of conflict of interest; but in proportion as the authority of government sanctions regulation by industrial combinations, the inevitable tendency is toward monopoly, with elimination of the small business."[11]

Needless to say, neither the report nor the special and supplementary report of the Review Board were well received by members of the NRA, especially its administrator, Gen. Hugh Johnson. The third report of the National Recovery Review Board concluded that all of the codes that were examined offered an "opportunity for the more powerful and more profitable interests to seize control of an industry or to augment and extend control already obtained" and "in instances mentioned, the codes . . . not only permit but foster monopolistic practices and the small enterprise is not only oppressed but in many cases its exit is accelerated from the field of business."[12] Members of the NRA charged that the reports of the Review Board were one-sided and superficial.[13] Conflicts developed within the NRA between those members who supported the findings of the Review Board and those who thought the reports were without basis in truth. Critics within the NRA received support from other state agencies, such as the Federal Trade Commission, which argued that the policy of the NRA supported monopolistic growth.[14] The conflicts that developed within the NRA mirrored wider conflicts between monopoly and nonmonopoly capital and political conflicts between state administrators over the monopoly issue and the nature of competition. Supporters of the NRA argued that the codes of fair competition had actually aided small-scale capitalists by regulating competition. Opponents argued that the larger, more profitable firms within the various branches of industry dominated the code authorities and set price and production quotas that hurt small-scale capitalist firms.

Probably the most illustrative statement about the conflicts that developed between the NRA and the Review Board is the letter of resignation of William O. Thompson, a member of the National Recovery Review Board. Thompson resigned as a member of the board on 13 June, after the special and supplementary report was filed along with the first report. Thompson's resignation included a scathing critique of the class character of the NIRA and its administration through the NRA. Thompson argued that the response of General Johnson and the Labor Advisory Board to the first report of the Review Board was an unjustified attack on the committee for doing what it set out to do—namely, to investigate and report on the complaints of small businessmen. Thompson argued that the purpose of the attack was to "divert public attention from the clear content of our findings which showed the growing encouragement of monopolistic combinations and practices by the National Recovery Administration."[15] He also criticized the NRA's announcement of a new price-fixing policy that could curb the tendency toward monopoly, calling it a device to calm "an aroused public realization of the extent of monopolistic practices." He argued that such a policy was not a change but rather was a continuation of the policy of the code authorities. Thompson concluded that the trend of the NRA continued to be toward the encouragement and development of monopoly capital—that even the participation of AFL labor leaders in the code-making process served to bolster the interest of "big business"—and, as a result, that rising prices had caused workers to suffer as consumer goods had become more costly. Thompson illustrated how monopoly growth had actually lowered the standard of living for the majority of workers and had instituted more speed-ups and stretch-outs—an increase in the rate of exploitation. He advocated a fundamental change in class relations as the solution to the problems of monopoly growth, of eliminating small businesses, and of a better standard of living for the masses of working-class people. For Thompson, the NRA was clearly a class agency that was advocating and implementing policies that were detrimental to the majority of the population.

Thompson's letter of resignation stated, in a rather direct fashion, what he perceived as the major problem with the administration of the NRA and the NIRA. By pointing to the class character of the NRA, he correctly pointed out the contradictions in the so-called intent of the NIRA and in the implementation of the codes of fair competition. However, there were some differences of opinion as to the exact extent to which the NRA represented the fractional interest of monopoly capital, thereby ensuring that neither Thompson's letter of resignation nor the report of the Review Board would be seriously acted upon. In short, many of the recommendations of the Review Board were largely ignored as they became enmeshed within the bureaucratic structure of the state. The executive branch abolished the National Recovery Review Board soon after Thompson resigned.[16]

The recommendations of the Review Board were never wholeheartedly acted upon, but they did crystallize the conflicts within the capitalist class and within the NRA over the issue of monopoly growth. The reports of the Review Board did stimulate some reorganization within the NRA which was concerned about improved compliance with the codes, the prevention of competitive abuses, and the simplification of authority. Although there was some reorganization administratively, conflicts persisted inside the NRA. Small-scale capitalists and antitrusters continued to complain that the NRA was a tool of monopoly, and even leaders of organized labor became increasingly disillusioned with the agency when the NRA failed to enforce the labor provisions of the NIRA. In late August 1934 Roosevelt asked General Johnson to resign as administrator and replaced him with a board. This action was perceived as appeasement of those critics of the NRA who placed on Johnson the majority of blame for the problems arising within the NRA. Johnson was steadfastly in support of what the NRA was accomplishing, and he was inflexible when dealing with opponents of the recovery agency. The board that replaced Johnson included agents of monopoly capital, as well as Sidney Hillman of the Amalgamated Clothing Workers to represent organized labor.[17] The replacement of Johnson with a board of administrators changed little in the actual operation of the NRA and proved to do even less in appeasing the critics of that agency.

The new National Industrial Recovery Board assured business concerns that there would be no broad changes in industrial policy without first consulting the industries concerned. The board assured capitalists that the goal of the administration of the NRA was cooperation with industrial concerns rather than with government-mandated industrial-recovery programs. The only significant difference between the new Industrial Recovery Board and Johnson was that the new leadership was more adept in handling the divergence between stated policy and practice.[18] However, conflicts within the NRA continued to develop, and conflicts intensified between members of the capitalist class—mostly small-scale, nonmonopoly capital—and the NRA. The authority of the NRA had come to be openly challenged by 1935 and, in many instances, was simply ignored by industrial capitalists. The compliance machinery of the NIRA bogged down, and the administrators of the NRA were not sure of their own popular approval or of their legal grounds to take a strong stance in enforcing the various codes.[19]

The actual implementation of the NIRA brought strong criticisms from small-scale, nonmonopoly capital, with the backing of the National Association of Manufacturers and the Chamber of Commerce. The implementation of the NIRA aided monopoly capital without accruing similar benefits to nonmonopoly capital. Nonmonopoly capital's criticisms of the price and production controls of the NRA were reinforced by the reports of the National Recovery Review Board. The Roosevelt administration did not attempt to revive the NIRA after it was declared unconstitutional in May 1935. However, the issue of monopoly growth did not disappear with the demise of the NIRA and the NRA.

The Monopoly Debate

The implementation of the NIRA did not run counter to the process of the concentration and centralization of capital, and it provided little by way of economic recovery. Hence, small- and medium-scale capitalists, along with anti-big-business state administrators and legislators, placed the blame for the economic depression on large-scale corporate capital. After all, it appeared that monopoly capital was the only element that was able to withstand the economic crisis and even benefited within certain limits. The end of the NIRA did not subdue the debates among capitalists and state administrators over the "monopoly problem." Moreover, the 1937/38 recession brought with it a revitalization of the concern over monopoly growth within the domestic accumulation process among both capitalists and members of the state administration. As economic conditions took a turn for the worse in late 1937, members of the state administration looked toward antitrust revision as a method of handling monopoly growth and as a solution to the economic downturn. The conventional wisdom among state administrators and, more specifically, members of Congress was that the tendency toward monopoly growth in the United States meant a decline in competition that would lead to higher prices for consumer goods. Hence, a policy of antitrust revision would restore the competitive market. Moreover, after the 1937 recession, the Roosevelt administration sought an expanded spending program in an attempt to increase purchasing power so as to overcome obstacles in the accumulation process.

Roosevelt was advised that the strategy of increased spending, combined with trust busting, would aid overall capital accumulation. Leon Henderson, an economic advisor, argued that full employment and sustained production were dependent upon both a balance of prices and a balance between savings and investment. While the former could be achieved by politically dislodging monopolistic controls over the competitive market, the latter required governmental investment to offset the decline in private investment. Antitrust action, Henderson argued, would also add to the effectiveness of spending by breaking down restrictions on production and economic expansion. At the same time, spending would facilitate antitrust action by arresting deflationary forces, thus reducing the trend toward monopolization.[20]

By early 1938 the administration and liberal democratic leaders of Congress had become convinced of the need for a spending program coupled with an antimonopoly program to combat the economic crisis. In early April 1938 Roosevelt sent a special message to Congress, in which he requested the spending or lending of more than $3 billion for relief and work programs and aid to local and state governments. In addition, he asked for the release of $1.4 billion in idle gold and the lowering of reserve requirements for Federal Reserve banks. Roosevelt was asking Congress for a Keynesian spending program in which the market forces would be manipulated in order to restore purchasing power. The proposed Recovery Relief bill was passed by Congress in mid June after a long debate. Congress thus endorsed the administration's decision to use governmental spending as a force in stimulating economic activity.[21]

Two weeks after his message to Congress, Roosevelt and his advisors worked on another message, one concerned with a revision of antitrust legislation as part of an antimonopoly program. Although labeled "antimonopoly," the program did not seek to curb monopoly growth; rather, it was aimed at regulating the competitive practices of large-scale business concerns. The view that monopoly growth caused a decline in competition led many congressmen to believe that the process of monopoly growth had to be politically controlled. In reality, however, the process of the concentration and centralization of capital was a basic tendency within the law of accumulation; the process of monopoly growth could not be curtailed if accumulation were to continue. What might be politically controlled was competition between firms. The entire debate over the growth of monopoly firms was essentially concerned with the political regulation of competition. The so-called antimonopoly message to Congress was carefully worded so as not to lose the confidence of the business community. Henry A. Wallace, secretary of agriculture, was particularly cautious; he warned Roosevelt that "these men still controlled the bulk of flow of private capital and, at the present juncture, it was absolutely necessary to induce the flow."[22] After sixteen leading capitalists had indicated their willingness to cooperate in a policy designed to regulate monopoly growth, Roosevelt on 29 April told members of Congress that the country was controlled by a clique of private individuals who regulated and/or dominated every branch of the economy. Roosevelt implicitly argued that this tight-knit group was able to determine the performance of the economy as a whole, with little concern for anything other than their own profitability. In order to change the situation, Roosevelt asked Congress for more funds for antitrust prosecutions, further banking legislation, and $500,000 for a study of the concentration of economic power.[23] The goal of such an antimonopoly program would be to politically restore and regulate the rhythm of capital accumulation for the country as a whole.

The congressional debate over Roosevelt's message was not centered either on spending or on the investigation of monopoly growth; rather, it was centered on the extension of *executive powers* over the investigation of monopoly in contrast to the *congressional powers* of the committee to investigate the growth of monopoly capital. In his message, Roosevelt made no mention of congressional participation in the investigation of monopoly control. This was quickly noted by senators, particularly Joseph O'Mahoney, who emerged as the leading sponsor of the investigation. What ensued was a proposal, initiated by O'Mahoney, that called for a congressional committee made up of four congressmen and three members from the executive branch. The Roosevelt administration countered this proposal by suggesting a separate congressional committee, to be assisted by a temporary commission from the executive agencies.[24] A compromise was reached after O'Mahoney met and spoke with representatives of the administration. The investigative committee included twelve members, equally divided between Congress and the executive branch. On 16 July, after some debate over the extension of executive power into the investigation of monopoly growth, the Temporary National Economic Committee (TNEC) was formed.[25] The formation of the TNEC signified that state agents agreed to investigate economic concentration in the United States and to recommend legislation to control abuse by industry. Little agreement, however, existed within the committee on the approach to take or on the goal that was desired. The broad goal was clearly that of the resumption of profitable accumulation; the strategy to accomplish this remained vague and contradictory.

The investigation into economic concentration meant an investigation into the extent of the centralization of capital in the domestic process of accumulation. Concentration, as defined by the state administration, meant that fewer and fewer firms were controlling a larger share of the market and that the ownership and the control of such firms were in the hands of fewer and fewer capitalists. The TNEC was charged with investigating the degree of centralization of capital within the various branches of industry. In theory, based on the findings of the committee, legislation could be formulated to politically regulate the form that competition would take.

The experience of the TNEC was not dissimilar to that of the NRA and the National Recovery Review Board before it. The experience of the Review Board had shown that any investigation into the extent of monopoly growth and any recommendations for legislation would all be conducted within the confines that would make the accumulation of private capital profitable. The members of the TNEC were divided over the monopoly issue; they represented views as divergent as national planning, anti-big-business, and pro-monopoly capital. The TNEC mirrored the conflicts within the state apparatus itself—conflicts between those capitalists and agents of capital who stressed a more planned national economy and those who desired a return to competitive capitalism. The divergent views between members of the committee, on the one hand, and the members and researchers, on the other hand, indicated that the TNEC was split over the monopoly issue along similar lines to Congress and the administration.

The actual operations of the TNEC, like those of the NRA before it, were confused.[26] In July 1938, after having received requests from two members of the TNEC, Berle prepared a memorandum of suggestions for the investigation of business organizations and practices. In his memorandum Berle suggested that a clear goal of the investigation into the extent of monopolies be delineated so that the investigation and further recommendations of the committee would be taken seriously and would aid in the shaping of legislation.[27] Berle began by suggesting that the investigation should essentially be a search to find an organization of business that would actually work—that is, what particular form of organization would provide adequate employment, goods, and services at a fair price, eliminate waste, and assure a "fair" profit. Berle argued that all of these questions would have to be determined by actual data on various branches of industry and that some concentration of power might be more desirable in some branches than in others. He cautioned the TNEC against making incorrect assumptions about small business; he argued that small-scale enterprises were not necessarily "competitive," "humane," or "efficient." According to Berle, the charge against monopoly could not be made that size alone determined desirability with respect to economic performance. Berle also warned that the outcome of the investigation of monopolies should clearly state why an additional degree of state regulation of industrial activity should be undertaken. He suggested that the reasons should be to provide more, better, and cheaper goods; to provide more, better-paying, and steadier jobs; to continue ready access to capital financing necessary to create and maintain additional plants; and to provide for the continued development of the arts of industrial production.

Berle's memorandum in many ways outlined the position of national economic planners, of monopoly capital, and of those state agents who believed that monopoly was a normal outcome of the accumulation process and that monopolistic forms of business organization were not necessarily evil. These capitalists and state agents recognized that the purposes of the committee were essentially to gather facts and to figure out the manner in which capital could continue to accumulate at the fastest and most desirable rates. These people realized that competition could be politically regulated in order to balance the profit rate between branches of industry as well as possible. Regulated competition was perceived as the solution to industrial bankruptcies and to bottlenecks within the accumulation process.[28]

Unlike the National Recovery Review Board, the TNEC gathered facts and figures concerning the growth of monopoly capital in the United States, but their recommendations were not based upon assumptions about the need to abolish monopolies or about the desirability of a nonmonopolistic form of economic organization. Nevertheless, businessmen in general, as well as agents of capital, severely criticized the TNEC for holding an investigation that could undermine business confidence. Some persons, such as Raymond Moley, argued that business should be allowed to expand at will, rather than being politically attacked for its "successes."[29]

Monopoly Growth

In late 1938 the TNEC initiated its study and investigation of the "concentration of economic power." The TNEC met until April 1940. In the seventeen months of its existence, the committee heard 552 witnesses who filled 31 volumes with testimony and exhibits. The economists who were retained by the committee submitted an additional 43 special studies which were published separately.[30] The reports and studies constituted the most extensive state-supported investigation into the mechanisms of capital accumulation within the industrial sector. After gathering facts upon facts, the committee presented no recommendations for major changes in the antitrust laws. In Hawley's words, "The investigation, after all, was essentially an escape mechanism, a way to deal with a fundamental policy conflict that could not be resolved. The scene of controversy was simply shifted from administrative bureaus and congressional halls to the committee hearings in the hope that somehow, by writing down all the facts, an answer might emerge."[31]

Although the committee did not make any major recommendations for legislation concerning monopoly growth, the reports and hearings of the committee did document the growth and importance of monopoly capital in the capital-accumulation process. During the economic crisis itself, the larger, more concentrated, and centralized firms tended to grow and profit at a much more rapid rate than smaller-scale nonmonopoly capital. The process of concentration and centralization of capital, which was so evident during the 1920s, continued during the world economic crisis of the 1930s. During the 1920s, most monopoly growth was due to mergers and acquisitions, but the increased dominance of monopoly firms during the depression was due to a higher rate of attrition among smaller firms that were less able to withstand the competition because they had smaller financial reserves. The largest 317 manufacturing corporations increased their share of net working capital from 39.0 percent in 1929 to 43.2 percent in 1933, with a further advance to 47.0 in 1938.[32]

The increased competition among capitalist firms within a given branch of industry, increased competition between branches of industry, and the negative impact of this competition on small-scale capitalist enterprises were well documented throughout the TNEC hearings. One monograph of the TNEC was devoted to the problems of small business within a generalized accumulation process dominated by monopoly capital. Frequent complaints by small-scale capitalists against the monopolistic practices of competitors were: (1) price controls; (2) the control of distribution channels; (3) labor coercion in the nature of racketeering; and (4) miscellaneous practices, including the control of location, the development of special brands, and similar devices. Small-scale capitalists complained to the Federal Trade Commission that these practices were common and that they operated unfairly against the small, independent entrepreneur, making it difficult for him or her to survive. It was further argued that state policy had been affected by business interests of large-scale corporate capital and, while seeking to protect the small-scale capitalist, had actually not helped small-scale capital at all. This was a result of the fact that state, local, and federal policies were so uncoordinated that larger-scale capitalists had a greater impact on national economic policy. The lack of coordination among pieces of protective legislation for small-scale capitalist firms was claimed to be the root cause of economic chaos and business mortality.[33]

At the very outset, the TNEC hearings documented that some branches of industry were more centralized than others and that the basic industries were far more concentrated and centralized than the more competitive branches of industry. In the automobile industry, 3 firms controlled 86 percent of the output in 1937; in the copper industry, 4 firms controlled 78 percent of the output in 1935; and in the steel industry, 3 firms controlled 60.5 percent of the industrial capacity in 1935.[34] The process of the concentration and centralization of capital, which is manifested in fewer and fewer firms' controlling a greater share of the market within the various branches of industry, was not blocked during the economic crisis. Indeed, part of the reason for the greater centralization was that during an economic depression the ensuing competition tends to drive smaller-scale capitalist enterprises out of the market. This was most certainly the case in heavy industry.

While many small- and medium-scale capitalist firms in the highly competitive sectors of industry suffered during the 1930s, the large, more monopolized firms actually profited during the years after the stock-market crash in 1929. For example, General Electric had a net income of $24,052,000 in 1934 and $78,207,000 in 1935; General Motors went from a net income of $110,353,000 in 1934 to $256,853,000 in 1937; the net income of Goodyear Tire and Rubber Company increased from $8,502,000 in 1934 to $11,942,000 in 1937; and United States Steel's net income grew from $11,078,000 in 1934 to $129,653,000 in 1937.[35] Sales, profits, and profit margins for the large monopolistic firms all showed significant increases during the 1930s.

The automobile industry, which grew tremendously after World War I, was essentially controlled by three large-scale monopolistic firms—General Motors, Ford Motor Company, and Chrysler Corporation. By the beginning of the crisis of the 1930s, Ford and General Motors were more or less equal in their total share of the automobile market, with General Motors taking the lead in 1931. All three of the major automobile firms profited to a significant degree during the depression. General Motors' net sales for its consolidated operations more than tripled (from $440,899,312 to $1,439,289,940) between 1932 and 1936; net profits before taxes increased approximately thirtyfold (from $8,824,212 to $283,696,144); and net profits after taxes multiplied by more than twenty-eight times (from $8,359,930 to $239,550,075). For the motor-vehicle portion of its business, General Motors converted its 1932 loss into a 1936 profit of approximately $163 million before taxes, a rate of return of 37.93 percent. Sales of cars and trucks to dealers in the United States almost quadrupled between 1932 and 1936 (from 472,859 to 1,682,594), the firm's total employment almost doubled (from 116,152 to 230,572), and its payroll jumped 168 percent (from $143,255,070 to $384,153,022).[36] Ford's production declined from 1,870,257 motor vehicles in 1929 to 395,956 in 1932. Sales recovered between 1935 and 1937 but declined again in 1938, a year in which Ford sold only half as many cars as General Motors did.[37] However, the decline in Ford's production did not mean a loss in profits. Chrysler Corporation, the third-largest automobile manufacturer, also grew during the depression; Chrysler, Ford, and General Motors controlled more than 80 percent of the automobile market. Sales and profits increased steadily between 1934 and 1937 at Chrysler. Sales increased from $371,657,000 in 1934 to $769,808,000 in 1937, which meant an increase in net income, or profit, from $13,723,000 in 1934 to $63,031,000 in 1937.[38]

The steel industry was also heavily concentrated and centralized. Eleven steel firms supplied 83.94 percent of steel output for the entire industry, with the top three firms—U.S. Steel, Bethlehem Steel, and Republic Steel—accounting for more than 60 percent of the total market. United States Steel Corporation, the leading firm within the steel industry, accounted for 35.31 percent of steel capacity in 1938. Its sales rose from $591,609,000 in 1934 to $1,395,550,000 in 1937; and its profits improved from a deficit of $11,078,000 in 1934 to a net income in 1937 of $129,653,000. Hence, during the period of the NIRA, U.S. Steel actually improved from suffering a deficit to making a large profit. Bethlehem Steel accounted for 13.75 percent of the annual capacity of the steel industry in 1938; it increased its rate of return on total investment from 1.21 in 1934 to 6.92 percent in 1937. Republic Steel, which in 1938 accounted for 8.9 percent of the total annual steel capacity, increased its annual rate of return on total investment from a loss of 0.08 percent in 1934 to a positive 5.65 percent in 1937.[39]

The rubber industry, a major basic industry since the rise in the importance of the automobile to the national income, was also largely in the hands of four major corporations: the United States Rubber Company, Goodyear Tire and Rubber Company, B. F. Goodrich Company, and Firestone Tire and Rubber Company. In 1929 the combined sales of these four corporations was more than

$750 million. Goodyear Tire and Rubber Company was the leader; in 1930 it showed a net income of $9.9 million. In the same year, U.S. Rubber showed a deficit of $6.96 million, Goodrich had a deficit of $5.2 million, and Firestone had a net income of $7.7 million.[40] During the depression, Goodyear Tire and Rubber increased its sales from $136,801,000 in 1934 to $216,175,000 in 1937 and increased its net income from $8,502,000 in 1934 to $11,942,000 in 1937. United States Rubber also profited during the depression, increasing its sales from $105,477,000 in 1934 to $186,253,000 in 1937 and increasing its net income from $3,546,000 in 1934 to $55,820,000 in 1937. Firestone Tire and Rubber also increased its sales during the depression—from $121,671,000 in 1935 to $156,823,000 in 1937; its net income increased from $8,131,000 in 1934 to $12,567,000 in 1937.[41]

Heavy industry was not the only highly monopolized branch of industry during the 1930s. The leading firms in practically every branch of industry not only survived the economic crisis and economic decline but actually emerged from the crisis stronger in terms of market share and profitability. The falling away of competitors, the increased difficulty of access for new firms, and a state economic policy that favored monopoly capital—all combined to make the economic crisis a period of relative success for monopoly capitalists.[42]

Monopoly Capital, Nonmonopoly Capital, and the State Apparatus

The TNEC's investigation into the extent of the centralization of capital and the restoration of the competitive market never analyzed the process that had led to the growth of firms and to increased centralization in the first place. The committee never examined the effects of growing monopolization on economic efficiency, labor displacement, and the like. Although the TNEC was operating on the loose assumption that monopolization was the cause of economic decline and economic dislocation, the testimony gathered and the facts and figures collected simply reported the incidence of centralization without presenting an explanation or an analysis of the economic forces that lead to a highly concentrated and centralized industrial sector.[43]

The TNEC did, however, recognize the growth of monopoly capital within the domestic accumulation process:

> While no final evaluation is possible concerning the amount of competition and monopoly present in our economy, certainly monopoly has greatly increased in American industry during the last 50 years because of the lax enforcement of the anti-trust laws, the impetus of price-fixing given by World War I, the tremendous development of trade associations during the twenties which increased price-fixing, the N.R.A. experience in 1933, and the great merger movements from 1898 to 1905 and 1919 to 1929.[44]

Nevertheless, the dominance of monopoly capital within the accumulation process and its increasing dominance on the political level more likely than not placed limits on the policy recommendations of the TNEC. It was nearly impossible for the TNEC to recommend major changes in the antitrust laws which would inhibit large-scale enterprises from increasing profits, since the profitability of large-scale capital had an impact on overall economic stability. The TNEC did not recommend any basic alterations in the process of capital accumulation, and it made no final evaluation of the extent of monopoly growth and its repercussions on overall economic relations in the United States. The very fact that the TNEC made no serious recommendations for reforming economic activity, after concluding that the industrial sector was highly concentrated and centralized, bears evidence that the interest of monopoly capital, as a class fraction, was gaining political dominance.

If anything, the collection of "facts" about the growth of monopoly capital within the industrial sector forced state administrators, elected officials, and the public to acknowledge the changing structure of the accumulation process. Instead of altering the process of capital accumulation, state administrators sought to alter political relationships that would coincide with the changing economic relations. Changes in the methods of production, which required state economic intervention of a new kind, had been recognized by economists and academics by the mid 1930s.[45] In the words of Arthur R. Burns:

> State participation in the administration of economic resources is urged as a means of securing greater efficiency than the partially competitive and partially monopolistic system of the past has been able to offer. It requires the frank recognition of the conflicts of interest between groups and individuals and serious effort to compromise these conflicts. This compromise can be made, however, only on the basis of a clear conception of the objectives of society. . . . In both the political and economic sphere the greatest of all contemporary problems is that of deciding how great a concentration of power shall be permitted. . . . [t]he problem is one of designing patterns for the distribution of power.[46]

This quotation from Burns illustrated the meaning of monopoly capital's dominance vis-à-vis nonmonopoly capital. The investigation into the concentration of economic power and the 1935 Supreme Court decision that ruled that the NIRA codes of fair competition were unconstitutional were the very compromises made to nonmonopoly capital at a time when monopoly capital was being organized as the dominant class fraction on the political level. The conflicts between the various fractions of capital made it clear to Burns that the political alliance of capital needed to be organized and unified by the state. Moreover, Burns's quotation illustrates his recognition that the accumulation process had changed since the turn of the century and that capital, in turn, needed to be reorganized under the hegemony of monopoly capital if the accumulation process was to continue and the long-term interest of capital as a whole was to be secure. In Poulantzas's words:

> Contradictions among the dominant classes and fractions—or in other words, the relationship of forces within the power bloc—are precisely what makes it necessary for the unity of the bloc to be organized by the State. They therefore exist as *contradictory relations enmeshed within the State.* As the material condensation of a contradictory relationship, the State does not at all organize the unity of the power bloc from the outside, by resolving class contradictions at a distance. On the contrary, however paradoxical it may seem, the play of these contradictions within the State's materiality alone makes possible the State's organizational role.[47]

The state administration did not seek to alter the profitability or the rate of accumulation for the large-scale monopoly firms; it did seek, however, to aid in altering the social relations of production within firms and the structure of the state to correspond more coherently with changes in the accumulation process. It was even acknowledged during the TNEC hearings that social relations lagged "behind developments in our economic life."[48] It appears that the state administration's strategy to rationalize economic activity in order not only to recover from the economic depression but also to prevent future economic crises favored monopoly capital. Although debates about monopoly growth continued throughout the years of the economic crisis, although the National Recovery Review Board reported a high rate of incidence of monopoly growth under the NIRA codes of fair competition, and although the TNEC verified monopoly growth, no serious political actions were taken to curb monopoly growth or the process of concentration and centralization of capital. Instead, relationships between capital and the state were altered. Monopoly capital was able to withstand political debates on the assumption that monopoly growth had been the reason and the cause for the economic decline by turning economic and political setbacks that resulted both from intracapitalist conflict and the gains made by working class struggles during the decade of the 1930s into advantages for itself in the post–World War II period. The debates and controversy surrounding the NIRA and the administrative activities of the NRA serve to support the claim that the NIRA actually provided the mechanisms that aided the process of the concentration and centralization of capital, helped to create monopolistic forms of business organization in certain branches of industry, and began the process of establishing the conditions for new social relations between monopoly capital and wage labor and between capital and the state.

CHAPTER SIX

Industrial Labor and the Struggle for Union Recognition

The N.R.A. has promised increased commodity prices to be supported by shorter hours and higher wages. You ask the whole-hearted support of labor in your campaign.

So far I have received shorter hours, increased commodity prices, but lo, and behold, as usual I am the sucker. Instead of higher wages I receive less. I must feed the same family, as much food as ever, and receive less pay. It's a great riddle, please tell me the answer.

—*Sparrow Point Steel Worker*

The second reason they expect disorder is that the Communists have imported some 1,500 people from Chicago who are hopped up with cocaine and are really professional strikers—they are the type that killed Arthur Lyman the other day. Mr. Rand has watched this closely and says that at least 1,500 have drifted in from Illinois the last two days.

—*Keith Merrill*

I might mention that during the riots, I shot a long-range projectile into a group, a shell hitting one man and causing a fracture of the skull, from which he has since died. As he was a communist, I have no feeling in the matter and I am sorry that I did not get more.

—*Joseph M. Roush*

The Rejuvenation of Labor Militancy

The inclusion of section 7a in the NIRA was an attempt by the Roosevelt administration to sidetrack the Black Thirty Hour bill.[1] However, as I have already argued, this concession actually heightened class contradictions and intensified class struggle between industrial capital and industrial labor. The labor provisions of section 7a of the NIRA guaranteed the right of industrial workers to organize unions, to engage in collective-bargaining arrangements, and to set maximum hours of work and minimum rates of pay. Significant portions of the industrial working class perceived that section 7a provided the legal mechanisms for union recognition and thereby would force industrial capital to provide better terms of employment. Capitalists, however, systematically opposed section 7a and vigorously fought its enforcement for the duration of the NIRA. The National Labor Board, which was established by the federal government to implement section 7a, lacked the necessary legal machinery to enforce the labor provisions of the act. As a result, capitalists largely ignored the provisions of section 7a.

The lifting of political repression and the commitment to reform under the Roosevelt administration's first term in office, the growing strength of Communist and Socialist organizations within the ranks of the working class, and the refusal of industrial capitalists to abide by the provisions of section 7a of the NIRA led to the rejuvenation of labor militancy.[2] A weak trade-union movement that was unable to counteract antiunion campaigns and to adjust itself to the changing composition of the labor force and changes in the labor process was transformed into a militant industrial labor movement that not only was capable of organizing workers in mass-production industry but also was strong enough to force significant political concessions. Unskilled mass-production workers joined with dissident craft unionists to demand not just better wages or shorter hours but also a qualitative change in working conditions. The struggle for union recognition gave direction to the dynamic of the class struggle between labor and capital during the first half of the 1930s. This struggle continued throughout the decade and, in the words of Mike Davis, was the "highwater mark of the class struggle in modern American history."[3]

The bargaining rights of labor and the enforcement of section 7a surfaced as major political issues and resulted in bitter and brutal struggles between industrial wage labor and capital. These aspects of the class struggle shaped the future course of capitalist development in the United States. The struggle for industrial unionization, the shortening of the workday, higher wages, and the eventual introduction of social services such as unemployment insurance and social welfare altered the social relationships within industrial firms, along with political relationships between organized industrial labor and the capitalist state apparatus. The result of the protracted struggle for industrial unionization and the state's response to it was the alteration of the terms of the rate of exploitation within unionized firms and of political structures in such a fashion as to integrate organized industrial labor within the national political-bargaining process.

The labor provisions of the NIRA provided the legal mechanisms for the initial growth of unions in mass-production industries. The labor struggles during the NIRA period necessitated the formulation and passage of additional labor policy. The National Labor Relations Act (NLRA) was enacted in July 1935. The NLRA went beyond the provisions of section 7a and *protected* workers' right to join unions; it also provided legal sanction for industrial unions and legal recourse for workers against employers. Contrary to its design, the NIRA provided the conditions under which new forms of labor struggle (the rise of industrial unions) were simultaneously created, given a certain amount of political space (government-sanctioned industrial unions and institutional mechanisms for settling worker discontent through the NLRA and National Labor Relations Board), and eventually (in the post–World War II years) incorporated into the political-bargaining process via the Democratic party.[4]

Labor's Response to the NIRA

Established trade unionists and significant portions of workers in industries that were untouched by the craft-styled organization drives of the American Federation of Labor (AFL) generally welcomed the inclusion of section 7a in the NIRA. The labor provisions of the NIRA implied that industrial workers had the right to organize, join unions of their own choosing, and bargain collectively. In addition, the labor provisions provided for the regulation of minimum wages and maximum hours of work. The industrial codes of fair competition fixed maximum hours of work and minimum rates of pay in those industries which did not have collective-bargaining agreements. Representatives of both labor and capital initiated the formulation of the industrial codes. In short, the labor provisions of the NIRA carried the implied promise of better terms of employment for the industrial work force.

The promise of the NIRA had the initial impact of stimulating drives for unionization. During the two years of the act, trade-union membership increased, especially in mining and cloth manufacturing, where efforts were made to organize industrywide. Membership in all unions, including unions that were not affiliated with the AFL, grew from 2,973,000 in 1933 to 3,608,600 in 1934 and to an estimated 3,888,600 in 1935. (The figure for 1935 includes 1,022,100 members in the Committee for Industrial Organization, which eventually split from the AFL and become the Congress of Industrial Organizations, or CIO.) Membership in the AFL itself rose by some 300,000 between 1934 and 1935; between 1933 and 1934 it had gained 712,500 members.[5] The largest increases in union membership occurred in those industries which had been previously untouched by the craft-styled organizational drives of the AFL. Craft unions grew only 13 percent, compared to the growth of 132 percent by the AFL's four industrial unions and 126 percent for the AFL's semi-industrial unions.[6]

The greatest increase in union membership occurred in the industrial unions of the United Mine Workers, the United Textile Workers, the International Ladies Garment Workers, and the Amalgamated Clothing Workers. These unions together accounted for approximately 700,000 new members. In addition to the established unions, more than 1,100 federal and local unions, affiliated with the AFL, were formed in mass-production industries such as automobiles, rubber, aluminum, and lumber. Membership in this group of unions grew from 10,396 in 1933 to 111,489 in 1935.[7]

The increase in union membership in mass-production industries, which ultimately formed the basis for the CIO, coincided with the growth in company unions in mass-production industries such as steel, automobiles, and rubber—

all of which had remained untouched by the old craft unions. The National Industrial Conference Board investigated the growth of company unions of one form or another: of the 3,314 manufacturing and mining concerns (employing a total of 2,585,740 workers), 653 concerns (employing a total of 1,163,575 workers) had company unions. Only 416 concerns (employing 240,394 workers in all) recognized trade unions.[8] According to a survey made by the Bureau of Labor Statistics, membership in company unions rose from 1,263,000 to about 2,500,000 in 1935.[9]

The rise in union membership did not, in any sense, guarantee union recognition. Industrial capitalists systematically fought union recognition and often employed brutal force to prevent independent unionization. (The extent to which capitalists tried to undercut organizing efforts will be discussed in greater detail in chapter 7.) Capitalists used labor spies, blacklisting devices, and weapons when propaganda campaigns and plans for company unions failed to distract workers from unionization efforts. The rise of company unions is only one manifestation of the attempts to stop the organizing of independent unions.

The passage of the NIRA and the inclusion of section 7a were used as mechanisms for the great increase in union membership. However, section 7a could not be used as a guarantee for union recognition. Debate over the interpretation of section 7a raged between capitalists and workers and between members of the state administration. Organized labor argued that section 7a outlawed company unions, and most capitalists argued that collective-bargaining arrangements and union affiliation included company unions. As a result, where the provisions of section 7a were opposed, company unions were encouraged.

The most instrumental industrial association to promote company unions was the National Association of Manufacturers (NAM). As early as 1933, a committee of the association was organized to take charge of the promotion of "employee-representation" plans. A special $7,000 fund was raised for this purpose. About $4,000 of this fund was spent for newspaper and magazine publicity, and most of the balance was appropriated for the printing and distribution of a pamphlet of employee-representation plans. As a result of this effort, a study of 126 companies found that in 11.2 percent of the cases, company unions were formed with the desire to improve personnel relations; in 24.8 percent of cases, they were formed as a result of the influence of the NIRA; in 22.4 percent, because strikes were in progress or had recently ended; and in 41.6 percent, company unions were introduced because trade unions were making headway in the particular plant or locality.[10]

The labor provisions under the NIRA which gave labor the right to organize were rarely enforced either by the federal government or by individual capitalists. The other provisions of the act which regulated wages and hours of work through the establishment of industrial codes were also, to a great extent, circumvented by capitalists. Capitalists used rather ingenious mechanisms to circumvent the labor provisions of the codes of fair competition. Some examples of ways in which capitalists manipulated wage and hour restrictions to their own benefit were (1) withholding wages to force buying in a company store; (2) employing people at low classifications and rates of pay and using them for much of their time in some other classification—for example, using a delivery boy as a clerk; (3) using the learners and apprenticeship clause to escape paying minimum wage; (4) using systems of speed-up; (5) using systems of deductions and loans; (6) blacklisting and firing employees for filing complaints; (7) paying less than the minimum wage and justifying this to employees on the grounds of an inability to pay the minimum wage and remain in business, thus eliciting employee acquiescence; (8) firing employees and then rehiring them at a lower wage; (9) leasing plants to employees so that they no longer would be called employees; (10) making employees partners and forming bogus cooperatives; (11) deducting uniforms, insurance, stock, breakage, short change, and so forth, from wages; (12) paying by check and then charging a fee for cashing it; and (13) having employees use time cards to check out on time but then having them finish the work at home.[11]

Within less than one year from the official enactment of the NIRA, large numbers of workers began to criticize the inadequacy of section 7a and the inability of the industrial codes to improve working conditions.[12] The bulk of the discontent was directed against lower wages, longer hours of work, deteriorating working conditions, and noncompliance of companies with the requirements to recognize unions and to develop collective-bargaining agreements. The promise of the NIRA was never realized for the majority of workers. In early 1934, various public hearings were held on the effect that the NIRA was having on employment in general. At a public hearing in February a member of the Furniture Workers Industrial Union claimed that under the furniture and allied codes, hours had been increased, wages had been reduced, and employment had decreased. Company unions had been established, and the labor-conciliation apparatus was unsympathetic to labor. At the same hearing, a member of the AFL stated that workers in the automobile industry who expressed a desire for outside unions had been discharged and that company unions were being forced upon workers. The employers had a comprehensive system of espionage, and they brought workers from other cities to displace union labor. Hours far exceeded the maximum, and wage increases were nullified by stretch-outs, speed-ups, and revamped rates for piecework.[13]

The state agencies and labor boards that were established to enforce the NIRA and to ensure that labor would get a "new deal" were unable to satisfy the demands of workers. The discontent of the rank and file grew as governmental officials proved unable to enforce the labor provisions of the NIRA. Along with the discontent directed against governmental officials there was a growing dissatisfaction with the legalistic approaches that the AFL leadership was taking to secure the due rights of labor. With the realization that bargaining rights and better terms of employment would not occur with the passage of a law, the rank and file made use of the strike as the weapon to obtain what had supposedly already been given to them by the labor provisions of the NIRA.

Labor Militancy under the Blue Eagle

The dissatisfaction of workers with the implementation of section 7a led to the use of work stoppages, slowdowns, and sit-downs as economic weapons designed to force capitalists to abide by the provisions set forth in the NIRA.[14] Strike activity during the six months after the signing of the NIRA included 1,695 work stoppages that involved more than 1,117,000 workers. Man-days lost had not exceeded 603,000 in any month during the first half of the year, but they increased to 1,375,000 in July and 2,378,000 in August.[15] The main cause of most of these work stoppages was the protest against the violation of NIRA codes that provided for minimum wages and conditions for employment. Approximately 35,000 members of the Amalgamated Clothing Workers Union went on strike in New York City against proposed codes; they were soon joined by 60,000 dressmakers of the International Ladies Garment Workers Union. At least twelve strikes occurred in the automobile industry, and more than 50,000 silk workers in Paterson, New Jersey, and elsewhere went on strike over proposed minimum codes.[16] Workers also went on strike against proposed codes in the mining industry. In August and September, more than 70,000 miners walked off the job in protest against proposed codes, and the situation in the coal-and-steel industry became "critical" as a result of the strikes.[17]

Strike activity was greater in 1934 than in 1933; it involved 1,470,000 workers in 1,856 strikes. A total of 2,014 work stoppages occurred in 1935, involving 1,170,000 workers. The major cause of the pre-1934 strikes had been the desire for higher wages and better hours, but the main issue in the majority of the strikes in 1934/35 was the desire for union recognition.[18] Four strikes in 1934 were of particular significance. The strike at the Electric Auto-Lite Company in Toledo, Ohio, the longshoremen's strike along the West Coast, the truckers' strike in Minneapolis, and the strike of textile workers along the East Coast not only involved workers at the point of production but also overflowed to other segments of the working class. These strikes are significant because leftist political organization played a significant role in the unfolding of the conflicts that surrounded the strikes. Before examining some of the highlights of these strikes, it is first necessary to make a brief examination of the general relationship between the strategies and tactics of the Communist party and the labor struggles of the 1930s.[19]

The Communist Party and the Labor Movement

The Communist party saw itself as the vanguard party of the working class during the early years of the depression. The prime focus of the Communist party during the NIRA period was in organizing previously unorganized workers into revolutionary unions. Prior to the strikes of 1934 the policy of the Communist party was not to work within the already established AFL unions but to establish rank-and-file organizing committees in the basic industries and eventually to create "revolutionary unions" that would become part of the Trade Union Unity League (TUUL), an organ of the Communist party that was formed during the period of dual unionism.[20] By 1934 the TUUL had moved towards forming independent unions in the needle trades, coal, and steel, and it was applying new tactics to unions such as the auto workers in which it already exerted substantial leadership.[21] In 1933 the Communist party reported 1,301 members of revolutionary trade unions, and in 1934, membership in revolutionary unions was recorded at 10,421.[22] It was the task of Communists, working within the trade-union movement, to seek out the most "advanced workers" and to conduct all strikes under the leadership of the Communist party.

The Communist party continued its dual unionization efforts after the passage of the NIRA. It publicly criticized the NIRA and section 7a as a fascist plan designed to co-opt labor. The Communist party argued that corporate self-regulation and the establishment of government-sanctioned labor unions that were easily co-opted into bourgeois political rule could possibly lead to fascism. However, by the middle of 1934 the rise of rank-and-file militancy independently of the AFL and the TUUL led the Communist party to move away from its hard-line stance on the NIRA. As a result, in many cases the Communist party was instrumental in organizing already discontented workers. By 1935 the Communist party had completely abandoned the policy of dual unionism, and it dissolved the unions that were associated with the TUUL.[23] Henceforth, the Communist party directed its energies at building industrial unions, and it became an influential force in the establishment of key CIO unions.[24]

The Communist party gained strength and influence within the ranks of the working class, despite the lack of enthusiasm among workers for the TUUL and the constant dissemination of anti-Communist propaganda by the AFL and the National Civic Federation.[25] Membership in the Communist party grew rapidly throughout the decade, increasing tenfold between 1930 and 1938. Between 1930 and 1935 alone, the membership increased from 7,545 to 35,356. Although membership in the Communist party may appear miniscule compared to the number of workers, these figures do not include all who actually joined the party during those years; the rate of membership fluctuation was high. Party membership in December 1933 was 28,849. However, if all the recruits had remained, party membership would have been 52,300.[26] During the first four months of 1934 the party recruited 9,601 new members, but the total membership actually decreased. The turnover for six months of 1934 was almost 100 percent. Excluding an eighteen-month period for which no recruiting figures are available, between 1930 and 1938 the Communist party actually recruited a minimum of 134,006 new members.[27] In 1935 alone, about 23.8 percent of the total membership of the Communist party was composed of workers located in industries such as steel, metal, railroads, mining, and automobiles.[28]

There is some debate as to why so many people who had joined the Communist party eventually left it. Some historians, especially those of the New Deal period, argue that workers who joined the Communist party essentially did not fully understand the party's position on American politics or that workers quickly became disenchanted with party polemics. However, Robert J. Alperin, on the basis of careful research, found that few who left the party cited political disagreements and that most of them continued to work closely with the Communist party in mass organizations or union caucuses that included Communists; very few were bitter or disillusioned.[29] James Robert Prickett suggests several reasons why people who were not disillusioned with the Communist party eventually resigned their official membership. First, Communists faced extensive repression. Second, given the intense pressure under which Communists worked, personal conflicts within a unit could be decisive in whether members remained in the party. Third, racism within units drove blacks out of the party. Fourth, a worker might disagree with an aspect of the party's line without rejecting the overall perspective of the party.[30]

The membership and recruitment figures of the Communist party somewhat underestimate the actual number of workers that were recruited to the party. Many applications for membership were either delayed or actually lost. In 1934, 2,680 applications for membership were lost in New York alone before they could be assigned to units and included in total membership counts. In other cases the drawing power of the Communist party far surpassed its ability to contact and assign the potential party members. In sum, in 1934 only 61 percent of those who applied for membership were actually assigned to party units. Furthermore, the party's membership figures do not take into account those nonmember workers who actually worked with Communists in union drives and essentially followed party leadership in various strikes. Part of the reason for this is that the members of the Communist party, especially after 1935 and during the campaigns that gave rise to the CIO, frequently neglected to combine party recruiting efforts with other activities such as building the union and leading strikes. Increasingly, Communists appealed to workers on the basis of the latter's skill as union leaders, and argued that their membership or nonmembership in the Communist party was irrelevant.[31]

Although membership in the Communist party was small, the party did exert considerable influence in the industrial-union movement. With the change in policy regarding dual unionism, Communist party members played an increasingly important role in organizing the new industrial unions in the maritime, electrical, and automotive industries and were crucial to the struggles for union recognition in the steel industry. In those unions in which Communists did not play a leadership role, Communist militants nevertheless provided the resources from which to carry on the long struggle for union organizing and building viable CIO unions. Nelson Lichtenstein has said: "In the thirties union consciousness was radically uneven; militancy proved an episodic and sometimes ephemeral phenomenon. To build the CIO out of this material required a corps of militants energized by a vision that far transcended the goals of even the union movement itself. The Communists and those who worked closely with them composed by far the largest resource of this sort."[32]

The influence of Communists in the formation of industrial unions and the role Communists played in newly established unions did not go unnoticed by employers, leaders of the AFL, or state administrators. The lifting of political repression during Roosevelt's first term in office provided a milieu in which Communists could openly engage in trade-union work. However, when the political climate changed in 1938 and when the Communist "resource" was no longer needed for organizational reasons, political tolerance of Communist activity declined.[33] Whether or not the influence of Communists in the industrial-union movement was a necessary factor in the gains accrued to industrial workers through the CIO unions or in altering the relationship between labor and capital within mass-production industries remains an unanswered question. What is certain is that the success of many CIO unions was undoubtedly aided by the organizational work of Communist trade unionists.

The Strike Wave of 1934

The four major strikes of 1934 involved unorganized workers and were waged against powerful antiunion employers. In three of the four cases, leadership of the strike was in the hands of leftists. The textile strike along the East Coast resulted in a defeat for the workers. However, strikes in Toledo, Minneapolis, and San Francisco were successful and gave hope to workers in mass-production basic industries that the strike could be used as a potent weapon. The successful strikes of 1934 paved the way for successful organizing drives in mass-production industries in the latter half of the 1930s. Moreover, the strike wave of 1934 represents the beginning of the formation of the Congress of Industrial Organizations (CIO). Finally, it was the intensity with which the labor struggles were waged that finally led to the passage of the National Labor Relations Act.

The Electric Auto-Lite Strike. The first drive for auto unionization in Toledo, Ohio, occurred in August 1933, when workers at Electric Auto-Lite and its subsidiaries, Bingham Stamping and Tool and Logan Gear, formed a local union which received a charter directly from the AFL as Federal Local Union (FLU) Number 18384. In early 1934 Electric Auto-Lite Company was paying less than the minimum wages provided for by the NIRA code, and it refused to recognize any noncompany union. By early February 1934, Local 18384 demanded a 10 percent wage increase, a system of seniority, and union recognition from Auto-Lite. The company rejected all of the union's demands, and on 23 February, 4,000 workers, not all of whom were union members, walked off the job. After the union had threatened to call a national strike that would affect the entire automobile industry, the federal government established a federal mediation board, and Auto-Lite agreed to a settlement granting an immediate 5 percent wage increase in addition to an agreement that a contract would be negotiated between the company and the union by early April.[34]

Early in April the company not only refused to negotiate but also fired workers who were involved in the February strike. The subregional labor board did nothing on the workers' behalf. On 11 April about 400 workers at Bingham Stamping and Tool Company went on strike, demanding that the Electric Auto-Lite Company negotiate a contract with the United Auto Workers Union Number 18384. On 11 April the union called a strike, and on 13 April approximately 1,000 workers went on strike at the Electric Auto-Lite Company. On 17 April, workers at Logan Gear Company followed.[35] The number of strikers was not enough to close down the manufacturing of automobile parts and accessories, and production went on as usual in Toledo with the employment of more than 1,800 strikebreakers.[36]

On 17 April, workers formed picket lines at the Electric Auto-Lite Company and attempted to prohibit strikebreakers from entering the struck plant. On the following day, all three struck companies filed an injunction to restrain picketing at the plants. The court reserved its decision because union and company representatives were to meet on 23 April with the Auto Labor Board—the federal mediation board that had been established by the state administration for the purpose of settling the strike in Toledo. The meeting with the Auto Labor Board resulted in the companies' refusal to arbitrate with the union, and a few days later the companies reported that a normal day shift was working in all three plants.[37] The court eventually issued an injunction that prohibited picketing by all outside parties such as the Unemployed Council, the Unemployed League, the Socialist and Communist parties, and all others not working at the struck plants. Picketing was limited to the actual strikers.[38]

By the beginning of May the Lucas Company Unemployed League (led by members of the American Workers Party), the Unemployed Council of Toledo, and the Young Communist League were involved in the strike. All of these "outside" forces organized unemployed workers in the Toledo area to picket with the striking workers, called for mass picketing, and urged workers to ignore the injunction. Almost fifty people were arrested for picketing the Electric Auto-Lite Company, but they were all acquitted after the Unemployed League staged demonstrations against the arrests.[39]

According to a Secret Service report, "On May 22 and 23, conditions in vicinity of Electric Auto-Lite plant became such that the strikers and sympathizers were in complete control."[40] The local police of Toledo—because of disaffection in the force and because of widespread sympathy with the strike—could not be relied upon to protect the property and interests of the Electric Auto-Lite Company. As a result, the sheriff hired special police who were subsequently paid by the Auto-Lite Company. On 23 May approximately 10,000 pickets attempted to block 1,500 strikebreakers from leaving the plant. The special police force responded by dropping tear-gas pellets from the roof and from upper story windows onto the people in the streets below. What followed was a seven-hour exchange of gas bombs and stone and bricks thrown by pickets. There were no reported deaths, but a number of persons were seriously injured.[41]

Late on the evening of 23 May the sheriff called in the National Guard to restore order at the Auto-Lite factory. National Guardsmen evacuated the strikebreakers from the factory early the next morning. However, by the afternoon a crowd of 20,000 people confronted the National Guardsmen. The 1,400 National Guardsmen that were in the area of the strike fired tear gas into the crowd to stop the advance of the pickets to the factory gates. The crowd outside the factory gates threw bricks and gas bombs back at the troops in retaliation. The guardsmen used their bayonets to force the people back from the gates, and eventually they fired their rifles directly at the crowd. Two men were killed and some fifteen others were wounded.[42] After several weeks of violence, the Electric Auto-Lite Company agreed to close the plant and to submit the dispute to federal mediation. The National Guard troops were withdrawn from the area.

Large demonstrations were conducted against the atrocities of the strike, and a general strike was threatened to be held in Toledo on 4 June. The Electric Auto-Lite Company finally acceded to the demands of the union and signed a six-month contract which included a 5 percent wage increase with a 5 percent minimum above the auto-industry code, and FLU Number 18384 was named as the exclusive bargaining agent in the plants that were struck. In the words of Art Preis, a participant in the struggle:

> This was the first contract under the code that did not include "proportional representation" for company unions. The path was open for organization of the entire automobile industry. With the Auto-Lite victory under their belts, the Toledo auto workers were able to organize 19 plants before the year was out, and before another 12 months, were to lead the first successful strike in a G.M. plant, the real beginning of the conquest of General Motors.[43]

The direct causes of the strike in Toledo were the refusal of management to grant a 10 percent wage increase and the violation of section 7a of the NIRA. What is peculiar to the strike at Electric Auto-Lite was the ability of the Unemployed League and the Unemployed Council to organize unemployed workers to provide physical support for the strike when needed and to refrain from taking jobs from strikers. In other words, the unemployed were organized to demonstrate in support of striking workers as opposed to demonstrating for their own immediate interests. Furthermore, members of the Communist party and the American Workers party (under the leadership of A. J. Muste) formed a united front against the injunction and jointly staged the demonstrations that followed. However, there were problems within the united front. Members of the Communist party criticized the American Workers party for monopolizing the demonstrations and attacked it for "selling out" to capital. The AFL leadership in the area, although it originally called the strike, initially advised workers to obey the injunction and, according to the Communist party's district organizer for Ohio, pointed out members of the Communist party to the special police force.[44] It seems clear that the auto workers in Toledo would not have made the gains they did without the support of the American Workers party and, to a lesser degree, the Communist party by aiding in the picket line and by organizing demonstrations in support of the striking workers. The Electric Auto-Lite Company was not about to concede to the strikes on its own accord. Only masses of organized demonstrators were able to act as a counterforce to the armed company guards and the special deputies hired by the Electric Auto-Lite Company.[45]

The Minneapolis Truckers' Strike. Minneapolis, Minnesota, was known to be an open-shop city. The Citizens' Alliance, an employer association in Minneapolis, essentially controlled the city. The purpose of the alliance was to prevent labor organization, and the association used any means necessary to prevent unionization, including industrial espionage, propaganda, the planting of stool pigeons in unions, the hiring of thugs to beat up labor leaders, the tampering with grand juries, and the use of industrial munitions.[46] Consequently, organized labor had not been very successful in Minneapolis. However, with the passage of the NIRA and the labor provisions of section 7a, the last six months of 1933 saw a renewal of organizing attempts in Minneapolis by truck drivers.[47]

One of the two most important unions in the city was the International Brotherhood of Teamsters, which at the end of 1933 had 800 to 900 members organized into separate locals of milk, ice-wagon, local cartage, and other specialized drivers at a time when most homes were heated by coal, iceboxes were more common than electric refrigerators, and dairy products were delivered daily to private dwellings. The second was the General Drivers Local 574, which had been chartered by the international with a jurisdiction that was so loosely defined as to allow for an industrial form of organization. In the fall of 1933, Local 574 was under the leadership of members of the Communist League of America, a Trotskyist splinter group of the Communist party in the United States. Local 574 began its organizational drives in the coal yards. Employers in the coal yards systematically refused to recognize the union, thus violating section 7a, with the result that 700 workers walked off the job at 65 of the town's 67 coal yards. It was a well-organized walkout, and the entire coal industry in Minneapolis was virtually shut down. The walkout caught the Citizens' Alliance and the coal companies by surprise, and the struck companies quickly signed a union contract which granted the workers a wage increase. Ironically, a letter from the national president of the Teamsters Union, which refused to sanction the strike, was received two days after the strike had been won.[48]

Local 574's victory in the coal yards helped the unionization campaigns for drivers and inside warehousemen. Local 574 had enlisted 3,000 new members by February 1934. With the Regional Labor Board mediating, Local 574, in accordance with section 7a, demanded union recognition, seniority in layoffs and rehiring, nondiscrimination against union membership, shorter hours, an average wage of $27.50 a week, and premium pay for overtime. The trucking companies would not agree to the demands of the union and absented themselves from the federal mediation board. The trucking companies, supported by the Citizens' Alliance, joined forces and on 7 May systematically rejected all of the union's demands. On 12 May the membership of Local 574 voted overwhelmingly to strike the trucking industry. On 15 May, 5,000 drivers and warehousemen left their jobs and gathered at a large garage that had been rented by the union for use as strike headquarters.[49]

From the outset the strike was exceptionally well organized. Strike headquarters included a dispatching center in which four telephone lines brought messages on truck movements from picket captains stationed all over the city, an auditorium in which anywhere from 2,000 to 20,000 people gathered nightly for speeches and entertainment, a kitchen with a dozen stoves that fed as many as 10,000 people daily, a hospital with two doctors and three nurses, and a repair shop, where 15 mechanics kept about 100 trucks and squad cars in repair. The first few days of the strike were relatively calm. More than 35,000 building-trades workers, cab drivers, and streetcar workers joined the strike. The AFL endorsed the strike, and thereafter the only vehicles moving on the streets were those driven by the already organized drivers of ice wagons and drivers for beer, milk, and coal companies. Pickets blocked almost every entrance to the city, thus stopping ordinary trucking movements. Farmers were even barred from bringing vegetables to the central marketplace.[50]

The Citizens' Alliance prepared for an all-out confrontation with strikers and strike sympathizers. Members of the Citizens' Alliance opened an office from which they wrote press releases and copy about the strike for full-page ads. They argued that the strike was due to Communist outsiders and that if the strike were not stopped, a revolution would probably occur. The alliance anticipated a food shortage because of the lack of movement in the city, which they expected would cause mass support against the strike. Two thousand businessmen met at the office of the Citizens' Alliance and selected a committee to enlist doctors, lawyers, clerks, salesmen, and other businessmen for a citizens' army. The local authorities designated this special army as a police force, thereby giving the army official sanction. The Citizens' Army opened its headquarters and prepared for battle with the strikers and strike sympathizers.[51]

The first act of violence occurred when a spy, placed in the union headquarters by the Citizens' Alliance, led a number of strikers down an alley where they were encircled by police and armed guards. Nearly all of the strikers were injured, and three women suffered broken legs. The confrontation between strikers and members of the so-called Citizens' Army continued for the next two days. Police and deputies clashed with strikers on 21 May after an attempt was made to move perishable goods from the central market area. One driver drove a truck loaded with twenty-five pickets headlong into the police to prevent the latter from using their guns. Thirty police were hospitalized, and casualties among union members included one broken collarbone, a few broken ribs, and one cracked skull. However, no trucks were moved.[52]

On 22 May more than twenty thousand people met in the central marketplace and prepared to confront the Citizens' Army. After a minor incident in which a window was broken, fighting broke out between the strikers and the Citizens' Army. Within an hour the strikers had won control of the marketplace. Fighting spread throughout the city as strikers confronted the disintegrated police and remnants of the Citizens' Army. The casualties of the day included two members of the Citizens' Army killed and at least fifty wounded. The governor threatened to call in the National Guard, and a truce was achieved between strikers and the Citizens' Army. The Regional Labor Board formulated arrangements for mediation. On 25 May the trucking companies agreed to the full reinstatement of the strikers to their former jobs, a minimum wage, and arbitration over future increases and seniority rights. The question of union recognition of Local 574, however, remained ambiguous with respect to inside workers. The union accepted the terms, and trucking operations resumed in Minneapolis, at least for the time being.[53]

By July it had become clear that the trucking companies would not recognize "inside workers" as members of Local 574. The union demanded recognition, negotiations over wages, hours, and conditions, and the retroactivity of wages to 26 May. The trucking companies refused the demands, and the union voted to strike on 16 July. The trucking companies, in collaboration with the police, planned to provoke a riot by the strikers in order to get the governor to call out the National Guard. The police sent out a truck with an armed convoy in an attempt to cause trouble. The police responded to a striker's attempt to stop the truck with a barrage of shotgun fire. In ten minutes the police shot sixty-seven people, many in the back, killing two. The governor called out the National Guard, imposed martial law, raided the strikers' headquarters, and arrested the leadership of Local 574.[54]

The federal mediation board presented a new plan to the strikers and the trucking companies. The trucking companies and the Citizens' Alliance were forced on 21 August to accept the plan and the unionization of inside workers. After a bloody conflict that lasted almost four months, the trucking companies conceded to the truckers the right to be represented by their own union. Victory was achieved despite the use of the state militia, the armed Citizens' Army, the condemnation of the strike leaders by the president of the national Teamsters as Communists and revolutionaries, and the widespread use of anti-Communist propaganda. The organizational abilities and efforts of the leftist leadership were the decisive elements in the workers' victory.[55] It is doubtful that the truckers would have been able to combat the vast resources of the Citizens' Alliance without the leadership abilities of the Left.

The truckers' strike in Minneapolis, like the Toledo strike, was a direct result of capitalists' refusal to comply with the provisions of the NIRA and specifically section 7a. The role played by Communists was crucial in the truckers' strike. The leadership of Local 574 was clearly dominated by Trotskyists working within the teamsters' union. The Trotskyists in Local 574 gained the support and loyalty of the membership, and consequently, the anti-Communist propaganda of the AFL's national teamster leadership did not carry much weight. The Communist party did not support the strike until rather late—it called the first settlement a sellout and did not join the picket lines until July. The observation of the organizational successes of the Trotskyists led the leaders of the Communist party to reevaluate their own position. They criticized its membership for not working within the AFL union and for not becoming involved in the struggle of the truck drivers much earlier. The Communist party learned from this mistake and chose to participate in the struggle of the longshoremen on the West Coast. However, Trotskyists remained unchallenged in their leadership within Local 574.[56]

The San Francisco Longshoremen's Strike. A revival in union organization occurred in San Francisco among longshoremen and waterfront workers during the months following the passage of the NIRA. Between 1919 and 1934 the Industrial Association of San Francisco almost totally controlled the industrial activity there. The Industrial Association of San Francisco was an employers' industrial association, quite similar to the Citizens' Alliance in Minneapolis. The open-shop drive of the National Association of Manufacturers, which got under way as early as 1920, actually reached its greatest peak in the Industrial Association of San Francisco. The strikes immediately following World War I particularly were disastrous for the maritime union of the West Coast. In a series of employer victories between 1919 and 1923 the union movement among longshoremen and maritime workers was essentially eliminated. San Francisco, which prior to World War I had become the first closed-shop city in the United States, now became open shop. San Francisco workers had previously been among the highest paid in the United States, but in 1926 they were among the poorest paid. The AFL International Longshoremen's Association was replaced on the waterfront by the so-called Blue Book company union.[57]

The demand for a union among waterfront workers was rekindled in 1933 with the enactment of section 7a. A group of former longshoremen retained the charter of the International Longshoremen's Association (ILA) local which had been destroyed in the 1919 strike. The ILA's international president confirmed the status of ILA Local 38-79 and established a Pacific Coast District, thus enabling Local 38-79 to gain autonomy from the international.[58] ILA Local 38-79 attracted a large number of workers. In July 1933, members of the local formed the Committee of 500 in an effort to expand the ILA to include all waterfront workers and warehousemen, as well as to demand from employers an end to the Blue Book, a union hiring hall, and better hours and wages.[59]

In February 1934, after an ILA convention of West Coast workers, the ILA demanded the abolition of the "shape-up system"—the particular form of hiring practices on the waterfront—and its replacement by the union hiring hall, wage-and-hour proposals, and most of all, union recognition. The ILA was prepared to strike on 23 March if the employers did not accept its demands. Employers rejected all demands put forth by the ILA. A federal mediation board was established to investigate, and the strike was postponed. Negotiations took place between ILA officers and the Waterfront Employers' Union, which represented San Francisco waterfront employers under the auspices of a federal mediation board. Negotiations failed, and on 9 May the ILA went on strike. Longshoremen struck in Bellingham, Seattle, Tacoma, Aberdeen, and Grays Harbor, Washington; Portland and Astoria, Oregon; San Francisco, Oakland, Stockton, San Pedro, and San Diego, California; and the small ports along the West Coast. One hundred percent of the unionized longshoremen on the West Coast walked off the job.[60]

Waterfront employers attempted to operate their businesses despite the strike. However, the hiring of strikebreakers did not diminish the effectiveness of the strike. Teamsters refused to haul merchandise to or from the docks. Consequently, whatever cargo the strikebreakers might load or unload was destined to stay on the piers or in the ships' holds. On 26 May the Seamen's Union of the Pacific Coast and ten other maritime unions went on strike in sympathy with the longshoremen. These unions had previously demanded union recognition. A conference to discuss union recognition was denied by the employers. Hence, the strikes of these unions were not only in sympathy with the longshoremen but they also constituted an effort to enforce their own demands. Shortly after 30 May the striking unions made an agreement that none of the unions would go back to work until all of the demands of all the striking unions had been satisfied. By June the entire western waterfront was immobilized.[61]

Frightened by the impact that the longshoremen's strike would have on business activity, the governors of Washington, Oregon, and California appealed in mid May for federal intervention on the matter of the maritime strike. Assistant Secretary of Labor Edward F. McGrady arrived in San Francisco to mediate between the employers and the striking unions. All efforts to mediate the strike failed. The leaders of the ILA international were willing to enter into an agreement with the waterfront employers, but the rank and file of the ILA refused arbitration over the issue of hiring halls. Finally on 16 June the president of the international ILA ignored the demands of the rank and file and entered into an agreement with the Waterfront Employers' Union to end the strike. The agreement did not include provisions for the closed shop, as demanded by the strikers, and the hiring halls were to be jointly administered, rather than falling under union control. The rank and file refused to abide by the agreement, and the employers, backed by conservative Hearst newspapers, went on the offensive.[62]

Businessmen in the Pacific Northwest wrote letters to the Labor Department and the White House; they protested that the maritime strike was led by Communists and that it ruined economic activity. The Hearst newspapers and the Industrial Association of San Francisco blamed the strike on the "Communists" and suggested that the strike was not a struggle between labor and capital but was, rather, a strike between anti-Americans and those who had American ideals. The rank and file's opposition to the agreement that had been made by the president of the ILA provided fuel for the anti-Communist campaign. A letter from an associate of the Hearst newspapers makes this point clear:

> If the officials in Washington think Ryan [president of the ILA] can iron out differences they are badly mistaken. He has lost control of the organization to communist leaders who don't want any settlement under any circumstances. This thing is very serious and unless newspapermen are able to mold public opinion against communistic leaders or unless government steps in with a strong hand there is going to be hell to pay in San Francisco.[63]

Furthermore, on 22 June, William Green, president of the AFL, confirmed the rumors that the situation on the San Francisco waterfront was being led and controlled by Communists. He argued that because of the Communist influence, trade unions everywhere were being "threatened."[64]

The charges of Communist involvement in the maritime strike were not without some validity. To be sure, the Communist party supported the strike. In accordance with the change in the party line with regard to dual unionism, the party emphasized working within the ILA and dissolving the TUUL affiliated Maritime Workers' Industrial Union in an effort to strengthen the ILA's Local 38-79. The leaders of the San Francisco longshoremen's strike, if not party members, had close ties with members of the Communist party. One of the leaders, the Australian-born Harry Bridges, openly and actively accepted financial help from the Communist party. The party did offer its organizational abilities to the ILA. Ironically, the charge that the San Francisco maritime strike was being led by "illegal aliens" of "Communist influence" was not taken too seriously by Secretary of Labor Frances Perkins. An investigation of Bridges conducted by the Immigration Department concluded that Bridges had no close links to the Communist party. The only direct link to the party was a witness at Bridges's citizenship proceedings who turned out to be a candidate for a public office on the Communist party's ticket![65] There is reason to believe, however, that Bridges did in fact have close links to the Communist party and that the party did have a presence within the ILA.[66] The police constantly harassed strikers in San Francisco throughout the months of May and June. Police attacked striking pickets on the waterfront, raided the homes of strike leaders and strike participants, and raided union halls.[67] On 3 July the Industrial Association of San Francisco armed some seven hundred men with tear-gas bombs and riot guns in an attempt to move cargo from the waterfront. These men were supposed to drive trucks to load and deliver the stationary cargo. Strikers and sympathizers, largely organized by the Communist party, met the trucks and their police escorts. Eighteen trips were made to the warehouses despite the violence that erupted. Pickets threw bricks at the trucks, and the police and armed drivers responded with night sticks, tear gas, and bullets. The pickets retreated, overcome by tear gas, after four hours of fighting which left a total of twenty-five people hospitalized.[68]

Newspapers reported on 4 July that the port was open for trade. On 5 July thousands of pickets and sympathizers grouped at the waterfront where they met 800 heavily armed police who were assigned to protect ten new trucks which would attempt to move the idle cargo. Fighting continued all day. Hundreds of pickets, police, and onlookers were injured; at least 115 were hospitalized; and 2 strikers were killed. The governor of California called in 1,700 National Guardsmen. The guardsmen placed machine guns and barbed wire along the waterfront and prepared armored cars to police the area.[69]

Strikers and sympathizers focused their attention for the next few days on the slain strikers. More than 25,000 San Francisco workers marched in a funeral procession. Teamsters, butchers, machinists, welders, laundry workers, and others in San Francisco walked off their jobs. Representatives of 115 unions voted on 14 July, by a conclusive tally of 315 to 15, to call a general strike. San Francisco was at a virtual standstill by 16 July. The general strike was led by the more conservative AFL unions, and after four days, most of the workers returned to work.[70]

All fractions of the capitalist class joined forces against the strike. The biggest attack, as was to be expected, was centered against the Communist party. Roger Lapham, owner of the American Hawaiian Steamship Company, reported to the secretary of labor that the strike was due to "communistic" and other "radical influences" and urged that federal action be taken against the "alien" influences.[71] The redbaiting was most evident in the local press, where every article and ad attacked the Communist party and the "communist influence" for leading the strike. Hugh Johnson, now head of the National Recovery Administration, while giving a speech at the University of California at Berkeley, condemned the strike for being led by a "subversive element" and urged the labor movement to "run these subversive influences out of its rank like rats." What he said was happening was not a strike; rather, it was a "bloody insurrection" by "one-half of one percent of our population to try to strangle the rest of us into submission."[72]

The Red scare was successful in instigating an attack of repressive forces against the strike. Bands of vigilantes attacked Communist-party headquarters. Both police and private citizens, moved by the anti-Communist propaganda, attacked and arrested members of the Marine Industrial Workers' Union and harassed all so-called Communist organizations. An account of the police raids on unions is captured in the following statement:

> I was sitting in the union room at 65 Jackson Street on July 17 typing, when the police came through the hall and drove us out the back of the hall, with clubs, into waiting patrol wagons. Several of the men were beaten during the arrests. We were taken to Central Station, and they booked me as a $1,000 vag, although they did not tell me what the charge was. I was afraid to ask what the charge was against me because of the violence used by the police.[73]

The acts of repression and redbaiting helped the conservative leadership of the San Francisco AFL to gain leadership of the strike, and by 18 July the strike was virtually ended. On 21 July the ILA agreed to arbitration. The seamen and other maritime unions accepted arbitration a week later.

The ILA did not win all of its demands, but the solidarity displayed among workers in San Francisco was never totally destroyed. The National Longshoremen's Board acted as mediator over discussions in which the waterfront employers agreed to fire all strikebreakers and to rehire the strikers without discrimination. The final agreement provided for union recognition, a 30-hour work week, a wage raise of 10 cents an hour, to 95 cents, and a joint operation with employers of central hiring halls in each of the seventeen West Coast ports. The union was permitted to pick the dispatchers in each of the halls, which resulted in effective union control and created a situation closely akin to a closed shop.[74]

The significance of the longshoremen's strike lay not only in the degree of solidarity shown by other maritime workers but also in the fact that the strike was conducted under rank-and-file leadership. The ILA Local 38-79, aided by the Communist party, was able to gain union recognition and to contribute to a developing tradition of strong unionization and worker solidarity. This was achieved despite opposition from the Industrial Association of San Francisco and all waterfront employers. The struggle of the ILA included other maritime unions and began the move away from craft unionization to a broader-based industrial union. A statement contained in the files of the 1934 strike in the ILWU archives sums up the assessment of the strike itself:

> In a year which has witnessed more widespread and dramatic industrial conflict than any since 1919, the general strike of last summer in San Francisco Bay Region stands out as a highlight, not because of its size or violence . . . but because of the nature of its challenge and the reaction

> which it invoked in a society which has ceased to believe in its own stability. One cannot have lived in California through the summer of 1934 . . . without being forced to the conclusion that if the working class of this country were only half as convinced of the possibility and imminence of social revolution as is the employing class, the battle would be half won.[75]

The East Coast Textile Strike. The strike of the United Textile Workers was the largest strike of 1934. This strike during the fall of 1934 differed from the somewhat localized strikes of truckers in Minneapolis, auto-parts workers in Toledo, and maritime workers in San Francisco in that it involved workers in the entire textile industry along the eastern seaboard. The significance of the textile strike was threefold. First, the strike included workers in the entire textile industry. Second, although the strike involved the largest number of workers of any strike in 1934, it did not develop any leadership and/or support from any leftist political group. The strike was led and controlled by a conservative leadership group associated with the AFL. Third, the textile strike was a total failure. Not one of the demands presented by textile workers was met by textile employers. Mill owners did not concede to union recognition. Finally, the failure of the strike illustrated that the combination of employer resistance and local military force not only was capable of wearing down strikers but also was capable of pressuring federal mediators to rule in favor of the mill owners.

The cotton-textile industry, which had been in decline since the end of World War I, was the first industry to adopt a Code of Fair Competition under the provisions of the NIRA. The code included provisions to deal with overcapacity in the industry, and in addition to the full provisions of section 7a of the NIRA with regard to labor, it included a 40-hour workweek and minimum wages, differentiated by employment in the North and the South. A special executive order provided for the investigation of the stretch-out, the system by which work loads were increased. The cotton-textile code helped to increase output and employment. During the code's first few months, both production and labor conditions improved rapidly. Child labor was eliminated from the industry, hours of work were reduced from an average of fifty-three per week to a maximum of forty, wage rates were raised from precode levels of $8.00 to $10.00 per week to a minimum of $12.00 and $13.00 per week. During the first months of the code, average hourly earnings increased by 70 percent. Payrolls and employment in the industry rose rapidly.[76]

Before the adoption of the code, there had been little labor organization in the textile industry, with the exception of the National Textile Workers (NTW), a TUUL affiliate. The NTW never had a significant impact on the unionization of the industry. The United Textile Workers (UTW) of the AFL was basically a conservative union; prior to the code it had a membership between 15,000 and 20,000 in an industry that employed 400,000 to 450,000 workers. The UTW undertook a campaign to organize the industry in response to the adoption of the code for the cotton-textile industry and the provisions of section 7a of the NIRA. By May 1934 the UTW increased its membership to include 300,000 workers in the cotton-textile industry alone.[77] Union membership grew simultaneously with an increase in worker discontent over the inadequacy of section 7a, over the ineffectiveness of the labor provisions of the code, and over an increase in work loads and the continuation of the stretch-out. The cotton-textile industry suffered a business decline during the fall of 1933. Consequently, the benefits that had accrued to workers under the code were eliminated. Mill owners reclassified workers as "learners," cut the wages of higher-skilled people to near minimum, and continued the stretch-out. The issue of the stretch-out was the most prominent complaint voiced by workers. In one mill the management had increased the quota of looms per weaver from 24 to 72, then to 100. When workers complained that a quota of 100 looms imposed an intolerably heavy burden upon them and therefore threatened to strike, the management yielded and reduced the quota from 100 to 84 looms.[78]

The Cotton Textile National Industrial Relations Board, which was controlled by the cotton-textile industry, was established to examine the labor problems of textile workers. Thus, workers had no "legal" recourse for their grievances. The board systematically failed to handle any labor problems. Complaints by workers were forwarded to the workers' employer, who usually would fire the worker for registering a complaint.[79] Furthermore, the board was inept in putting into practice the provisions of section 7a. Most mill owners refused to negotiate with the UTW and claimed that although the UTW represented 300,000 workers, the union was not a representative of the majority of the workers in the industry. One mill owner even went so far as to suggest that all labor unions should be abolished and that one organization, under the auspices of the Labor Department, should represent all laborers.[80]

Worker discontent mounted when all institutional mechanisms to handle worker complaints failed. On 18 July 1934, officers of the UTW called a special convention to consider the question of a possible strike in the face of the inadequacy of section 7a and the cotton-textile code of fair competition. On 14 August 500 delegates of various UTW locals met in New York City and voted for a general cotton-textile strike, which was to take place on 1 September. The fundamental issues involved in the strike were recognition of the UTW, methods of collective bargaining, machinery for handling complaints of violations of section 7a and other labor provisions of the cotton-textile code, hours of work, wages, and the stretch-out.[81]

By 4 September the work stoppage of the UTW had spread to almost every textile center in the country. Textile workers in Alabama, North Carolina, Georgia, South Carolina, Tennessee, Virginia, Pennsylvania, Rhode Island, Massachusetts, New Hampshire, and Maine all joined the general strike. Silk workers walked off the job in New Jersey. Mills in New Bedford, Massachusetts, were completely shut down. Elsewhere in that state the textile industry in Fall River was crippled, and woolen workers in Lowell walked off the job. It has been estimated that more than 376,000 textile workers went out on strike.[82] The effectiveness of the walkout was made possible by the organizational tactics used to shut down plants along the entire East Coast. Regional directors of the UTW took charge at Providence, Rhode Island; Cohoes, New York; Philadelphia, Pennsylvania; and Greenville, South Carolina. The "flying squadron" tactic was especially successful in the southern mills. The members of a squadron would move from town to town and from factory to factory, helping to shut down production in one place and then moving on to other towns and factories that needed their help. The arrival of the squadron frequently hastened a walkout in less organized mills. The UTW refused support from leftist political groups and made no effort to call citywide or statewide strikes. The only strike support received from other unions came in the form of financial support—mostly from the more industrialized unions within the AFL.[83]

Mill owners responded to the strike by importing armed guards and industrial spies. Mill owners also pressured public authorities to evict strikers' families, to cut off relief, to terrorize union leaders and sympathizers, and above all, to have governors in the textile states mobilize the National Guard. During the first week of the strike, one striker was killed and twenty were wounded in Georgia, six strikers were killed in South Carolina, and two strikers were killed and twenty were wounded in the states of Rhode Island, Connecticut, and Massachusetts combined. By the second week of the strike, with the help of National Guardsmen and special militia, mills were being kept open in Alabama, Mississippi, Georgia, and North and South Carolina. In the South, union organizers were forced out of town, mills were protected with machine guns and armed guards, telegrams for union officials were intercepted by mill owners, and relief was discontinued for the families of striking textile workers.[84] The governor of Rhode Island called in the National Guard to many towns, blamed the strike on Communists (although in this case, Communists really had nothing to do with the strike), and attacked Communist-party headquarters. Within three days, special militia and the National Guard had shot fifteen strikers and killed one. Although the violence was instigated by the state militia, the governor of Rhode Island was convinced that the Communist party was behind the "rioting." He subsequently demanded that President Roosevelt send in federal troops. However, an FBI report from J. Edgar Hoover indicated that there was "no probability of any serious violence or outbreaks in that vicinity . . . there is not now even a remote possibility of a necessity for the stationing of Federal Troops in Rhode Island."[85] No federal troops were sent to Rhode Island.

After numerous letters had been sent to various agencies and to the White House in protest against the use of National Guardsmen and state militia in the textile strike, Roosevelt appointed the Board of Inquiry for the Cotton-Textile Industry and empowered it either to make recommendations for the resolution of the issues of the strike or to act as an arbitrator if requested to do so by both the workers and the mill owners.[86] On 20 September the board sent its recommendations to Roosevelt. On 22 September the UTW accepted the recommendation, and the strike was called off. The recommendations of the Board of Inquiry represented a stunning defeat for the UTW. The strike ended without recognition for the UTW, the stretch-out remained unchanged, and wages were not increased. As a result, UTW membership dropped drastically. Although it was recommended that the employers rehire the strikers, UTW records show that 113 northern and 226 southern mills refused to do so. Strikers in mill villages were evicted from company houses. The new Textile Labor Relations Board was appointed by Roosevelt, but by the time the board had finished making its recommendations, the NIRA and all of its provisions for industrial labor were on the way to being declared unconstitutional.[87]

The textile strike involved the largest number of workers in any strike of 1934. The number of workers involved and the financial support from sympathetic trade unions were not enough to offset the tremendous force of militia and National Guardsmen in almost every state along the East Coast. By refusing to work with leftist political groups, the leaders of the AFL-associated UTW rejected a potentially useful organizational support group that was committed to the objective interests of the textile workers. Furthermore, the state-appointed Board of Inquiry made recommendations that were favorable to mill owners. The UTW and the conservative leadership were not strong enough to reverse these recommendations. Mill owners neither recognized the UTW as a bargaining agent nor conceded to increased wages and reduced hours; this resulted in a setback for union organizing in the entire cotton-textile industry. The combination of repression and the conservative leadership of the UTW left the trade-unionization efforts of cotton-textile workers at the mercy of mill owners long after the labor upsurges of 1934.

One of the major differences between the textile strike and the other significant strikes of 1934 is that even though the textile strike involved more workers than any of the other strikes, the strikers were presented with severe physical force to break their strike. Simply put, the United Textile Workers were not able to muster enough strength to withstand either the military force of special state militia and the National Guard or the economic hardships that mill owners placed on the striking workers. The balance of forces in the textile strike were clearly in favor of the mill owners by the time the Board of Inquiry made its recommendation to President Roosevelt. In contrast to the situation in Toledo, Minneapolis, or San Francisco, the mill owners retained control over their laborers. The decision of the Board of Inquiry merely reflected the balance of forces in the textile industry.

The AFL and Labor Militancy

Throughout the existence of the NIRA, the AFL remained the conservative force within the labor movement.[88] The conservative nature of the AFL is most evident in its lack of support for the strike wave of 1934 and in the anticommunism of its leaders. The enthusiasm of rank-and-file workers in mass-production industries for unionization was not sufficient to induce the AFL to abandon its narrow policy of craft unionization. The leadership of the AFL fought industrial unionization and only granted charters to industrial-based unions when the demand was overwhelming. Even then, the AFL leadership retained the authority to break the so-called federal union into many craft unions. The AFL primarily represented skilled workers; it made no attempt to organize the less skilled. In fact, the militancy of new AFL members during 1933 and 1934 worried the AFL leadership. By 1934, hundreds of workers were striking against the wishes or consent of the national leadership. These workers were often labeled as "irresponsible" or just plain "rubbish."[89]

The AFL welcomed the passage of the NIRA, and it sought to take advantage of section 7a by initiating a massive campaign for unionization. However, its craft orientation weakened the ability of the AFL to organize mass-production industries in the face of intense resistance on the part of employers. AFL union drives failed most notably in the automotive, rubber, and steel industries, where federal locals were initially established but eventually were broken up into craft unions. The AFL was very reluctant to use the weapon of strikes; it favored conciliation through a federal mediation board.

The AFL did little in an activist way to improve the lot of the masses of workers during the early years of the economic depression. The AFL proposed no real alternatives to state policies; it even dropped the demand for unemployment insurance in 1931. In addition, the AFL deserted unemployed members who could not pay dues. The AFL was not concerned in working with the unemployed.[90] By 1935 the AFL was losing its legitimacy among the rank and file. The experience of the 1934 strike wave and the awareness of the gross inadequacies of section 7a led most AFL unionists to become critical of the NIRA, but the AFL leadership continued to support section 7a and even tried to curtail attempts to challenge this policy.[91] From the point of view of the rank and file, the AFL was "out of touch" with the situation. Membership in the AFL had fallen drastically by 1935. Its membership within the automotive industry had fallen from approximately 100,000 in 1934 to 10,000 by the winter of 1935. Its membership within the steel industry declined from approximately 100,000 in 1934 to 5,300 in 1935.[92] The decline in union membership did not represent workers' loss of interest in unionization; rather, it represented the unwillingness of the rank and file to join unions that were basically ineffective.

The AFL leadership's attack on industrial unionization was surprisingly similar to the antiunionism of industrial capitalists. Most notably in 1933 and 1934, the AFL tried to disrupt any form of industrial unionization, and it resorted to anti-Communist propaganda in an attempt to lure workers away from such unions. Furthermore, the AFL informed various state officials about the potential "menace" of industrial unionism. During 1933 and 1934, powerful craft unionists "raided" members from the industrial locals, directly affiliated with the AFL, that had been successfully organizing factory workers.[93] Part of the AFL's plan to discredit industrial unions was to single out to state authorities various members as Communists or Communist sympathizers. In March 1934 a report of the AFL leadership intimated that the Ladies Garment Workers, the Textile Workers, and the United Mine Workers were the unions that had been most heavily infiltrated by Communists or by Communist sympathizers.[94] In February 1935 a special report was submitted to William Green, president of the AFL, which indicated trade-union work on the part of the Communist party.[95] What is interesting about this report is that it was dated 12 December 1934 and that it was written in the manner of an interparty correspondence. Apparently, the AFL had informants within the Communist party. After receiving the report on Communist activity in the trade-union movement, Green forwarded the report to Roosevelt in order that "proper action" might be taken against radicals and "subversive" elements within the labor movement. A more striking example of the anticommunism of the AFL can be illustrated by a statement that a former member of the Communist party made to Green: it implied that the industrial unions were infiltrated by Communists, and it furnished the names of people who allegedly had links with Communist organizations and were affiliated with industrial unions.[96] The statement was intended to give Green the necessary ammunition to discredit all attempts at industrial unionization. However, the AFL's attempts to destroy industrial organization and to discredit the activities of the Communist party within the trade-union movement failed—at least temporarily.

A National Policy for Industrial Labor

The potential benefits of the labor provisions of the NIRA were never fully realized by workers. After the Supreme Court's decision declaring the NIRA unconstitutional, hours were increased and wages were reduced in most industrial enterprises except for the large-scale firms and in those concerns that had strong labor organizations. During the month of June 1935, the National Industrial Recovery Review Board submitted reports to Roosevelt which documented changes in hours and wages after the suspension of the NIRA. These reports indicated that in general, wages had decreased and hours of work had increased.[97] Even during the NIRA period, workers gained only minimal improvements in working conditions and benefits. The NIRA codes, in spite of a gain in manufacturing production of 14 percent, stimulated little increase in jobs between October 1933 and May 1935. In industries that employed 57 percent of the total number of workers, provisions in 84 percent of the codes allowed a basic forty-hour workweek. However, in 64 percent of the codes, covering 61 percent of the total number of workers in the codified industries, provisions permitted a workweek of forty-eight hours or longer. The abuse in the application of loosely drawn provisions with regard to hours of work reduced the extent of reemployment which the codes were intended to accomplish. Although the codes of the NIRA provided for minimum wages, increases in the average yearly incomes for workers were minimal, especially after allowing for the rise in the cost of living. Between October 1933 and May 1935, average weekly earnings increased by 8 percent, although in a significant percentage of industries, there was actually a decrease in the average weekly earnings. The annual earnings in mining, manufacturing, and construction went from $874 in 1933 to $1,068 in 1935. The total money income of workers rose from $1.627 million in June 1933 to an average of $2.022 million in the last five months of the NIRA. However, the increase in the cost of living nearly canceled out the increase in real wages.[98]

Although the labor provisions of the NIRA included minimal benefits for workers, the gross inadequacy of section 7a set off the spark for labor militancy. The suspension of the provisions of the NIRA, and consequently section 7a, did not mean that the struggle for union recognition would cease. Rather, it forced the state administration to develop a new labor policy. Within five weeks of the Supreme Court decision that declared the NIRA unconstitutional, Roosevelt signed the National Labor Relations Act.

In the spring of 1934 Senator Robert Wagner introduced a bill in Congress to establish a new labor-relations board. Unlike the national labor board under the supervision of the National Recovery Administration, this proposed board would possess enforcement machinery. At the time the bill was introduced, nearly all capitalists opposed the bill, and the Roosevelt administration did not support it. In its place the Roosevelt administration established the National Labor Relations Board. However, within one year, Wagner reintroduced his bill to Congress with some minor revisions. After a year of increased labor militancy and perhaps because of the hope that the bill would control labor radicalism and unrest, the bill gained support in both the House and the Senate.[99]

The major argument in favor of Wagner's bill was that changes within the industrial sector that would result in highly concentrated and centralized industrial branches would give the employer an advantageous bargaining position over the worker. Both recovery and long-term economic prosperity depended upon a greater level of wages, which would increase purchasing power and thereby balance economic activity. Proponents of the bill argued that collective bargaining, preferably industrywide, would promote a more balanced economy. Some proponents argued that the state's protection of collective bargaining would reduce the threat of revolutionary trade unions and would provide labor with a legal means to express economic grievances with their employers. Opponents of the bill essentially argued that the bill was unconstitutional and that it would discriminate against employers. Opposition to the bill was mild at best within Congress, and the major opposing force was located within the National Association of Manufacturers.[100]

With no great opposition, the debate in the Senate over Wagner's bill was uneventful. The bill passed the Senate in May 1935 with a vote of 63 to 12. Opposed to the bill were 4 Democrats and 8 Republicans. Irving Bernstein has argued that the speed with which the bill was passed in the Senate was due to the "feebleness" of the opposition. Moreover, the influence of labor was at its height by the spring of 1935, and many senators were dependent on labor's vote in the upcoming elections. Convinced that the Supreme Court would declare the bill unconstitutional, some senators voted for the bill in order to gain labor's political support. These senators believed that the measure would not take effect until after the Supreme Court had ruled on its constitutionality.[101]

Although Roosevelt did not initially support the bill, the suspension of the labor provisions of the NIRA, rising labor militancy, and passage of the bill in the Senate forced him to take a position on the Wagner bill. According to Leuchtenburg, "after calling in Wagner to work out certain differences with members of the administration, the President abruptly announced, for reasons that are not wholly clear, that he not only favored the Wagner bill but regarded it as a 'must' legislation."[102] By the end of June, with little debate, the bill passed the House, and on 5 July 1935 Roosevelt signed the law, which is referred to as the National Labor Relations Act (NLRA).

The NLRA stated that workers had the right to form unions. Proceeding a step further than section 7a of the NIRA, the NLRA stated that employers could not interfere with the attempts of workers to form unions. In addition, it outlawed the establishment of company unions, and it demanded that employers bargain over terms of employment with unions that had been selected by a majority of workers. The National Labor Relations Board was established as an independent agency, empowered to enforce the provisions of the NLRA and to rule on "unfair" labor practices. Unlike the NIRA and the labor provisions of various codes that differed for workers who were employed in different branches of industry, the NLRA applied to all nonagriculture workers regardless of their industrial affiliation. The NLRA represented a prounion stand on the part of the state administration.

A prounion stand should not be confused with a pro-working-class stand.[103] On the contrary, by providing both legal sanction for unions, especially industrial unions, and legal recourse for workers' complaints against employer attempts to subvert unionization, the NLRA provided an institutional mechanism for settling worker discontent in a peaceful and often depoliticizing form—that is, depoliticizing insofar as collective-bargaining arrangements remain within the confines of bourgeois political rule and tend to isolate workers' political struggles from economic struggles. Although the NLRA represented a victory for workers, in that they received government sanctions to settle shop-floor conflicts, the NLRA continued and solidified the process that turned a union movement that was previously suspicious of governmental interference into a "semi-public unionism whose organization was part of a government program."[104]

The struggle for union recognition and the right to bargain collectively did not end with the passage of the NLRA. Industrial capitalists did not readily accept the provisions of the NLRA; they defiantly resisted industrial labor's organizational rights. What followed from the law's enactment was a "new period" of labor struggles. The course of this new period of struggle is what altered relationships between labor, capital, and the state and provided the context for a new social structure of accumulation.

CHAPTER SEVEN

Industrial Unionization and the Political Scene

> Bill Green who betrayed the interest of the auto, steel, textile, and now rubber workers, must be prevented from repeating this in the future. Take up in your local union immediately the transformation of the present form of federal locals into industrial unions and form an International union in the rubber industry, controlled by honest, militant, rank and file workers.
>
> —*Communist Party leaflet*

> AFL and CIO [are] organizing a war.
>
> —*J. R. Steelman*

Rifts in the Labor Movement and the Emergence of the CIO

The National Labor Relations Act provided industrial labor with the legal space to organize mass-production industries.[1] Moreover, the favorable relationship between the Democratic party and the emerging industrial-union movement gave industrial wage labor the political space to make further gains. Nevertheless, the industrial workers' movement of the mid 1930s did not emerge as a unified class movement. Although the balance of class forces was certainly changing in that industrial labor was on the offensive against industrial capital, the labor movement itself faced serious internal problems, which prevented industrial labor from sustaining its offensive struggle. These problems, internal to the labor movement, focused on the issue of industrial unions and surfaced within the American Federation of Labor. Many workers became disillusioned with the ineffectiveness of the AFL and the conservative role that the AFL's leadership played during the 1934 wave of strikes. Although the leadership maintained that it granted charters to industrial unions, the AFL was hostile to the establishment of industrial unions in areas where craft unions still existed.[2]

Significant numbers of workers were employed in the concentrated mass-production industries, so it is no surprise that by 1935 a large number of workers within the AFL supported industrial unionization. At the 1935 convention of the AFL these workers proposed resolutions that would fundamentally have changed the craft characteristic of the AFL itself. The resolutions called for the establishment of "pure" industrial unions with charters that would not include craft jurisdictions. For example, in the automotive industry the craft unions for machinists, parts workers, and the like would be abolished and brought under the charter of the industrial union.[3] The resolutions were defeated at the national convention. Under the instigation of John L. Lewis of the United Mine Workers, a group of industrial unions within the AFL formed an opposition group—the Committee for Industrial Organization—to support industrial unionization and to embark on an industrial-organization drive.[4] The stated purposes of the committee were to help organize the unorganized mass-production workers and to bring them into the AFL. Within a few days after the formation of the Committee for Industrial Organization, Green, president of the AFL, warned the AFL membership that the committee would cause cleavages in the labor movement. He argued that the committee's intentions would cause confusion and would result in a dual organization. Nevertheless, the committee attracted many new unionists. By 1936 the AFL's leadership had suspended from the AFL the unions associated with the Committee for Industrial Organization, which in 1938 formally split from the AFL and became the Congress of Industrial Organizations, or CIO.[5]

Thus a full-scale drive was launched to organize the mass-production industries that had remained untouched by craft-unionization drives. At the same time, the Communist party officially changed its policy of dual unionism because of developments in the international Communist movement and changes in the domestic situation. With increased numbers of workers joining unions, especially the new unions connected with the CIO, the Communist party began to work within the industrial-union movement, applying its considerable organizational abilities to the building of the CIO. The party worked with CIO unions to build and strengthen unionization in basic mass-production industries. Aided by the Communist party and other radicals, the CIO was able to build durable industrial unions by successfully combining rank-and-file militance with organizational skill and was able to succeed in organizing unions in basic mass-production industries such as rubber, steel, and automobiles, where AFL craft unionism had failed.[6]

Part of the reason for the Communist party's contribution to the development of CIO unions was that the leadership of the CIO willingly accepted the party's support. Unlike the leadership of the AFL, that of the CIO did not attempt to purge Communists from its ranks and, in fact, hired known members of the Communist party to work in organizing drives. The CIO needed all the available organizational help if it was to be successful in organizing the mass-production industries that were controlled by monopoly capital and ones that had been citadels of the open shop. The publicity director and the general counsel for the CIO's Steel Workers' Organizing Committee, who was later to be the general counsel for the CIO, were both members of or sympathizers with the Communist party. Moreover, of the two hundred full-time organizers in the Steel Workers' Organizing Committee, sixty were members of the Communist party. The party had a more extensive presence in the organizing drives in the steel and automotive industries than in the other CIO organizing campaigns.[7]

The CIO had grown and made considerable progress in basic industries by 1937. However, the 1937/38 recession witnessed a halt in the major offensive of the CIO as unemployment rose, capitalists increased their class struggle with industrial labor, and the AFL experienced a resurgence in the field of industrial relations. By 1938, mass-production industries had become far more organized than in 1935, and in the political climate of the time the CIO began to purge Communists from its membership. In its anti-Communist and anti-industrial drives the right-wing trade unionism of the AFL allied with capital by entering into a number of "back door" contracts negotiated between capitalists and AFL affiliated unions.[8] According to Sidney Lens,

> at Consolidated Edison in New York, for example, where the United Electrical and Radio Workers, CIO, had thoroughly taken over an AFL local, management hastily signed a contract with the AFL to freeze out the UE. . . . In Kansas, Oklahoma, and Missouri, where the CIO Mine, Mill, and Smelter Workers had unionized thousands of miners who had formerly been forced to join the Blue Card Union, a corporation-run organization, the AFL chartered the company union under the name Tri-State Metal, Mine and Smelter Workers.[9]

The changing political climate, the resurgence of the AFL, and the victories of the CIO combined to provide labor disunity. This labor disunity, particularly the weakness of the labor Left as a consistent force within the trade-union movement, had made it possible to isolate CIO leftists by the end of the 1930s.[10] Official governmental sanctioning of the CIO during the last few years of the 1930s and during the war years provided organized industrial labor with the protection needed from antiunion employers. State sanctioning of industrial unions and the "marriage" between industrial organized labor and the Democratic party overpowered Communist and radical militant influence within the CIO.[11]

The Struggle for Unionization Continues

The drive to organize workers in basic mass-production industries was strengthened by court rulings that declared the National Labor Relations Act constitutional. Increases in union membership coincided with an increase in work stoppages between 1935 and 1937. In 1935 there were 2,014 work stoppages involving 1,120,000 workers; in 1936, 2,172 involving 789,000 workers; and in 1937, 4,740 involving 1,860,000 workers. The major issue in the majority of these strikes was union recognition.[12] Eight unions with a membership of 900,000 formed the

CIO in November 1935. By September 1938 the CIO had grown to include thirty-two international unions with a membership of 3,718,000. Total AFL membership in September 1938 was estimated at 3.6 million, an increase of more than one million new members in two years.[13] The growth of trade-union membership was not necessarily brought about simply by the legalization of unionization under federal law; rather, it was the success of the organizing campaigns of the CIO in building strong unions in mass-production industries such as rubber, automobiles, and steel. Trade-union membership only grew when unions were powerful enough to threaten an interruption in the production process, thereby forcing capitalists to abide by the provisions of the NLRA.[14]

A successful tactic of the CIO unions was the sit-down strike, which involved the possession of property not protected under the NLRA. Sit-down strikes entailed having the workers stop their machines or work, sit down in the factory or plant, and refuse to move until all demands had been met by respective employers. In 1937 alone, the Bureau of Labor Statistics estimated that there were 477 sit-down strikes involving 398,117 workers. The sit-down found immense support in the rubber, steel, and automotive industries. In fact, the tactic of the sit-down was so powerful in the automobile industry that it proved indispensable to the unionization of the entire auto industry.[15] Unlike the walkout, the sit-down entailed taking possession of the means of production and preventing them from being used by strikebreakers to continue production. In 1936 and 1937 the CIO was concentrated chiefly among rubber, steel, and automotive workers. The sit-down strikes and their relative successes in these mass-production industries were decisive for the growth and organization of the CIO. The following is a brief examination of the major strikes during the first few years of the NLRA and the formation of the CIO. A review of those strikes indicates how working-class militancy indirectly served to aid in the organization of the working class and resulted in increased union growth.

The Rubber Workers' Strike

The first major strike after the passage of the NLRA occurred in Akron, Ohio; it involved rubber workers at the Goodyear Tire and Rubber Company. By the time the CIO had been formed, many union rubber workers had left the AFL union because of the ineffectiveness of the union in establishing a presence among rubber employers. In 1935 at the Goodyear plant only two hundred out of fourteen thousand workers paid dues to the United Rubber Workers. CIO organizing drives began in January 1936, and many rubber workers returned to union membership.[16]

The first incident of strike activity in the rubber industry occurred in the Firestone plant in January 1936, when workers began a sit-down strike over the dismissal of a union worker. The sit-down, which lasted for three days, was quite successful. Firestone reinstated the union worker and agreed to reduce the speed-up which had been a constant source of complaint among the workers. As a result of the strike, four hundred Firestone workers rejoined the union.[17]

In the Goodyear plant, 3,000 workers struck in February 1936. The immediate cause of the strike was the dismissal of 137 workers. However, worker discontent had been evident in the Goodyear plant as early as October 1935, when a federal mediation board settled an agreement between the rubber workers and the rubber companies. This agreement resulted in the postponement of a threatened strike. The major issue was the lengthening of hours of work in violation of the agreement made between the workers and the rubber companies before the NIRA had been suspended. Moreover, the rubber companies had never abided by the recommendations of the federal mediation board and did not recognize the AFL union as the sole bargaining agent of the rubber workers.[18] In February, despite federal recommendations, Goodyear laid off 137 workers. On 17 February, thousands of rubber workers left the Goodyear plant and established an eleven-mile picket line around the company's fences and gates. By the second day of the strike, 10,000 workers had both joined the walkout and rejoined the union.[19]

Goodyear obtained a restraining order against mass picketing. However, the restraining order was never enforced because the labor unions of Akron threatened a general strike if physical force were used to break the strike. In late February, negotiations began between rubber workers and rubber companies, but no agreement was reached. The former mayor of Akron enlisted 2,500 residents of Akron to act as vigilantes to break the strike.[20] Unlike the vigilante associations connected with the 1934 strike wave, the Akron Law and Order League gained little support among the residents of Akron. The strike ended after a month when Goodyear agreed to recognize the United Rubber Workers, reinstate the discharged workers, grant seniority rights, and reduce the work week to thirty-six hours. Nevertheless, Goodyear continued to negotiate with the company union. However, the company union was discredited, and the United Rubber Workers gained a significant number of new members. Workers staged at least 180 sit-down strikes in rubber plants during the ten months following the Goodyear strike, and almost every one of the strikes entailed some gain for unionists and new members for the United Rubber Workers of America.[21]

The strike at Goodyear was the first CIO-led strike. The CIO was able to revive unionization in the rubber industry by early 1936. The slight economic upturn from 1935 until the fall of 1937 restored some self-confidence among wage labor, and the passage of the NLRA, along with Roosevelt's seemingly prolabor position, provided a political climate that reassured workers that their rights would be protected.[22] The workers' victory in the rubber industry signified the growing importance of the CIO as an industrial-union organization that was able to win major battles from large-scale monopoly industrial capital. Victories in the rubber industry stimulated the great offensive of CIO-affiliated unions.

The Automotive Workers' Strike

During the NIRA period, many auto workers joined AFL-affiliated federal unions. However, under the policies of the AFL and consequent governmental conciliation in the automobile industry, not to mention the incredible amount of industrial espionage in that industry, total membership in unions had declined by early 1935 to 5 percent.[23] However, the passage of the NLRA in mid 1935 and the organizing campaigns of the CIO caused many auto workers to join the United Auto Workers (UAW), a union that was now affiliated with the CIO. By late 1936 the UAW had become strong enough to confront General Motors and demand union recognition as sole bargaining agent for auto workers.[24] With the success of the rubber workers in Akron, the auto workers were determined to win union recognition.

Auto workers staged a series of sit-down strikes during the first four months of 1937.[25] The largest and most notable of these was in the General Motors plant in Flint, Michigan. Workers were contemplating a strike in the G.M. plants because management had dismissed workers who wore union buttons. The Flint strike was called after a worker reported that G.M. was shipping material from the Flint plant to a weakly unionized plant to minimize the consequences of a possible strike. The UAW called a strike on 30 December, and workers in the Fisher Body plant in Flint occupied the assembly line. G.M. responded the following day by stating that negotiations would not take place so long as workers retained "illegal possession" of the property of G.M. The company also obtained an injunction ordering strikers to leave the plant, restraining picketing, and allowing strikebreakers to leave the plant. Workers refused to leave; they held the plant until 11 January without any incidents of violence. On 11 January, company guards, reinforced by Flint police, tried to prevent sympathizers from delivering food to the workers inside the plant. A battle between police and the strikers ensued. Workers responded to the tear gas and guns with fire hoses, door hinges, bottles, and stones. By the end of the day, fourteen strikers had been injured, thirteen by gunshots, and one had died; but the plant had been held.[26]

On the next day the governor of Michigan, accompanied by National Guard troops, arrived in Flint. He urged G.M. to negotiate with the auto workers. Negotiations took place, and strikers agreed to evacuate the plant on the condition that G.M. not resume operations for fifteen days, during which negotiations would be continued. However, as the UAW was preparing to leave the plant, a press release indicated that G.M. had no intentions of negotiating solely with the UAW. Therefore the strikers did not leave the plant, and the occupation continued. A court order also called for a prohibition of picketing. As the deadline to the court order approached, thousands of workers marched outside the plant, where several hundred "special police" hired by G.M. and National Guardsmen armed with machine guns were stationed. However, at 3:00 P.M. the sheriff announced that no attempt would be made to evict the strikers until G.M. had sought a writ of attachment against them for remaining in the plant.[27]

On 3 February, negotiations resumed, but little progress was made on the main issue of union recognition. On 9 February, still with no agreed-upon settlement, the governor of Michigan threatened to use troops to clear the plants. The threat did not work, strikers remained in the plant, and G.M. finally agreed to bargain solely with the UAW for a period of six months. With the recognition issue settled, the union agreed to evacuate the plant while negotiations on other matters continued. The strike was over. General Motors had been forced to recognize the UAW.[28] Within a few weeks after the G.M. settlement, auto workers in the Chrysler plants, supported by mass picketing, staged a sit-down and held the plants for thirty days. An agreement was reached in April between the UAW and Chrysler. The strikes at G.M. and Chrysler induced other automobile companies to settle worker grievances with the UAW before any strike activity took place in their respective auto plants. Ford was the only major auto company to successfully resist the efforts of the UAW in 1937.

The General Motors strike was a tremendous victory for the UAW and for the CIO as well. In some ways, the victory at G.M. was the "testing ground" for the CIO and for the future of industrial unionism in other basic mass-production industries. The favorable outcome of the G.M. strike was the result of the tremendous dedication and organization of the auto workers. Communist militants were particularly influential in inspiring the sit-down, organizing the shops, and participating in publicity, relief, entertainment, negotiation, and legal work. Roger Keeran has argued that Communists had a great deal to do with the entire strategy of the sit-down at G.M. The victory of the UAW at G.M. represented a significant triumph not only for the UAW and the CIO, but for mass-production workers in general. Moreover, the G.M. sit-down strike led to major CIO breakthroughs outside of the automotive industry, particularly at U.S. Steel. Successful organizing at G.M. helped to establish the CIO as a permanent factor in the industrial unionization of basic mass-production industries.[29]

The Steel Workers' Strike

Between 1933 and 1934 the steel industry responded to workers' demands and grievances by incorporating 90 percent of the 500,000 steel workers into company unions. By early 1935, however, workers became dissatisfied with the inadequacy of the companies' union structure. By the summer of 1936 the Steel Workers' Organizing Committee had infiltrated company unions in an effort to sign workers up in the Organizing Committee. The Steel Workers' Organizing Committee (SWOC) was affiliated with the CIO and was largely under the leadership of members of the Communist party. In November 1936 the SWOC announced that 82,315 workers had signed membership cards. U.S. Steel responded with a 10 percent wage increase and offered to sign contracts only with company unions. However, company-union leaders, who for the most part had been drawn from the SWOC, refused to sign. The SWOC had established 150 locals with 10,000 members by March. The company unions were thus essentially destroyed, and U.S. Steel signed up with the CIO union without a strike.[30]

U.S. Steel probably accepted bargaining with the SWOC for several reasons. First, the SWOC was strong among a significant number of workers in U.S. Steel plants and had the potential of crippling steel production if a strike were called. Second, U.S. Steel probably was not interested in fighting a losing battle along the lines seen in the sit-down strikes in the automotive industry. Third, as early as 1934 the vice-president of U.S. Steel had indicated a preference for an industrial union over a craft union, although he continued to defend the open shop. This resulted from the recognition that if U.S. Steel were to be an AFL closed shop, it would have to deal with thirty-nine separate unions, which would make it difficult to ensure labor discipline. Hence U.S. Steel preferred to negotiate with a single industrial union.[31] Finally, at the time of the SWOC organizing drives in steel, the Senate was conducting investigations of industrial-espionage activities in the steel industry. Signing a contract with the SWOC without a strike appeared to be the best alternative available to the world's largest steel corporation.

The companies that comprised "Little Steel"—Bethlehem, Republic, Youngstown Sheet and Tube, Inland, and National—refused to sign with the SWOC and continued their antiunion campaigns. Workers in the Little Steel companies went on strike in May and June 1937. In May alone, approximately 110,000 workers walked off the job in Republic plants and in the Youngstown Sheet and Tube plants.[32] The walkout in Little Steel resulted in a bloody battle which left a total of 18 workers dead, 160 people wounded, hundreds of people sickened by tear gas, and hundreds more arrested. Of the 18 workers who died, 10 were shot outside the Republic Steel plant in Chicago.[33] The Memorial Day Massacre, the name given to the brutal killing of workers outside the Republic Steel plant in Chicago, was one of the bloodiest labor battles of the decade. Although the workers had lost the strike by mid July, the brutal tactics used by the steel companies, especially Republic Steel, would be condemned by a state investigation. By the fall of 1941, after a strike at Bethlehem, the companies constituting Little Steel finally recognized the SWOC.

For the SWOC the defeat of the Little Steel strike illustrated that the CIO could not expect quick, nonviolent victories. Moreover, because FDR was unwilling to criticize the brutal force employed by Republic Steel and because Chicago's Democratic mayor condoned the use of such force, the limits of New Deal political support for industrial labor's unionization efforts were made clear. Those industrial capitalists who were adamantly opposed to unionization would use any means necessary to halt labor's gains in the field of industrial relations.[34]

Capital's Class Struggle against Labor

Between 1936 and 1940 a Senate subcommittee—known as the La Follette Civil Liberties Committee—conducted an extensive investigation of alleged violations of civil liberties and undue interference with the right of labor to organize and bargain collectively. By 1938 the committee had amassed a body of testimony that constituted an incredible indictment of American industrial capitalists. In the words of Jerold S. Auerbach, "The La Follette Committee did not warn of the imminence of class warfare, it documented its existence."[35]

The La Follette Committee exposed numerous capitalist antiunion activities that had frustrated organizing attempts for decades, including industrial espionage, the stockpiling of industrial munitions, strikebreaking, and private police. As the committee noted, between the years 1933 and 1936 a list of selected corporations had spent $9,440,132.15 for the use of spies, strikebreakers, and munitions.[36] When industrial espionage failed, capitalists invested in tear gas, machine guns, gas bombs, and billy clubs in anticipation of labor trouble. When spies and munitions failed to keep workers from organizing, capitalists employed detective agencies to provide strikebreakers and strike guards. Some capitalists also employed private police to assure "industrial peace."

Munitions companies and detective agencies profited greatly from the attempts by capitalists to attack workers for organizing labor unions. General Motors alone paid the Pinkerton Detective Agency $419,850.10 between January 1934 and July 1936 for labor spies and strike guards.[37] Munitions companies tried to increase the demand for their goods by portraying every impending labor crisis as a call for "revolution." Munitions salesmen carried copies of antiunion and anti-Communist propaganda to show to prospective customers. Pamphlets such as "The Red Network" and "The Red Line of Crime and Disorder" were distributed by Federal Laboratories, the largest manufacturer of tear gas; these pamphlets were given to prospective customers in an attempt to prove that the strikes were part of a Communist "menace" that had to be stopped.[38] It was also in the economic interest of detective agencies to prolong strikes and deliberately to provoke violence so that more strikebreakers and/or strike guards would be hired. Detective agencies kept themselves informed of any impending strike or industrial unrest that could potentially lead to a strike. They then personally solicited prospective capitalists to hire their services. Some detective agencies had their own spies in labor unions, and they attempted to provoke strikes so that the particular detective agency could be the first to warn capitalists of impending labor unrest and to suggest the need for their services.[39]

The organizing efforts of various labor unions were paralleled by expenditures made by capitalists for industrial espionage. For example, Republic Steel increased its espionage activities when the SWOC began its drive for unionization.[40] The chief providers of spies to industry were (1) private detective agencies that sold their services to capitalists at a profit; (2) employers' associations that, along with other activities, rendered spy services to their employer members who may have requested it; and (3) corporations that provided their own spy systems. Spying on workers and unions was also occasionally performed by the industrial squads of various city and state police departments. General Motors spent $994,855.68 between June 1934 and July 1936 on detective agencies for spy services. At times, as many as 200 spies were reporting on the activities of the workers in sixty G.M. plants. Many of the spies in unions sought to destroy the unions. Almost one-third of the 304 Pinkerton operatives that held membership in unions also held union offices of varying importance. This labor spy system proved beneficial for G.M., as union membership often decreased. In 1934 the Federal Automobile Workers claimed 26,000 members in the G.M. plant in Flint, Michigan. Three labor spies sat on the union's executive board, and consequently, membership in the Flint local had dropped to 120 members by 1936.[41]

Capitalists also made heavy investments in munitions. More than $450,000 worth of gas munitions was sold to industry in the years 1933 to 1936.[42] The largest purchasers of gas munitions were firms either involved in or threatened by strikes and law-enforcement agencies in localities affected by strikes. Of the seventeen largest gas purchasers among employers and groups of employers, seven were from the steel industry, four were from the automobile industry, four were groups of employer associations (three representing important shipping interests and one representing coal mines), and two were from the rubber industry. About $21,000 of the $24,000 that G.M. spent on gas munitions was spent during the wave of strikes for union recognition during the spring of 1935 and early in 1937. All but $12 out of the total of $11,000 spent by Electric Auto-Lite Company for gas munitions was expended between April and July 1934—the period of the strike over union recognition and a wage increase. Goodyear spent more than $22,000 for munitions and arms from 1933 to 1936, and U.S. Steel owned more than $62,000 worth of gas equipment and at least three Thompson submachine guns. During the Little Steel strike, Republic Steel and Youngstown Sheet and Tube together had a total of 1,881 guns of all types, 153,930 rounds of ball ammunition, 10,234 rounds of shot-cartridge ammunition, and 10,064 items of gas ammunition. Republic Steel bought four submachine guns in 1933 and purchased 1,000 rounds of ammunition for submachine guns in 1934. As of May 1935, Republic possessed 552 revolvers; 64 rifles, with 1,325 rounds of ammunition; 245 shotguns, with 5,784 rounds of shotgun shells; 143 gas guns, with 4,033 gas projectiles; and 2,707 gas grenades.[43]

Strikebreakers hired by capitalists did their utmost to produce resentment, bitterness, violence, and bloodshed among strikers. Most strikebreakers were armed, but capitalists never really had control over the tactics that the strikebreakers employed. Private police often proved more useful to capitalists because they were totally under the control and discipline of the capitalists themselves. The use of private police was more common in company towns, although this was not always the case. A few examples will illustrate the tactics used to stop union organization. A group of miners who belonged to the United Mine Workers planned a march to mines near Birmingham, Alabama, for the purpose of organizing. People who were connected with the mines placed charges of dynamite under the road that the union organizers were expected to travel, while riflemen hid along the sides of the road. One organizer was killed. In May 1935 the Republic Steel Corporation terrorized strikers, pickets, and local people throughout the community during a strike at its subsidiary, the Berger Manufacturing Company in Canton, Ohio. Members of Republic's police force rode through the streets of the town indiscriminately firing tear gas and shotguns. A pregnant woman who had no connection with the strike was shot by company guards outside her home, almost two miles from the plant. An elderly man, sitting on the steps of his home, died after being struck in the head by a tear-gas shell.[44] The private police force of Republic Steel constantly hounded people, harassed union organizers, and blocked the distribution of union literature. In almost all of the other large steel companies, one of the functions of the company police was the obtaining of information on union-related activities of the workers. Steel companies often exchanged undercover information with regard to union organizing in the steel industry.[45]

Capitalists also waged a major propaganda campaign against union organizing. Capitalists used the "threat of communism" as the rationale for discouraging unionization. As mentioned earlier, the National Association of Manufacturers was instrumental in sponsoring antiunion campaigns. The NAM spent more than $790,000 a year for the preparation and distribution of propaganda material which included booklets that endorsed various strikebreaking mechanisms.[46] Propaganda campaigns were also waged by munitions salesmen and by the United States Chamber of Commerce.

In short, the findings of the La Follette Committee constituted a devastating condemnation of the so-called partnership between capital and labor, as New Deal policy makers had anticipated. Although industrial capital was clearly divided over a strategy for economic recovery, industrial capitalists were in agreement in their position on unions. Yet, in contrast to the workers' collective action for unionization, industrial capital primarily responded individually to workers' offensive organizing drives. While industrial capital might have indeed shared information on union organizing in an effort to halt unionization within an entire branch of industry, individual capitalist firms engaged in antiunion activities to stop collective organization among their particular work forces.[47] A reexamination of the labor struggles of the 1930s reveals that most industrial capitalists were not the least bit willing to concede union recognition, and they brutally resisted any attempts by workers to establish recognized unions. Union recognition and the right to collective bargaining were not outcomes of a growing consensus among capitalists; rather, they were outcomes of the militant struggles of the industrial working class with the backing of legal support from the NLRA. Indeed, the right to collective bargaining and union recognition marked a great victory for industrial labor over industrial capital.

Industrial Labor and the Political Scene

The National Labor Relations Act significantly altered the relationships among capital, labor, and the state apparatus. It provided state sanctioning of industrial unionization and provided the federal mechanism by which organized labor could be incorporated into the political structure of the state apparatus. The class struggle between industrial wage labor and industrial capital was national in scope, and the NLRA was the federal response to this struggle. Unlike previous periods of heightened class struggle, the working-class struggles of the 1930s crossed state and regional lines and necessitated concessions from the federal government. Comprehensive labor policies came under the jurisdiction of the federal government, with less dependence on local state jurisdiction and local economic and social policies.[48]

State labor policies were not enough, however, to incorporate organized industrial labor within the political structure of the state apparatus. It was the changing relationship between organized labor and the Democratic party that provided for the political incorporation of organized industrial labor into the national process of political bargaining. It was through the Democratic party that organized labor formed a linkage with the state apparatus. Simply put, the class struggle between industrial labor and industrial capital was channeled through the party system. While recent work on New Deal labor policies has stressed the significance of party alignment in legislating prolabor policies, this same work has ignored the process by which class forces shaped party alignment and realignment and, in turn, were shaped by them.[49]

The Realignment of the Democratic Party

The realignment of the Democratic party during the 1930s, particularly the 1936 Democratic landslide, brought about a political recomposition of the party with a strong working-class base. The rise of a second-generation ethnic working-class voting bloc, heightened with a switch of formerly Republican blacks, served to produce a working-class base for the Democratic party.[50] The peculiarity of the political scene in the United States rests on the fact that the two-party presidential regime produces political parties that are heterogeneous and nonhierarchical. In other words, although the two parties present platforms, individual party members are not bound by any particular party discipline. The Republican and Democratic parties do not present themselves as class organizations per se, which allows for the class base and the class affiliation of the two major parties to change over time. This peculiarity permits major parties to undergo realignment in times of heightened class struggle, which results in a greater class affiliation of the dominated classes. Because the parties themselves are divided along class lines and regional and ethnic differences, neither of them ostensibly presents any one class interest or identifies as a class organization; therefore the working class can be affiliated with either of them. For this reason the class character of political parties in the United States has been masked by incorporating popular demands into party platforms during crucial historical periods.

The 1936 presidential election reflected the realignment in the Democratic party. The extraparliamentary struggles of the industrial working class forced Democratic congressmen and senators to take a more liberal position within congressional debates, thereby moving the Democratic party to the left on the political spectrum. The Democratic party continued to stress the importance of a balanced budget and high profits, and Roosevelt signed measures for the extension of federal subsidies to various industrial concerns. But by the time of the 1936 presidential election, workers were perceiving the Democratic party as the party that had passed the National Labor Relations Act and the Social Security Act and were identifying it with progressive taxation, support for labor, antitrust action, old-age pensions, unemployment insurance, and relief.[51] The class struggle, which was national in scope during the 1930s, needed a place in national politics and found it in the Democratic party. The record of the Roosevelt administration's first term provided the conditions for a form of class-based voting behavior in the 1936 presidential election.[52]

The voting results of the 1936 election indicated that Roosevelt and the Democratic party did best in working-class neighborhoods. This is no surprise, because those who were hardest hit by the depression perceived the Democratic party as the party that aided the working class. Organized labor became a major element in the 1936 presidential-campaign process. By 1936 the labor vote had become crucial. The formation of Labor's Non-Partisan League in April 1936 indicated that organized labor was officially entering national politics. The league was a union campaign organization that worked through local union members to gather support for Roosevelt and the Democratic party. Organized industrial labor campaigned for Roosevelt and contributed almost $750,000 to the Democratic campaign. As contributions from large-scale capital fell, labor's contributions enabled the campaign of 1936 to take a definitively prolabor stance.[53]

The Democratic party was able to incorporate organized labor into its ranks while incorporating second-generation ethnic working-class people and blacks. The 1936 election was the first presidential election in which the black vote decisively shifted from the Republican party to the Democratic party.[54] As the migration of blacks to the northern industrial regions took place during the depression, more and more blacks perceived that their interests were best represented through the Democratic party. The Democratic administration and Congress passed legislation that was favorable to equal rights, regardless of race. Relief legislation attempted to make sure that blacks received the same relief as whites.

Equal pay for governmental jobs was at least legislated, if not implemented. Moreover, the Roosevelt administration appointed blacks to political posts, gave blacks their share of low-cost housing, and attempted to treat black workers in the same way as white workers, something that had not been the case in previous administrations. As workers, blacks aligned themselves with the prolabor stance of New Deal policies, and as blacks, they looked favorably on the civil-rights gestures of the Roosevelt administration.[55]

The 1936 presidential election proved that the leftward movement of the Democratic party was a politically astute move. The Democratic party was transformed into the working man's party. While gaining mass support of the working class during the 1930s the Democratic party, however, did not lose a significant amount of its traditional support; the class character of the party remained unchanged. The party had succeeded in incorporating southern traditionalists, urban political machines, industrial workers of all races, trade unionists, and many depression-hit farmers. The 1936 election further resulted in the Democrats' obtaining a clear majority in Congress—all but 19 seats in the Senate and all but 107 in the House.[56]

The leftward movement of the Democratic party during the 1930s did not mean that conservative elements had left the party. One of the peculiarities of the party system in the United States is that both parties are internally divided and do not present a consistent political strategy adhered to by all of its constituents. The recession of 1937/38 brought conservative Democrats to the forefront, and the last few years of the 1930s witnessed a split between liberal and conservative sentiments. With a conservative bloc in Congress, the Democratic party moved back to a centrist position after 1938. While the party continued to incorporate the demands of organized labor, blacks, and other poor urban minorities into its party platforms, the expression of its position became more moderate as recovery from the depression occurred with wartime preparations. Conservative Democrats joined with Republicans to form the political machinery for the corporate counteroffensive against the CIO. In an effort to form a majority consensus for new foreign-policy initiatives as war got under way on the European front, the Roosevelt administration gave up its program for social reform and civil rights. As Mike Davis has put it: "Thus from 1938 onwards, the maintenance of a bipartisan consensus in support for American imperialism overrode the exigencies of social legislation and political reform. By accepting the discipline of the Cold War mobilization, the unions and their liberal allies surrendered independence of action and ratified the subordination of social welfare to global anti-communism."[57]

In brief, while the Democratic party attracted a large working-class coalition between 1932 and 1936, the party did not entirely alienate its traditional class support. By the time of the 1936 presidential election, a greater proportion of workers had affiliated themselves with the Democratic party in comparison to the proportion of capitalists who had left the party and identified with the Republican party.[58] The realignment of the Democratic party concealed not only its own class character but also the class character of the state apparatus. The relationship between organized labor and the Democratic party provided the political apparatus by which organized labor was incorporated into national politics. Because of the class character of the party, organized labor entered into a structure of "unequal representation" within the national political-bargaining process.[59]

The Democratic Party and the CIO

The political alliance between the Democratic party and the CIO began with the formation of Labor's Non-Partisan League in 1936. The league effectively campaigned for Roosevelt and the Democratic party in the industrialized states of New York, Pennsylvania, Illinois, and Ohio. The CIO convincingly argued that the Roosevelt administration had brought to the American worker many social benefits and the protection of trade-union rights. Moreover, many members of the CIO perceived the Democratic party and the Roosevelt administration as having made it possible for their organization to emerge in the first place.[60] Widespread straight-ticket voting in the 1936 election proved to be beneficial in the Democratic landslide.

CIO support for the Democratic party continued after the 1936 election. In 1938 the CIO lobby supported Roosevelt's Supreme Court reform and efforts to purge conservatives from the Democratic party. In addition, the CIO published and distributed a bulletin called "How to Organize and Conduct a Local Political Campaign" in an effort to increase the electoral impact of an organized industrial labor. By 1940 the CIO's commitment to the Democratic party was secure enough not to pay heed to John L. Lewis's personal opposition to Roosevelt. Members of the CIO remained largely Democratic, and many CIO leaders participated as delegates to the Democratic National Convention that drafted Roosevelt for a third term.[61]

The political alliance between the CIO and the Democratic party was consolidated during the war years with the formation of the CIO's Political Action Committee (PAC). Through elaborate and highly bureaucratized operations, the PAC explicitly reflected the CIO's allegiance to the Democratic party and demanded from Congress not only a good labor record but also support for the entire New Deal program of labor reform. The PAC solidified a trade-union political apparatus that was becoming increasingly important for electoral success and attempted to provide a permanent place for the CIO within the Democratic party.[62]

The CIO's political alliance with the Democratic party was aided by the change in policy of the Communist party.[63] Still a crucial element in CIO unions, the Communist party, with a membership of more than 75,000 in 1938, worked with the PAC in support of the Democratic party. Critical support of Roosevelt and the Democratic party in 1936 became less important in 1938. The Communist party's positions on building a popular front and on uniting with liberal Democrats aided in the curtailment of labor militancy and in a union movement that was more willing to enter into a "partnership" with the state.

The "marriage" between industrial labor and the Democratic party might have transformed the party into a working man's party, but the partnership between the state and the union movement prevented the Democratic party from becoming a working-class party. Cleavages within the labor movement and splits within the working class continued and resulted in trade unions' becoming political bases for the Democratic left wing. The capacity of the unions to enact substantive prolabor reforms was constrained both by the Democratic right wing and by the growing tide of anticommunism and political repression.[64] The industrial-trade-union movement was under the direction of reformist leadership, and Communist elements subdued their politics in order to work with them. Political and industrial struggles were pursued in isolation from one another.[65]

The Organization of Basic Industry and Political Incorporation

The struggle for union recognition that continued during the first two years after the National Labor Relations Act was passed into law resulted in employer recognition of industrial unions. This struggle was aided by the state's sanctioning of industrial unions associated with the CIO. Moreover, state support for the rights of industrial workers was strengthened by the devastating evidence compiled in the Senate investigation of the violations of free speech and the rights of workers that were perpetrated by industrial firms. Whereas the state administration could essentially ignore the report of the National Recovery Review Board, the same could not be said of the Senate investigation. The industrial work force in mass-production industries was far more organized by 1938 than it had been at the time of the passage of the NLRA, and industrial workers already had proved themselves capable of interrupting production. The lack of response to many of the recommendations of the National Recovery Review Board had little consequence for economic recovery, whereas not taking the Senate investigation seriously could have had serious ramifications for industrial production and efforts for economic recovery.

The dynamic of the class struggle between industrial wage labor and capital was what directed the implementation of state labor policies. Labor support for the Democratic party was a key ingredient for the party's majority status. Hence, Democrats in Congress were willing to grant concessions to organized labor in order to maintain labor's dominance. Without the militant activity associated with efforts for unionization in mass-production industries, however, it is unlikely that even liberal Democrats would have supported such prolabor policies.

Primarily it was the struggle for union recognition that took place on the shop floor that had ramifications for changing political relationships. In turn, changing political relationships had an impact on further relationships on the shop floor.

The struggle for union recognition did not go beyond the struggle over the terms of the rate of exploitation. The union struggles of the period and the internal conflicts within the labor movement resulted in the institutionalization of collective-bargaining arrangements. The union struggles of the period were aspects of the economic class struggle and were not able to reach the level of a political class struggle.[66] The labor provisions of the NIRA and later the NLRA granted concessions to segments of the working class, such as the legal mechanisms to settle worker disputes. The concessions—while they were in opposition to the visible desires of the capitalist class—never threatened the continual reproduction of capitalist social relations of production. The political alliance between organized industrial labor and the Democratic party further provided the political mechanism by which organized labor was incorporated into the national political-bargaining process. In the words of Michel Aglietta,

> this . . . represents a moment . . . at which class confrontation can no longer be canalized by the previous structural forms, and give rise to a process of social creation which may be prompted by shifts in political forces, as with the New Deal. Such class struggles can then generate, in a political and ideological climate that does not threaten capitalism itself . . . those major transformations in the social organization of labor which can provide the basis for the conditions of a new and lasting accumulation.[67]

The industrial labor movement of the mid 1930s and the corresponding realignment of the Democratic party tended to unify an industrial working class that had previously been fragmented by religious, ethnic, racial, and regional divisions. Nevertheless, the class struggle in the United States during the mid 1930s did not emerge as a coherent class movement on the part of labor. The lifting of political repression and the split between the CIO and the AFL provided the context for a significant Communist and radical influence in the unfolding of working-class struggles. The Communist party, however, was not able to transform the trade-union movement into a class unified movement that was capable of politically challenging capitalist rule. By the spring of 1937 the economic struggles of the industrial working class had resulted in the favorable relationship between organized industrial workers and the state administration. As the industrial working class became more organized, the capitalist class became ever more divided. The balance of forces within the class struggle was such that industrial labor, including a significant Communist element, was on the offensive against industrial capital. The organization of basic mass-production industries and the political recomposition of the Democratic party with a strong working-class base represented a political and economic setback for industrial capital. However, the isolation of workers' political struggles from their economic struggles had made possible the resurgence of redbaiting and political repression by 1938. Communist and radical influence within the trade-union movement, which was so critical to the formation of many CIO unions, began to be purged in 1938, and a new wave of anti-Communist and antilabor repression began to sweep through the United States.

CHAPTER EIGHT

Foundations for a Restructuring of the Political and Economic Order

The object is not to tear down going concerns, but to improve if possible, the plans by which future structures may be built.

—*Robert E. Cushman*

History will pay its tribute to you as the Moses of the 1930s. We Americans will ever relate to our offsprings the tale of a Roosevelt that was greater in accomplishment, more supreme in Americanism, etc., than the great Teddy.

—*Bert E. Askern*

As a part of the post-war program, the United States must plan for, and bring about, an expanded economy which will result in a greater degree of security, employment, recreation, education, health and decent housing for all its citizens so that the tragic days which made necessary the New Deal of 1933, will not come again.

—*Samuel Rosenman*

Recession, Repression, and Political Incorporation

Industrial labor's offensive came to a halt during the recession that began in the summer of 1937 as unemployment increased, capitalists heightened their class struggle with industrial labor, the AFL experienced a resurgence in the field of industrial relations, and the conservative movement in Congress pushed Roosevelt and the Democratic party towards a less favorable stance in relation to militant trade unionism.[1] The 1937/38 recession and the 1937 sit-down strikes helped to create a new climate of frustration and anger between labor, leftists, and New Deal liberals; and it fostered renewed conflicts within the capitalist class, especially between nonmonopoly capital and the Roosevelt administration. Intracapitalist conflict over the monopoly issue combined with increasing tensions between industrial labor and industrial capital to provide the conditions for the emergence of a conservative bloc in Congress. The recession brought conservative Democrats to the forefront of the party and quelled further labor reforms. Organized industrial labor's support and presence within the Democratic party had not delimited the resurgence of redbaiting and political repression by 1938; the formation of the House Committee on Un-American Activities—known as the Dies Committee because its chairman was Congressman Martin Dies—was the first step in purging all leftists from the trade-union movement.

The Dies Committee focused largely on the Communist party, leftists within the CIO, and possible Communists within the Roosevelt administration. The committee investigated the alleged un-American activities of various congressmen and members of Roosevelt's cabinet and sought to link the activities of liberal politicians with pro-Communist connections. Hearings by the Dies Committee were marked by irresponsibility. For example, a representative of 114 patriotic organizations named 640 organizations as communistic and even suggested that the Boy Scouts and the Campfire Girls were serving subversive purposes. One witness before the committee suggested that the child movie star Shirley Temple had unwittingly served Communist interests by sending a greeting card to a French Communist newspaper. By the end of 1938, hundreds of organizations and thousands of individuals, without receiving any advance notice, had been named as Communists before the Dies Committee.[2]

The Dies Committee received widespread publicity, and as a result the CIO was assaulted by an unfavorable press, including the NAM leaflet depicting John L. Lewis holding a picket sign that read "Join the CIO and Build a Soviet America."[3] Congress followed the repressive sentiment of the Dies Committee by enacting the Foreign Agents Registration Act in June 1938, which required all persons as agents for foreign countries to register with the secretary of state and to file information on their relationship to the foreign principal involved. In June 1939, Congress passed a relief appropriations act which barred payment to any person "who advocates, or who is a member of an organization that advocates the overthrow of the government of the United States through force or violence." This measure was directed at Communist party members who received relief during the depression. Moreover, the Federal Writers' Project, a program of the New Deal, was alleged to be a group of subversives, and manuscripts were seized from the office of the New York City Writers' Project and were scrutinized for "red propaganda." Staff workers for a House committee investigating the Writers' Project planted Communist periodicals in the New York office in an attempt to produce photographs demonstrating that the Writers' Project was subversive. In August 1939, Congress enacted the Hatch Act, which included the provisions that no person who had "membership in any political party or organization which advocated the overthrow of our constitutional form of government in the United States" could gain federal employment of any type. The principle of guilt by association and the punishment for abstract advocacy of violence applied to all American citizens and was upheld by the federal government. Finally, in March 1940, Congress reenacted the Espionage Act of 1917 by increasing penalties and by making some provisions applicable in peacetime.[4]

The wave of political repression that began in 1938 curtailed Communist and Socialist influence within the trade-union movement. The influence of the Communist party became less tolerable after the 1939 Hitler-Stalin Pact, and a wave of working-class nationalism ensued during the war and culminated in the post-war cold war and McCarthyism.[5] Whereas political structures were altered in such a fashion that organized labor had a place in national politics, left-wing political groups were denied such access. The labor militancy of the mid 1930s declined significantly during the last few years of the decade. The resurgence of the AFL in 1938 increased redbaiting, political repression, disunity in the labor movement, and the purging of Communist influence from the CIO. The incorporation of organized industrial labor into the Democratic party provided the context in which an informal bargain was struck between large-scale industrial capital and organized labor: organized labor received union recognition, better terms of employment, and the promise of a higher standard of living, while large-scale industrial capital anticipated a relatively self-disciplined labor force. The organization of basic mass-production industries represented both a political and an economic setback for industrial capital. Monopoly capital, however, which itself was in the process of becoming the politically dominant fraction of capital during the 1930s, was able to adjust to these structural changes.

Working-class militancy and the struggle for industrial unionization led to the reorganization of basic industry. The course of the class struggle in the 1937–39 period illustrates that the economic class struggle was averted and that it never reached the political or ideological level to form a unified working-class movement. The tremendous class struggle on the part of wage labor for union recognition remained primarily an economic class struggle, and the incorporation of organized labor into the Democratic party served to isolate political struggles from economic struggles. The struggle for collective bargaining can be compatible with overall capital accumulation if (1) its Socialist and Communist leadership is not maintained and (2) the struggle for unionization is not seen as a critique of private property. These two factors were sustained in the period after the 1937/38 recession.

The realignment of the Democratic party did not transform that party into a labor party. The failure of Communists in the trade-union movement to perceive the political danger of working too closely with the Democratic party and to provide active Communist leadership to the trade-union movement made it relatively easy for the Democratic party and even segments of the working class to stand by and/or actively encourage the purging of leftists from the trade-union movement. The formation of the Dies Committee in 1938 was the first step towards the purging of all leftists from the trade-union movement, as well as within the Democratic party, which was undertaken during the post–World War II years under McCarthyism. The realignment of the Democratic party provided the political apparatus with which organized labor could participate in national politics. When the Democratic party became faced with militant trade unionists in its constituency and the potential of having them change the *class character* of the party, redbaiting and the purging of leftists within the party and within the labor movement took place. The Democratic party and the Roosevelt administration, in the context of intracapitalist conflict, became less tolerant of militant workers and Communists in particular. The realignment of the Democratic party, the purging of leftists within the trade-union movement, and cleavages within the labor movement converged to produce a reformist, politically docile labor movement during the post–World War II years.[6]

The Reorganization of the State Apparatus

Intracapitalist Conflict

The recession of 1937/38 not only brought industrial labor's offensive to a halt; it also intensified intracapitalist conflict. Politically, intracapitalist conflict not only aided in the resurgence of redbaiting and the political incorporation of the industrial labor movement; it also stimulated plans for the reorganization of the executive branch of the federal government. Capitalist opposition to the Roosevelt administration's prolabor policies was heightened by the series of sit-down strikes that followed the enactment of the National Labor Relations Act. The recession of 1937/38 furthered capitalist dissatisfaction with the New Deal recovery program and created a political climate that was not only tolerant of redbaiting but that also actually augmented anti-Communist sentiment. Moreover, the crisis of the 1930s made it plain that the accumulation process was so complex within the industrial sector that the state was forced to politically regulate the conditions under which profitable accumulation could occur. The increased concentration and centralization of capital meant that market mechanisms alone were no longer sufficient to bring about a general profit rate that would be beneficial to individual units of capital.[7] However, the organizational apparatus of the state made it difficult to initiate policies that would prove to be beneficial to the capitalist class by closely adhering to the direct benefits of monopoly capital. Intracapitalist conflicts in the years after passage of the NIRA stimulated plans for reorganizing the executive branch of the state apparatus, which entailed greater centralization. A more centralized state apparatus means that more decisions and more policy directives can be formulated within a limited range of political and economic concessions and/or compromises. Unlike the legislative branch, the executive branch makes policy decisions without having to deal directly with the divergent interests of dominated and dominant classes and of fractions of classes.[8]

The investigation of increased monopoly growth that was undertaken by various branches and agencies of the state apparatus coincided with increased intracapitalist conflict, which was manifested in antagonisms within the Congress and between the legislative and executive branches of government. Politicians who represented the interests of nonmonopoly capital pressured the state administration to regulate monopoly growth by strengthening the antitrust laws, arguing that large-scale centralized capital units were not a problem per se but that governmental regulation of monopoly competition was essential.[9] Intracapitalist conflicts that are manifested in antagonisms between the executive and the legislative branches are not as clear as the conflicts that are manifested in antagonisms within Congress. Theoretically speaking, the Roosevelt administration put forth policy proposals and a program of legislation that not only favored monopoly capital but also served to organize monopoly capital into the politically dominant fraction of capital. Monopoly capital was a fraction in formation during the predepression years and was still in formation as the dominant fraction during the economic crisis. In fact, one could argue that the state sought to organize monopoly capital at the same time that monopoly capital was often resisting programs and policies that would have served to consolidate its own political hegemony. Hence, although monopoly capital would most certainly have benefited from a more centralized executive branch of government, monopoly capital nevertheless joined with nonmonopoly capital in resisting such attempts. Monopoly capital simply did not have the foresightedness to understand the implications of various governmental policies.

The antagonisms between the legislative and the executive branches of government had less to do with direct intracapitalist conflict than with ideological issues, which resulted in a Congress that prevented a reorganization of the state apparatus that would have promoted a truly social-democratic program. Both monopoly and nonmonopoly capital were wary of the social programs put forth by the Roosevelt administration. The resistance of congressional members to executive reorganization, for example, reflects the fractional unity against a social-democratic possibility. The end result of executive/legislative antagonisms did, however, lead to executive reorganization. The final form of executive reorganization provided a wedge to expand the legislative powers of the executive branch in later years, thereby opening the organizational form of the state apparatus to benefit in a direct fashion the fractional interest of monopoly capital. In sum, the state administration during the world economic crisis not only promoted the fractional interest of monopoly capital; it organized the fraction and provided mechanisms for its dominance on the political terrain.[10]

As noted previously, the 1937/38 recession brought with it capitalist resistance to further New Deal reforms. The Democratic party, which was responsible for the reforms that were brought about by New Deal legislation, retained conservative elements even after the stunning 1936 Democratic victory. The 1937/38 recession brought conservative Democrats to the front to join with Republicans to form a conservative bipartisan bloc after the 1938 congressional elections. This conservative bloc worked to curtail further social reforms and even sought to curtail fundamental state reorganization. The conservative bloc represented primarily the interests of nonmonopoly capital, but both liberals and conservatives who represented monopoly and nonmonopoly capital resisted an encroachment of legislative powers by the executive branch.[11] By 1938, conservative southern Democrats had joined with congressional Republicans to curtail the power of the presidency, thereby delaying significant reorganization plans that would relate more smoothly with changes in the industrial sector. The Democratic coalition, which had previously embraced all classes of different ideological bents, appeared to be heading for disruption.

Executive/legislative antagonism over executive reorganization manifested political shifts within the fractional alliance of capital. Theoretically speaking, the Roosevelt administration furthered the fractional interest of monopoly capital, as the consequences of state-administration-sponsored policy reveals. The legislative branch was a mixture of agents of monopoly and nonmonopoly capital. The ideological struggle over executive reorganization merely indicated that nonmonopoly capital was not secure in its politically dominant position. Neither the Republican party nor the Democratic party represented definitively any particular fraction of capital, a condition that allowed a conservative bloc within Congress to embrace both Republicans and Democrats. Fractions of capital remained entrenched within both of the parties. One could argue that it was because fractional interests of both monopoly and nonmonopoly capital existed within the Democratic party that reforms during the early depression years were not extended during the last few years of the decade. Although it was commonly acknowledged that the industrial sector had undergone a major reorganization since the turn of the century, particularly during the period of economic crisis, members of Congress were unwilling to reorganize the state apparatus in such a fashion as to limit legislative powers.

A stronger executive branch of government would short-circuit debates about economic policies that would best serve the interests of monopoly capital. Yet despite the intense debates over executive reorganization, administrative reforms did take place that proved to be of benefit to monopoly capital. Intracapitalist conflict stimulated the Roosevelt administration to take seriously the fragmented and administrative weaknesses of state structures. In an effort to rationalize state policy, especially after the NIRA fiasco, the Roosevelt administration's strategy unwittingly provided the mechanisms for the dominance of monopoly capital on the political terrain. If the state were to provide conditions for uninterrupted and profitable accumulation, then clearly, state economic policy would have to serve the interests of monopoly capital, which was dominant economically. A stronger executive branch with administrative powers would be able to transcend any political differences that might surface between nonmonopoly and monopoly capital in Congress. Even though, therefore, debates over executive reorganization focused on issues in regard to the balance of governmental powers, the underlying issue at stake was one of the shifting political importance of fractions of capital.

Proposals for Reorganization

The proposals for executive reorganization that developed between 1936 and 1939 reveal the processes that induced reforms in the administrative arm of the state apparatus.[12] The debates over proposals for executive reorganization reveal the process of building and remodeling the policy infrastructure of the state in a fashion that corresponded with the political requirements of a changing accumulation process. The final outcomes of debates and the actual form that reorganization assumed shed light on changing relationships between capital and the state.

The expansion of governmental participation and legislation into economic and social arenas brought about a tremendous growth in the federal government during Roosevelt's first term as president. By the end of the administration's first term, and certainly by the middle of the second term, serious problems of administration had arisen between various branches and agencies of the executive branch that had been created by New Deal policies. By 1936, more than one hundred separately organized establishments and agencies were located within the executive branch and were reporting to Roosevelt directly. These included the ten "regular" executive departments, along with many boards, commissions, administrations, authorities, corporations, and agencies that were located within the executive branch but were not in any designated department.[13] Indeed, the chaotic nature of the information-gathering process made policy making anything but coherent. Clearly, as Margaret Weir and Theda Skocpol have pointed out, the fragmented nature of the state apparatus leads to administrative weaknesses.[14]

Proposals for the reorganization of the federal government did not originate with the Roosevelt administration. The earliest proposals for a reorganization emanated from Congress in the post–Civil War years with a stated purpose of promoting efficiency in policy-making processes and efficient state management. It is no surprise that proposals for reorganization took place when alterations within the capital-accumulation process were beginning to occur. The succeeding presidential administrations of Theodore Roosevelt, Woodrow Wilson, William Howard Taft, Warren G. Harding, Calvin Coolidge, and Herbert C. Hoover all proposed various methods of organizing the state apparatus in a more coherent structure that could more conveniently respond to changing economic conditions. Wilson and Hoover in particular saw the need for some form of executive reorganization. However, none of the proposals for reorganization were implemented to any significant degree. The Congress under Hoover did pass the Economy Act of 1932, which enabled the president to regroup agencies, subject to veto by either the House or the Senate within sixty days. Congress vetoed all of Hoover's recommendations for reorganization.[15]

In the summer of 1935, Louis Brownlow, of the Public Administration Clearing House in Chicago, and Charles Merriam, founder of the Social Science Research Council and a member of the National Resources Committee, suggested to Roosevelt the adoption of a measure that would coordinate all of the emergency activities of the branches, boards, and agencies of the executive branch of government; they proposed a study of a more effective method of executive administration management within the state apparatus. After some reservations and consideration, Roosevelt was convinced in March 1936 of the necessity of establishing a committee that would study effective measures of executive reorganization.[16] On 22 March 1936 a White House press release stated that Roosevelt had appointed a committee to make a careful study of the relation between emergency agencies and the regular organizations of the executive branch of government. The committee was composed of three men: Louis Brownlow as chairman, along with committee members Charles Merriam and Luther H. Gulick, who had been director of the Institute of Public Administration in New York since 1921. It was stated that the committee would serve as an adjunct of the National Emergency Council, which would provide the necessary office facilities and such personnel as the committee might require.[17]

In addition to the president's committee, Senator Byrd of Virginia chaired a select committee to study the reorganization of the executive branch, with particular emphasis on discovering any duplication of administrative functions and on reducing the costs of governmental administration. The Brookings Institution had the duty of undertaking the survey for the Senate Select Committee. In addition, the House set up its own committee to study reorganization, with James Buchanan of Texas as its chairman. Both of the congressional committees came into sharp disagreement and never worked together with the president's committee. Essentially, the congressional committees were wary of the potential power that the executive branch might assume over the legislative branch of the state apparatus.[18]

The president's committee conducted research into the many facets of executive reorganization and attempted to make proposals that would make possible a more efficient use of the executive branch of government in the administrative and policy-making processes. Most of the reports of the president's committee had been completed by late 1936. Roosevelt subsequently presented the report of the committee to Congress in January 1937. The research staff of the committee was composed of twenty-six academic political scientists who did not represent any overt political or business interest but who had either experience or contacts with various parts of the state apparatus.[19]

In his original draft of the reorganization of executive departments for the report of the committee, Luther Gulick stated that the many different agencies of the executive branch produced a "chaotic" condition, which made it no "surprise that there is duplication, waste motion, and at times conflicting policy. It is rather a miracle that anything is accomplished."[20] Gulick continued his report by stating that the lack of planning within the state apparatus had three fundamental defects: (1) the multiplicity of unrelated organizations was inherently inefficient, overlapping, and wasteful; (2) the existing structure of the state was a poor instrument for implementing effective policy, "that is, really doing the job expected of it by the nation"; and (3) control was lost in the "maze." In the draft of his report, Gulick argued that the basic problem with the structure of the executive branch was that it was unmanageable. Implicit in Gulick's draft was a clear and insightful recognition that the reorganization of the executive branch of the state apparatus was a continuous process that must change as increased state involvement became part of the changing economic and social scene.

One major area of executive reform that was researched was the issue of the independent regulatory commission that essentially implemented the policy of economic regulation. In a confidential memorandum, one member of the staff concluded that the numerous regulatory commissions that had been set up by the federal government caused a decentralized and chaotic form of administration. Because many areas of economic concern were not accountable to the executive office, they were exercising governmental powers under conditions of "virtual irresponsibility." The proposal for a more effective form of economic regulation was that the independent regulatory commissions be set up within the executive departments of the executive branch. However, the judicial aspects of the regulatory commissions would be placed outside of the executive branch of the state apparatus; only the administrative aspects—the policy determinations—would be placed within it.[21]

The final report of the President's Committee on Administrative Management, which was given to Roosevelt in late 1936 and was presented to Congress in January 1937, recommended four major principles for reorganization. The first principle was that the many branches, agencies, and commissions which were part of the executive branch but were in no special executive department be consolidated into twelve major executive departments by the addition of a Department of Social Welfare and a Department of Public Works. The second recommendation was to require and authorize the president to determine the appropriate assignment to the twelve executive departments of all operating administrative agencies and to place upon the executive the continuing responsibility and power for the maintenance of the effective division of labor among the departments. The third recommendation was to equip the president with the essential tools of management in budgeting efficiency research, personnel, and planning. The fourth was the extension of the principle of executive accountability to Congress through the development of a report of fiscal transactions, as well as through a simplification of the structure of the executive branch.[22]

In essence, the president's committee recommended that a more planned form of executive administration be undertaken in order to ensure the efficient manner in which policy, most importantly economic policy, could be implemented. Agencies would be consolidated within the vast chaos of the state apparatus, and a central planning agency would coordinate policy. Hence, the plan for executive reorganization would not only provide for a more centralized state apparatus but would also bestow a greater degree of policy-making and implementation power through the executive branch and would stimulate a greater trend toward state planning.[23]

Opposition to Reorganization

In January 1937 Roosevelt presented his committee's reorganization plan to congressional leaders, who were taken aback at both the substance of the proposal and the manner of its presentation. These leaders objected to Roosevelt's failure to consult with them and his desire to have the entire measure adopted without modifications. They particularly objected to raising the salaries of cabinet members and to placing the independent regulatory commissions within an executive department. On 12 January, Roosevelt sent his special message on executive reorganization to Congress, stressing the need for reorganization. Congressional response was generally lukewarm. Administration leaders and also leaders of the Democratic party admitted that reorganization would meet with a great deal of opposition.[24]

Congressional opposition to the various aspects of the reorganization proposals came from many directions. Republicans in general feared that the extension of the civil-service system would give permanent status to Roosevelt appointees. Other congressmen were opposed to the six new presidential assistants, arguing that this would only create more bureaucracy. Some opposed the measure on economic grounds. More widespread opposition stemmed from the fact that many congressmen wanted to protect particular departments that had treated them well in the past or whose authority they did not wish to see come under presidential scrutiny. Finally, many perceived the reorganization proposals as another method of strengthening the power of the presidency and the executive branch, thereby causing an imbalance between the executive and the legislative branches of the state apparatus. Some congressmen even went so far as to argue that the reorganization plans forwarded by Roosevelt would enable him to have dictatorial powers and that the measure was one step toward American fascism.[25]

During February, March, and April the joint committee that Congress had created scheduled sporadic hearings with the president's committee to discuss and debate plans for reorganization. The Joint Committee began to draft its version of a reorganization bill in June. However, a procedural rift between leaders of the House and the Senate emerged, and each chamber drafted a separate bill. The Senate bill was an omnibus bill, whereas the House bill was broken down into four separate measures. The Senate bill was introduced in August 1937 but was not voted on or even debated until 1938. Meanwhile, the House had passed two of its bills: one provided for six administrative assistants to the president; the other granted the president reorganizational powers similar to those granted in 1933 and created a Department of Welfare. The real issue of executive reorganization as recommended by the president's committee, however, was not debated until 1938. In the interim, various fractions of capital that were opposed to the reorganization effort mustered a significant degree of support.[26]

One of the major noncongressional groups that emerged in opposition to the reorganization bill was the National Committee to Uphold Constitutional Government (NCUCG). Frank E. Gannett, owner of the third-largest newspaper chain in the United States, which had a circulation of over 665,000, organized the NCUCG in an effort to raise public sentiment in opposition to the New Deal policies in general. In the leadership with Gannett were Amos Pinchot, a wealthy New York lawyer, and Edward Rumley, a producer of farm equipment. The sponsors of the organization largely included small-scale capitalists and farmers. When the Senate began hearings on the reorganization bill in early 1938, the NCUCG engaged in a massive mail campaign to urge people to write to their senators and congressmen in opposition to the bill. Largely, the NCUCG argued that the bill would give unlimited powers and possibly dictatorial authority to the president. The mailing reached more than 850,000 people who were thought to hold influential positions and some sort of community leadership roles. The distribution of this propaganda material was directed at nonmonopoly capital and the traditional petite bourgeoisie who shared similar interests to those of nonmonopoly capital.[27]

The propaganda campaign of the NCUCG was successful in stimulating thousands of letters to both the White House and to Congress from the "great middle class of America," expressing a deep desire to defeat the reorganization bill. Most of the letters expressed the fear of dictatorship and stressed the need to oppose the bill in order to maintain American democracy. The number of letters from people who opposed the bill far outweighed the letters that were sent to the White House and Senate in its favor.[28] The NCUCG was also able to secure by March 1938 a bloc of thirty-five senators who opposed the bill. The massive propaganda campaign that the NCUCG waged was well timed in that it coincided with a growing disenchantment with the inability of New Deal policies to offset the economic recession. This helped to foster congressional opposition against any form of executive reorganization.[29]

Father Charles E. Coughlin, a Detroit priest who had his own radio show, contributed to the propaganda campaign against the reorganization bill. Although he originally had supported the New Deal, Coughlin had become a critic by the mid 1930s and a strong supporter of nonmonopoly capital. Coughlin argued that the reorganization bill would set up a financial dictatorship in the person of the president and that it would put an end to democratic rights in the United States. The rising power of Hitler in Germany and of Mussolini in Italy helped to play on the fears of the American people. When the Senate was about to vote on the reorganization bill, Coughlin urged all of his listeners to send telegrams to their senators to vote against the bill. As a result, more than 300,000 telegrams were sent.[30] After the reorganization bill had been modified and passed in the Senate, Coughlin encouraged his listeners to form small groups and ride to Washington, like modern-day Paul Reveres, to urge congressmen to defeat the reorganization measures. Groups of "modern Paul Reveres" from Baltimore, New York, Philadelphia, and Boston arrived at the Capitol in Washington in mid April 1938. More than two thousand people gathered in Washington to demand that congressmen defeat the bill. Richard Polenberg has stated: "The ride of the Reveres was an exaggerated expression of the discontent which existed in the spring of 1938. The rapid expansion of German Fascism and the failure of American democracy to provide prosperity had produced widespread anxiety . . . the measure had come to symbolize executive power and radical change at a time when men, above all else, sought security."[31]

Many businessmen who represented nonmonopoly capital also expressed their opposition to the reorganization bill during the spring of 1938. Groups such as the Chamber of Commerce endorsed much of the program of the President's Committee on Administrative Management when it was first proposed in early 1937. However, by 1938, business journals and organizations were increasingly expressing opposition to the reorganization bill. As early as spring 1937, the Chamber of Commerce launched a vicious attack on the bill, claiming that it was a short step away from dictatorship. The Chamber of Commerce wrote letters to its potential supporters and financial contributors, lauding them for their aid in securing funds and urging them to continue their "fine work" in opposition to the reorganization bill. The Chamber of Commerce pledged to "further organize all Business Men of the country to decisively defeat the rule at Washington of *four men and a woman.*" Finally, the Chamber united around the political position that "all business *as a class* should be strongly organized to impose its will upon Congress."[32]

Nonmonopoly capitalists argued not only that the reorganization bill would potentially breed executive dictatorship and a form of government similar to that prevailing under communism, fascism, or nazism but also that the plan would entail wasteful spending. Fighting the recession should take precedence over executive reorganization. Nonmonopoly capitalists believed that the Roosevelt administration had, in the past, favored monopoly capital over nonmonopoly capital. Consequently, small-scale nonmonopoly capital generally perceived the Roosevelt administration as being hostile to "business interests."[33]

State administrators, to a large and significant degree, also opposed executive reorganization. State agents and state managers perceived executive reorganization as an abridgement of their own particular authority within the various bureaus and agencies that were, as yet, independent from the control of the executive branch. In essence, cabinet members, White House aides, commissioners of regulatory agencies, bureau chiefs, and regular federal employees all tried to avoid any plan for executive reorganization. Members of the executive branch of the government strongly resented any curtailment of their authority, and many were more concerned with their particular department than with overall administrative efficiency. Cabinet members also sought to defend their particular prerogatives against having bureaus shuffled out of the various departments. This was the specific complaint made by Perkins of the Labor Department when she opposed the shifting of the Employment Service out of the Labor Department. This particular line of opposition was also carried through by the AFL. Most of the members of the executive branch did not overtly seek to block the passage of the bill in Congress, but members of the independent regulatory commissions openly lobbied with congressmen to oppose the reorganization bill of 1938. Governmental agencies, such as the General Accounting Office and Civil Service, which were threatened by the proposed reorganization, worked together to block the passage of the plan. Moreover, bureau chiefs resisted change in their status with utmost tenacity, and governmental workers did their best to prevent a reshuffling of job assignments. In essence, more state managers, agents, and workers opposed reorganization than supported it. The opposition ensured that their particular position on the reorganization bill would be heard and taken into account.[34]

The situation in Congress was even more intense in 1938 than in 1937. In the midst of a recession, many congressmen, especially the more conservative elements, were not going to let another New Deal experiment take its course of failure. The more conservative members were apprehensive about the kinds of programs that Roosevelt and the New Dealers would generate and implement through a reorganized federal executive. They also were nervous about the possible administrative reorganization that would disrupt existing relationships among congressmen, state administrators, and capitalists in general. Liberals, including some members of Roosevelt's own cabinet, also opposed the reorganization bill because of similar fears of increased executive power or decreased personal (collective) authority. Senator Robert Wagner, who was so instrumental in introducing welfare and social legislation into the Congress and who was a trusted "admirer" of Roosevelt, also opposed reorganization. Wagner particularly wanted to preserve the administrative independence of the National Labor Relations Board; fearing what might happen to its policies if the secretary of labor or the president should gain more control over it.[35]

The issue that ultimately defeated the reorganization bill was not the threat of possible dictatorship raised by NCUCG and Father Coughlin; it was the opposition of state agents and state workers to departmental reorganization. State managers and people whose interests lay in one particular state agency were afraid that comfortable relations with existing governmental agencies would be disrupted if the agency were moved and if its work were appraised in a broad national context. The American Legion testified before congressional members that it did not want the Veterans Administration in the Department of Welfare. Physicians did not want the Public Health Service moved out of the Treasury

Department. Social workers did not want the Children's Bureau moved from the Labor Department to Human Welfare. Railway labor did not want the Interstate Commerce Commission moved to the Commerce Department. The secretaries of labor, interior, and agriculture; the chairman of the National Labor Relations Board; the heads of the General Accounting Office, the Corps of Engineers, and the Bureau of Fisheries—all openly opposed the reorganization bill as proposed by Roosevelt.[36]

After much debate, the Senate voted on the reorganization bill on 28 March 1938, approving it by a vote of 49 to 42. However, the bill passed by the Senate had been greatly modified from the original proposal of the President's Committee on Administrative Management. The bill limited the president's authority to make transfers to two years, and it excluded independent regulatory commissions and the Army Engineers. It extended the merit system, but not so far as to cover positions filled by the president with the advice and consent of the Senate; it eliminated higher-salaried positions; and it stipulated that the civil-service administrator was to be appointed without an examination. The bill also created an independent auditor general, and it eliminated the office of comptroller general, transferring its functions to the Bureau of the Budget rather than to the secretary of the Treasury. The bill set up a Department of Welfare but made no provisions for a Department of Conservation or a Department of Public Works.[37]

The opposition to the reorganization bill still had reason to believe that the bill could ultimately be defeated in the House. After the Senate had passed the bill, Roosevelt expressed his approval at a press conference, at the same time intimating that those who had voted against the bill had been "bought off" by an organized telegram drive that totally misrepresented the intentions of the bill. This statement by Roosevelt only angered those congressmen who were opposed to the bill and increased the resentment toward Roosevelt and the reorganization measure. Telegrams and letters expressing opposition continued to pour into the White House and to congressmen.[38] Many voters were equally outraged at Roosevelt's implication that they were dominated by devious organizations and that they had blindly urged their congressmen to vote down the bill. An example of such a telegram is one from Grace M. Aister to Roosevelt: "I personally protest against Reorganization Bill and against your remarks regarding protests to Senators. I am not dominated by any organization, and am only an American Citizen protesting against Dictatorship and demogogues."[39]

On 31 March 1938 the House began its debate on the bill. The debate was met with a wild uproar, "punctuated by boos, laughter and sarcastic comment." Many congressmen were already disgusted with various aspects of the bill, so the popular pressure only encouraged them to consider open revolt. Many thought it was safe to vote against the reorganization measure since support of the bill promised to please few voters. Congressmen passed so many amendments to the bill that it barely resembled what it had been in 1937, but the House did vote

204 to 196 to recommit the bill on 8 April. After six weeks of congressional debate, the reorganization bill died.[40]

The defeat of the reorganization bill in the House came about in large part because a significant number of congressmen wanted to reaffirm congressional independence from the executive branch and especially from Roosevelt. It also resulted from the willingness of congressmen to respond to popular pressure, which had been stimulated by extraparliamentary groups representing primarily the interests of nonmonopoly capital, to quell any attempt at executive reorganization. The conservative coalition that emerged to block the reorganization efforts demonstrated the concerted effort of nonmonopoly capital to prevent any further New Deal programs. Certainly the economic recession of 1937/38 served to muster support for opponents of New Deal reform and recovery measures. There was no consolidated bloc, representing monopoly capital or other class interests, to favor the bill and to blunt the opposition. In Polenberg's words:

> Congressmen who wished to restrict the Executive authority, protect pet bureaus, or inflict a defeat upon the president united against the measure. They were encouraged by powerful interest groups and ordinary citizens whose fear of dictatorship and resentment at the recession were exploited by opponents of the bill. The countervailing forces—Roosevelt's political skill, his influence over New Deal democrats, the need for reorganization—were offset by lapses in political strategy. Even in a diluted form, reorganization could not overcome these obstacles.[41]

Executive Reorganization

The defeat of the reorganization bill in 1938 did not stop Roosevelt from submitting a bill for reorganization in 1939. In 1938 Roosevelt began to discuss legislative strategy for a new reorganization bill with Luther Gulick, Charles Merriam, and members of Congress. In early 1939, without consulting the president's committee, Congressman Lindsay Carter Warren drafted a revised bill, which stood in sharp contrast to the measure that had been defeated in the House in 1938. It was rather mild, omitting almost all the controversial features of the previous bill. Moreover, it was drawn up by the legislative leaders who paid little attention to the recommendations of the President's Committee on Administrative Management. The reorganization bill of 1939 authorized the president to suggest plans for reorganization, subject to a veto by a majority of both the Senate and the House, and to appoint six administrative assistants. Proposals to modernize the civil-service system, renovate accounting procedures, and create new departments of the federal government were all dropped.[42]

The major revisions that were made in the bill meant that little, if any, opposition to the measure was anticipated. The House passed the bill on 8 March

1939 after a brief debate. The Senate did likewise on 20 March. The reorganization bill of 1939 did not reorganize anything, but it did give the president the authority to initiate reorganization plans subject to a sixty-day legislative veto. It also gave the president six administrative assistants.[43]

Although the president's committee had little to do with the drafting of the reorganization bill, the committee played a large part in the implementation of the Reorganization Act. The committee drew up a timetable for plans of reorganization within a few weeks following congressional approval of the act. Roosevelt sent Plan I to Congress on 25 April. This created the Federal Security Agency, the Federal Works Agency, and the Federal Loan Agency and placed related bureaus under them. Moreover, the plan established the Executive Office of the President and brought the White House Office, the Bureau of the Budget, and the National Resources Planning Board into it. On 3 May, Congress approved the plan. Plan II was presented to Congress on 9 May; it was concerned with the interdepartmental transfers of a noncontroversial sort. This plan also was upheld by Congress.[44]

Although the Reorganization Act of 1939 made no structural change in the executive branch per se, it did provide the basis for administrative reorganization in the years during and following World War II. The creation of the Executive Office of the President did enable the organization of a sort of holding company for the collection of councils and boards and individuals who worked near the White House. The act also provided for the continuing initiative of the executive branch to adjust its structure to correspond to the imperatives of the accumulation process. Although the structure of the executive branch was not significantly altered during the latter part of the 1930s, the struggle for executive reorganization does reveal shifting relationships between capital and the state and the attempt of the state administration to provide an organizational structure that would prove to be amenable to the interests of monopoly capital. The minor changes that were made in 1939 provided the basis for subsequent executive reorganization in which policy making could be implemented more easily, thus providing the structural conditions under which monopoly capital could assume a dominant position on the political terrain.

The proposal of the reorganization bill in 1937 signifies shifts in the power bloc. The tenacity with which the struggle over the bill was waged reflects fractional antagonisms between nonmonopoly capital and a state administration that was seeking to organize the hegemonic position of monopoly capital within the power bloc. The bill, as drafted, was designed to overcome many built-in obstacles to the pursuit by the state of a coordinated state economic policy. It called for the consolidation of federal administrative organs into functionally rationalized, centrally controlled cabinet departments, thus enhancing presidential powers of planning and policy coordination. It would have increased executive control vis-à-vis Congress over the expenditure of the budget; it would have established a central planning agency; and it would have expanded White

House staff directly responsible to the president. All of these measures were designed to reverse the fragmented nature of the United States' state apparatus. This desire to centralize the policy-making process would have had the consequence, however unwittingly, of politically benefiting monopoly capital. As previously illustrated, the accumulation strategy for economic recovery that was proposed by Roosevelt's Brain Trust met with barriers. These barriers on the surface level may have been due to the administrative inability of the state. But on a deeper level, the strategies for economic recovery were limited by intra- and interclass conflict and antagonisms. State administrators were not able to implement policy with impunity from pending class antagonisms. Hence, even the opposition to the reorganization bill by Congress and groups such as the Chamber of Commerce and the NCUCG, while ostensibly not presenting opposition based on stated class interests, nevertheless reflected the fact that intracapitalist conflict—specifically nonmonopoly capital's conflicts with a state administration that sought policy that would serve the interests of monopoly capital, *even when monopoly capital was not an active participant in the conflict*—would have to be reckoned with by state administrators. In many ways, the congressional struggle to prevent reorganization, while it ostensibly reflected a value conflict over congressional versus presidential powers, on another level reflected the backwardness of the political leadership, which lagged behind the changing imperatives of the accumulation process.

The state's attempt to organize the political alliance of capital under the dominance of monopoly capital provided the context of the ensuing class struggle. It was the course of the class struggle during the last few years of the depression and the war that resulted in the consolidation of the hegemonic position of monopoly-capital class fractions on the political terrain. The marginalization of the Left and the political incorporation of organized labor into the Democratic party provided the context in which an informal bargain was struck between monopoly capital and organized labor. The concatenation of executive reorganization and monopoly capital's adjustment to industrial unionization provided the conditions for the unchallenged political hegemony of monopoly capital, and thus the foundation for a new political and economic order in the post–World War II years.

The Restructuring of Capitalist Development

The world economic crisis of the 1930s provided the occasion for a fundamental restructuring of capitalist development in the United States. The dynamic of the class struggle and the manner in which state policies attempted both to resolve class conflicts and class antagonisms and to overcome obstacles to capital accumulation mediated the historical restructuring of capitalist social relations of production that proved necessary for the expanded reproduction of capital.

Restructuring involved at least three significant changes: (1) the unchallenged political hegemony of monopoly capital, (2) the diffusion of labor militancy into general ideological consensus for capitalist rule, and (3) the incorporation of organized labor into the political bargaining process and into a clearly subordinate position vis-à-vis monopoly capital.

The crisis of the 1930s represented three obstacles to capital accumulation in the United States: (1) too high a rate of exploitation, which resulted in problems of realization; (2) unregulated competition, which led to problems with capitalist investments; and (3) a political structure that was not responsive or structurally conducive to the imperatives of the accumulation process. Whereas the Hoover administration had done little to renew capital accumulation, the Roosevelt administration attempted to put into motion plans and programs for economic recovery by first concentrating on a policy that would alleviate antitrust provisions, regulate production, and control prices to stimulate investments. The National Industrial Recovery Act was formulated and implemented not only to overcome obstacles to accumulation but also to organize the capitalist class politically. Contrary to its design, the NIRA neither stimulated economic recovery nor organized the capitalist class politically. Rather, the implementation of the NIRA actually heightened the conflicts with the capitalist class and stimulated labor militancy. The accumulation strategy that was embedded within the NIRA had been limited by the balance of class forces by 1934. The capacity of the state to administer the NIRA was determined not simply by administrative weaknesses but also by intra- and interclass conflicts and antagonisms.

New Deal policies did not, in and of themselves, lead to a renewal of capital accumulation. By 1939, monopoly capital in particular was accumulating at a greater rate, and industrial capital in general was recovering from the economic downturn as a result of increased war production. Nevertheless, New Deal policies did provide the political conditions and the structural mechanisms for a renewed phase of capital accumulation in the post–World War II period. New Deal policies, by attempting to resolve class conflicts and class antagonisms, created the structural forms that regulated the objective conditions for capital accumulation and the conditions under which future class struggles and conflicts would be waged. These structural mechanisms and political conditions involved the reorganization of the state apparatus to correspond more effectively with the interests of monopoly capital. Because monopoly capital was dominant within the accumulation process, a political structure that was more in tune with the specific interests and needs of monopoly capital would not only further the interests of monopoly capital but would also strengthen capital accumulation for U.S.–based firms.

State policies provided the political and resulting economic conditions that were favorable to the growth and expansion of monopoly capital. Most capitalist industrial firms opposed the Roosevelt administration's New Deal policies. These businessmen carried out their concerted opposition to various state policies through all means available—for example, the news media and in-house publications. How, then, can one argue that the New Deal provided favorable conditions for capital expansion, particularly monopoly capital? First, both monopoly capital and nonmonopoly capital opposed the New Deal because it did not conform to their visions, their view, of what the various state agencies ought to do. These businessmen retained narrow sectional views of how the state administration ought to serve their own particularistic interests. However, the state administration—because it reflected the balance of class forces at the specific historical conjuncture—attempted to put into motion plans for economic recovery that represented the compromise not only between capital and labor but also within capital itself. Second, while the contours of the class struggle are not predetermined in some teleological fashion, the class struggle over the rate of exploitation is circumscribed within limits imposed by the accumulation process. The class struggle that occurred during the economic crisis of the 1930s never threatened the essential nature of the capitalist accumulation process itself, although industrial labor, through strikes, indeed did interrupt the industrial-production process. The industrial workers' movement for unionization never reached the political or ideological position from which it could directly challenge the capitalist system. The struggle for union recognition involved a struggle between portions of the industrial working class and industrial capital over the terms of the rate of exploitation. The struggle for union recognition was a struggle for better wages, for better working conditions, and for some day-to-day control over the organization of production and the labor process. The struggle never called into question the nature of the relations of production or of capitalist exploitation. The influence of Communists on the industrial trade-union movement was short-lived because of the increasingly divisive nature of the trade-union movement, because of political repression, and because of political mistakes made by Communists themselves. Consequently, the real and meaningful structural changes that were gained by segments of the working class were channeled into areas that were compatible with the overall accumulation of capital and that provided the basis for a new phase of capital accumulation.

The state's protection of unionization ultimately provided for the incorporation of significant segments of the working class—through the trade-union movement and its relationship to the Democratic party—into a clearly subordinate position vis-à-vis monopoly capital. The National Labor Relations Board brought organized labor's institutional representation within the national political arena. Finding political expression through the Democratic party, the industrial trade-union movement entered into an unequal relationship with monopoly capital at the level of representation within the state apparatus. The state's protection of industrial trade unionization, itself a product of labor militancy during the 1930s, made possible the institutionalization of collective-bargaining arrangements that overcame the problems with realization because of the bargaining rights of labor over the rate of exploitation. The purging of Communists from the trade-union movement and the nature of U.S. political parties provided the context through which collective-bargaining arrangements tended to isolate political struggles from economic struggles. The incorporation of the trade-union movement into the national political-bargaining process, via both the Democratic party and collective-bargaining arrangements, altered social relations *in* production and social relations *of* production. State activity sought to furnish active aid in altering the rate of exploitation. The dynamic of the class struggle was such that Communist and Socialist politics came to be less acceptable to significant portions of the working class. What developed was a general ideological consensus for capitalist rule.[45]

The trajectory of capitalist development in the United States took a different course as a result of the upsurge of workers' militant activities during the 1930s. Labor militancy in demanding and using collective bargaining made it possible to overcome large-scale capital's resistance to a fundamental reorganization of wages and consumption. Nevertheless, it was monopoly capital that was able to adjust to these working-class gains. Monopoly capital—in the long boom period of economic recovery and expansion that was first generated by World War II and then by the political hegemony that the United States enjoyed on a world scale from 1945 to the mid 1960s—not only passed on to consumers (internationally) wage gains and benefits that workers had acquired; it also used collective bargaining—particularly with the Taft-Hartley Act—as a way to ensure labor peace. In the process, monopoly capital was able to dominate crucial state agencies and to become the hegemonic fraction within the power bloc. Increased state intervention aided not only in the regulation of competition but also in further investment outlets. The obstacle to capital accumulation of too high a rate of exploitation was temporarily resolved through the institutionalization of collective bargaining and the incorporation of significant trade unions into the national political-bargaining process. Problems of unregulated competition were temporarily resolved through state policies that reflected the growing divisions between monopoly and nonmonopoly capital over the monopoly issue. The political structure was altered to correspond more closely with the imperatives of the accumulation process by having monopoly capital dominate key state agencies and by having the industrial trade-union movement incorporated into a clearly subordinate position vis-à-vis monopoly capital on the political level.[46] The incorporation of the industrial trade-union movement into the national political-bargaining process and into a more cooperative relationship via collective bargaining with monopoly capital, the purging of leftists and the resultant ideological consensus for capitalist rule, and the unchallenged political hegemony of monopoly capital—all combined to produce the conditions for a new phase of capitalist development within the United States.

The renewed phase of capital accumulation in the post–World War II period involved the following elements. Monopoly forms of competition resulted in having few firms dominate crucial branches of industry (steel, automobiles, rubber), thus making it virtually impossible for the entry of competing firms. New forms of competition meant that competition was no longer solely based on keeping down the cost of labor and reducing prices. This new form of competition involved the "appropriation of technology and information, control over specific markets, access to financial resources, and influences on sectors of the state apparatus."[47] Competition became based not only on control of the market but also on the capacity to create favorable conditions for investment. Increasing state activity in the regulation of competition aided monopoly competition and stimulated competition in the sphere of advertising. Competition between monopoly firms for a bigger share of the consumer market grew as a result of the reorganization of wages during the 1930s. In the same way that collective-bargaining arrangements altered social relations within large-scale basic industry, new forms of competition altered relationships between industrial firms.

Although the renewed phase of capital accumulation involved the political and economic dominance of monopoly capital, nonmonopoly capital continued to exist, albeit in a clearly subordinate position. Several factors explain the coexistence of monopoly and nonmonopoly capital within the industrial sector. First, nonmonopoly capital tends to occupy sectors that are currently of limited profitability, and it tends to take the risks associated with technological innovation. Monopoly capital may then expand into these new sectors of production, recouping technological innovations with minimal risk and at a lower cost than could have been associated with earlier experimentation. Second, nonmonopoly capital provides secondary lines of production that do not enter into the continuous large-scale flow of complex production units but that are necessary for the sale of a particular commodity. Finally, nonmonopoly capital has lower labor productivity and, generally, higher production costs. This enables monopoly capital to fix prices by reference to those of nonmonopoly capital, thereby producing increased profits for monopoly capital.[48]

Monopoly capital expanded rapidly during the post–World War II years, and the United States was consolidated as the hegemonic world power, opening up new markets and production sites abroad. Capitalist accumulation was strengthened within the United States. The change in consumption patterns of the home market combined with higher-priced domestic labor to encourage U.S.–based firms to increase direct investments abroad and to export capital. The internationalization of capital created greater linkages with the underdeveloped world and resulted in greater corporate profits for U.S.–based firms and greater economic dependency for the underdeveloped world. The crushing of Communist and Socialist tendencies within the working class during the 1950s provided capitalists with a seemingly docile labor force — a necessary condition for the expanded reproduction of capital, since it limits the struggle over the rate of exploitation. The expansion of state economic activity helped to offset overproduction and therefore aided in the profitable accumulation of capital. All of these elements combined to provide the conditions for a seemingly lasting profitable capitalist accumulation.

The course of capitalist development on a world scale consists of phases. Obstacles to capitalist accumulation in one phase may be temporarily resolved to enable the continued expansion of capital in another phase. This was the case in the United States during the world economic crisis of the 1930s. However, the process of capitalist development is a contradictory process, and the conditions that are created to overcome obstacles in one phase of capitalist development often come to present obstacles in a later phase. The class struggle that was waged during the 1930s directed the restructuring that took place in the post–World War II period. State policies, as mediated through the historical class struggle, created conditions that were necessary for the expanded reproduction of capital in the post–World War II years, but these same conditions also provided the preconditions for the economic downturn and the crisis of world capitalist development in the 1970s.[49] It must be stressed, however, that the working-class struggles of the 1930s were not fought in vain. The workers' movement did—through its efforts to alter the balance of the rate of exploitation in its favor—force certain *real and meaningful* structural changes (e.g., gaining the political right to organize and to bargain collectively with capital over the rate of exploitation). Renewed class struggle in the present conjuncture takes place from a new starting point and is able to build upon working-class gains that were achieved in the past. It still remains to be seen what course the class struggle will assume, what will be the outcome of the intensity of the current economic downturn, and what avenues will be available for the development of a new phase of capitalist expansion.

NOTES

Chapter One. The Capitalist State, Class Relations, and the New Deal

1. Donald Winch, *Economics and Policy* (New York: Walker, 1969), p. 219; Louis M. Hacker, *The Course of American Economic Growth and Development* (New York: John Wiley, 1970), p. 85; U.S. Bureau of the Census, *Historical Statistics of the United States, Colonial Times to 1970,* Bicentennial Edition, pt. 1 (Washington, D.C.: Government Printing Office, 1975), p. 135.

2. Bernard Bellush, *The Failure of the NRA* (New York: W. W. Norton, 1975), p. xiii.

3. For studies that perceive the New Deal as a new departure in state activity, representing "radical" innovations, see, e.g., William E. Leuchtenburg, *Franklin D. Roosevelt and the New Deal, 1932–1940* (New York: Harper & Row, 1963). Basil Rauch, *The History of the New Deal, 1933–1938* (New York: Creative Age, 1944), was one of the earliest scholarly histories of the New Deal that argued that the New Deal represented far-reaching reforms in domestic institutions. Similar arguments are found in Carl N. Degler, *Out of Our Past* (New York: Harper & Row, 1959), chap. 13, and Arthur M. Schlesinger, Jr., *The Coming of the New Deal* (Boston, Mass.: Houghton Mifflin, 1958), *The Crisis of the Old Order* (Boston, Mass.: Houghton Mifflin, 1957), and *The Politics of Upheaval* (Boston, Mass.: Houghton Mifflin, 1960). For studies that argue that the New Deal had "conservative" dimensions and was part of an earlier trend see Barton J. Bernstein, "The Conservative Achievements of Liberal Reform," in *Towards a New Past,* ed. Barton J. Bernstein (New York: Vintage, 1969), pp. 263–88; Paul K. Conkin, *The New Deal* (New York: Thomas Y. Crowell, 1967); and Ronald Radosh, "The Myth of the New Deal," in *A New History of Leviathan,* ed. Ronald Radosh and Murray N. Rothbard (New York: E. P. Dutton, 1972), pp. 156–87. Radosh differs somewhat with the analyses put forward by Bernstein and Conkin. Radosh argues that the New Deal was a conscious program put forth by corporate capitalists. For Radosh, the entire New Deal program was a series of well-thought-out pieces of legislation that were "of such a character that they would be able to create a long-lasting mythology about the existence of a pluralistic American democracy, in which big labor supposedly exerts its countering influence to the domination that otherwise would be undertaken by big industry" (p. 186). Aside from the rather general studies of the New Deal period, a number of studies have attempted to analyze specific themes or changes that have been attributed to the New Deal. These studies also, however, pose the question within the framework of continuity vs. change and liberal vs. conservative. See, e.g., Ellis W. Hawley, *The New Deal and the Problem of Monopoly* (Princeton, N.J.: Princeton University Press, 1966); Robert F. Himmelberg, *The Origins of the National Recovery Administration* (New York: Fordham University Press, 1976); and Sidney Fine, *The Automobile under the Blue Eagle* (Ann Arbor: University of Michigan Press, 1963).

4. Leuchtenburg, *Franklin D. Roosevelt and the New Deal,* p. 336; William E. Leuchtenburg, *The New Deal: A Documentary History* (New York: Harper & Row, 1968), p. xi.

5. Bernstein, "Conservative Achievements," pp. 264–65.

6. See, e.g., Leuchtenburg, *Franklin D. Roosevelt and the New Deal,* and Schlesinger, *Coming of the New Deal.*

7. See, e.g., Radosh, "Myth of the New Deal"; Bernstein, "Conservative Achievements"; Gabriel Kolko, *Main Currents in Modern American History* (New York: Harper & Row, 1976), chaps. 4–6.

8. Instrumentalist accounts of the New Deal have been referred to under the general rubric of a corporate liberal perspective. Corporate liberalism argues that a self-conscious capitalist class rationally pursued a set of policies that would allow them to control the political process as well as the economic processes of capitalism. Corporate liberalism implicitly operates from an instrumentalist view of the state.

9. Bob Jessop, *The Capitalist State* (New York: New York University Press, 1982), p. 226.

10. See Goran Therborn, *What Does the Ruling Class Do When It Rules?* (London: New Left Books, 1978), p. 169.

11. Ralph Miliband, *The State in Capitalist Society* (London: Quartet, 1973). The Poulantzas-Miliband debate is best summed up in the exchange between the two in *New Left Review.* See Nicos Poulantzas, "The Problem of the Capitalist State," *New Left Review* 58 (Nov.–Dec. 1969): 67–78; Ralph Miliband, "The Capitalist State: Reply to Nicos Poulantzas," ibid., 59 (Jan.–Feb. 1970): 53–60; Ralph Miliband, "Poulantzas and the Capitalist State," ibid., 82 (Nov.–Dec. 1973): 83–92; Nicos Poulantzas, "The Capitalist State: A Reply to Miliband and Laclau," ibid., 95 (Jan.–Feb. 1976): 63–83.

12. For an excellent review of recent Marxist literature on the state see Bob Jessop, *The Capitalist State.* Instrumentalism is best exemplified in the works of Ralph Miliband, *The State in Capitalist Society,* and *Marxism and Politics* (New York: Oxford University Press, 1977). Structuralism is best exemplified in the works of Nicos Poulantzas. See especially, *State, Power, Socialism* (London: New Left Books, 1978), *Classes in Contemporary Capitalism* (London: New Left Books, 1975), *Political Power and Social Classes* (London: New Left Books, 1973), *Fascism and Dictatorship* (London: New Left Books, 1974), and *The Crisis of the Dictatorships* (London: New Left Books, 1976).

13. See, e.g., Theda Skocpol, "Political Response to Capitalist Crisis: Neo-Marxist Theories of the State and the Case of the New Deal," *Politics and Society* 10, 2 (1980): 155–201; Fred Block, "The Ruling Class Does Not Rule: Notes on the Marxist Theory of the State," *Socialist Revolution* 33 (May–June 1977): 6–28; idem, "Beyond Relative Autonomy: State Managers as Historical Subjects," *Socialist Register,* 1980, pp. 227–42; Jill Quadagno, "Welfare Capitalism and the Social Security Act of 1935," *American Sociological Review* 49, 5 (Oct. 1984): 632–47; Kenneth Finegold and Theda Skocpol, "State, Party, and Industry: From Business Recovery to the Wagner Act in America's New Deal," in *Statemaking and Social Movements: Essays in History and Theory,* ed. Charles Bright and Susan Harding (Ann Arbor: University of Michigan Press, 1984), pp. 159–92; Theda Skocpol and Kenneth Finegold, "State Capacity and Economic Intervention in the Early New Deal," *Political Science Quarterly* 97, 2 (Summer 1982): 255–78; Margaret Weir and Theda Skocpol, "State Structures and the Possibilities for 'Keynesian' Responses to the Great Depression in Sweden, Britain, and the United States," in *Bringing the State Back In,* ed. Peter B. Evans, Dietrich Rueschemeyer, and Theda Skocpol (New York: Cambridge University Press, 1985), pp. 107–63; Theda Skocpol and Edwin Amenta, "Did Capitalists Shape Social Security?" *American Sociological Review* 50, 4 (Aug. 1985): 572–75; Jill Quadagno, "Two Models of Welfare State Development: A Reply to Skocpol and Amenta," *American Sociological Review* 50, 4 (Aug. 1985): 575–78.

14. Poulantzas, *State, Power, Socialism,* p. 132.

15. See Block, "Ruling Class Does Not Rule" and "Beyond Relative Autonomy."

16. Theda Skocpol, "Bringing the State Back In," in *Bringing the State Back In,* p. 5.

17. See, e.g., Weir and Skocpol, "State Structures," pp. 132–37.

18. Finegold and Skocpol, "State, Party, and Industry," p. 161.

19. See, e.g., Skocpol, "Political Response to Capitalist Crisis," Finegold and Skocpol, "State, Party, and Industry," Skocpol and Finegold, "State Capacity," Weir and Skocpol, "State Structures." Because of the great deal of attention that Skocpol has paid to New Deal legislation and the critique of existing frames of reference, I have paid more attention in my critique to Skocpol's analysis than to any other frame of reference.

20. See especially Skocpol, "Political Response to Capitalist Crisis," and Finegold and Skocpol, "State, Party, and Industry."

21. For an excellent composite picture of Poulantzian theory see Bob Jessop, *Nicos Poulantzas: Marxist Theory and Political Strategy* (New York: St. Martin's, 1985).

22. Jessop, *The Capitalist State,* p. 24.

23. See, e.g., Skocpol, "Political Response to Capitalist Crisis," pp. 169–81.

24. Jessop, *The Capitalist State,* p. 221.

25. Quadagno, "Welfare Capitalism and the Social Security Act of 1935."

26. Ibid., p. 646.

27. Ibid., p. 645.

28. Poulantzas, *State, Power, Socialism,* p. 132.

29. Poulantzas, *Classes in Contemporary Capitalism,* p. 144.

Chapter Two. The Process of Capitalist Development: Capital, Labor, and the State, 1890–1929

1. The first epigraph is cited by Willard L. Thorp in "The Changing Structure of Industry," *Recent Economic Changes in the United States,* Report of the Committee on Recent Economic Changes of the President's Conference on Unemployment (New York: McGraw-Hill, 1929), p. 181; the second is from "Labor Groups in the Social Structure," in *Recent Social Trends in the United States,* Report of the President's Research Committee on Social Trends (New York: McGraw-Hill, 1933), pp. 829–30.

2. David M. Gordon, Richard Edwards, and Michael Reich, *Segmented Work, Divided Workers: The Historical Transformation of Labor in the United States* (New York: Cambridge University Press, 1982), pp. 22–26.

3. See Ernest Mandel, *Late Capitalism* (London: New Left Books, 1975), pp. 120–21, 190.

4. Gordon, Edwards, and Reich, *Segmented Work,* p. 111.

5. For an interesting account of the manner in which capital resisted labor organization in the pre–New Deal period see Larry J. Griffin, Michael E. Wallace, and Beth A. Rubin, "Capitalist Resistance to the Organization of Labor before the New Deal: Why? How? Success?" *American Sociological Review* 51, 2 (Apr. 1986): 147–67.

6. See Gordon, Edwards, and Reich, *Segmented Work,* pp. 129–30; Paul H. Douglas, *Real Wages in the United States, 1890–1926* (New York: Houghton Mifflin, 1930), pp. 207–8; and Ada Beney, *Wages, Hours, and Employment in the United States, 1914–1936* (New York: National Industrial Conference Board, 1936), pp. 48–50.

7. For an interesting theoretical account of changes in the labor process associated with the intensive exploitation of labor see Brighton Labor Process Group, "The Capitalist Labor Process," *Capital and Class* 1 (Spring 1977): 3–26.

8. Gordon, Edwards, and Reich, *Segmented Work,* pp. 110–112.

9. See Stephen Skowronek, *Building a New American State: The Expansion of Na-*

tional Administrative Capacities, 1877–1920 (New York: Cambridge University Press, 1982), for a discussion of changes within the state for the period.

10. Lewis Corey, *The Decline of American Capitalism* (New York: Covici, Friede, 1934), p. 30.

11. Alfred D. Chandler, Jr., *The Visible Hand: The Managerial Revolution in American Business* (Cambridge, Mass.: Harvard University Press, 1977), p. 286.

12. Jurgen Kuczynski, *A Short History of Labour Conditions under Industrial Capitalism, vol. 2: The United States of America, 1789–1946* (New York: Barnes & Noble, 1973), p. 71.

13. Ibid., p. 72.

14. Edward C. Kirkland, *Industry Comes of Age* (New York: Holt, Rinehart & Winston, 1961), p. 165.

15. Harold U. Faulkner, *The Decline of Laissez-faire, 1897–1917* (New York: Holt, Rinehart & Winston, 1951), p. 115.

16. Ibid., p. 155.

17. Edwin F. Gay and Leo Wolman, "Trends in Economic Organization," in *Recent Social Trends in the United States,* p. 241.

18. George Soule, *Prosperity Decade: From War to Depression, 1917–1929* (New York: Rinehart, 1947), p. 142.

19. Gordon, Edwards, and Reich, *Segmented Work,* p. 129.

20. See Faulkner, *Decline of Laissez-faire,* p. 121; and Chandler, *Visible Hand,* p. 240.

21. Chandler, *Visible Hand,* pp. 240–41.

22. Faulkner, *Decline of Laissez-faire,* pp. 121–22.

23. Ibid., p. 122.

24. Ibid., p. 123.

25. Dexter S. Kimball, "Changes in New and Old Industries," in *Recent Economic Changes in the United States,* p. 80.

26. Louis M. Hacker and Benjamin B. Kendrick, *The United States since 1865* (New York: F. S. Crofts, 1932), p. 620.

27. Ibid.

28. Kimball, "Changes in New and Old Industries," p. 81.

29. Hacker and Kendrick, *United States since 1865,* p. 621.

30. Alfred Sohn-Rethel, *Intellectual and Manual Labour* (London: Macmillan, 1978), p. 148.

31. For a more detailed examination of scientific management see Harry Braverman, *Labor and Monopoly Capital* (New York: Monthly Review Press, 1974), pp. 45–152; Chandler, *Visible Hand,* pp. 272–83; Richard Edwards, *Contested Terrain: The Transformation of the Workplace in the Twentieth Century* (New York: Basic, 1979), pp. 90–162.

32. Sohn-Rethel, *Intellectual and Manual Labour,* p. 153.

33. Ibid., p. 157.

34. Michel Aglietta, *A Theory of Capitalist Regulation: The U.S. Experience* (London: New Left Books, 1979), pp. 114–15.

35. Daniel Nelson, *Managers and Workers: Origins of the New Factory System in the United States, 1880–1920* (Madison: University of Wisconsin Press, 1975), p. 162; see also Griffin, Wallace, and Rubin, "Capitalist Resistance," pp. 157–61.

36. Claus Offe, *Disorganized Capitalism* (Cambridge, Mass.: MIT Press, 1985), p. 178.

37. Nelson, *Managers and Workers,* p. 121; Griffin, Wallace, and Rubin, "Capitalist Resistance," pp. 155–65.

38. For an interesting discussion of regimes of accumulation see Aglietta, *Theory of Capitalist Regulation,* pp. 68–100. For Aglietta, "A regime of accumulation is a form

of social transformation that increases relative surplus value under the stable constraints of the most general norms that define absolute surplus value" (p. 68). Aglietta argues that the distinction between absolute surplus value and relative surplus value "denotes an articulation of social relations that induce different complementary practices" (p. 68). In brief, a regime of accumulation refers to the different social relations that are attributed to the different types of exploitation.

39. L. P. Alford, "Technical Changes in Manufacturing Industries," in *Recent Economic Changes in the United States,* p. 104.

40. Wolman and Peck, "Labor Groups in the Social Structure," p. 821; see also Albert Rees, *Real Wages in Manufacturing, 1890–1914* (Princeton, N.J.: Princeton University Press, 1961), pp. 120–27; and Stanley Lebergott, *Manpower in Economic Growth: The American Record since 1800* (New York: McGraw-Hill, 1964), p. 523.

41. Douglas, *Real Wages,* pp. 510–90.

42. Kuczynski, *Short History of Labour Conditions,* p. 183; Marjorie R. Clark and S. Fanny Simon, *The Labor Movement in America* (New York: W. W. Norton, 1938), p. 120.

43. See Kuczynski, *Short History of Labour Conditions,* p. 147, for a detailed computation of hours worked per week.

44. Wolman and Peck, "Labor Groups in the Social Structure," p. 445.

45. Alford, "Technical Changes in Manufacturing Industries," pp. 101–2.

46. Wolman and Peck, "Labor Groups in the Social Structure," pp. 806–8. For different estimates of levels of unemployment for the entire civilian labor force see Lebergott, *Manpower in Economic Growth,* pp. 403–12; and U.S. Bureau of the Census, *Historical Statistics of the United States, Colonial Times to 1970,* Bicentennial Edition, pt. 1 (Washington, D.C.: Government Printing Office, 1975), p. 135.

47. Faulkner, *Decline of Laissez-faire,* p. 249.

48. Wolman and Peck, "Labor Groups in the Social Structure," p. 806.

49. Ralph G. Hurlin and Meredith B. Givens, "Shifting Occupational Patterns," in *Recent Social Trends in the United States,* pp. 284–85.

50. Ibid., p. 286.

51. Ibid., pp. 295–96.

52. See Gordon, Edwards, and Reich, *Segmented Work,* pp. 100–164.

53. See David Montgomery, "Workers' Control of Machine Production in the Nineteenth Century," *Labor History* 17, 4 (Fall 1976): 485–509.

54. Milton J. Nadworny, *Scientific Management and the Unions, 1900–1932* (Cambridge, Mass.: Harvard University Press, 1955), p. 5, 102–3.

55. Ibid. and passim.

56. Brian Palmer, "Class Conception and Conflict: The Thrust for Efficiency, Managerial Views of Labor and the Working Class Rebellion, 1903–1922," *Review of Radical Political Economics* 7, 2 (Summer 1975): 33.

57. See, e.g., David Brody, *Steelworkers in America* (New York: Harper & Row, 1969), passim.

58. See Griffin, Wallace, and Rubin, "Capitalist Resistance," passim.

59. Faulkner, *Decline of Laissez-faire,* p. 296; see Offe, *Disorganized Capitalism,* pp. 170–220, for an excellent discussion of the differences between labor organizations and associations of capitalists.

60. See Albion Guilford Taylor, *Labor Policies of the National Association of Manufacturers* (New York: Arno, 1973), passim.

61. See Mike Davis, "Why the U.S. Working Class Is Different," *New Left Review* 123 (Sept.–Oct. 1980): 3–44; Robert Justin Goldstein, *Political Repression in Modern America, 1870 to the Present* (Cambridge, Mass.: Schenkman, 1978), pp. 44–101.

62. Soule, *Prosperity Decade,* p. 187.

63. Taylor, *Labor Policies,* pp. 167–68, 91, 73.

64. National Association of Manufacturers, "Evidence for the Open Shop," 28 Feb. 1927.

65. Soule, *Prosperity Decade,* p. 193; Brody, *Steelworkers in America,* passim.

66. Wolman and Peck, "Labor Groups in the Social Structure," p. 490.

67. Davis, "Why the U.S. Working Class Is Different," p. 43.

68. Goldstein, *Political Repression,* pp. 63–101.

69. James P. Cannon, *The First Ten Years of American Communism* (New York: Pathfinder, 1962), p. 33.

70. Melvin Dubofsky, *We Shall Be All* (New York: Quadrangle, 1969), pp. 448–49.

71. Goldstein, *Political Repression,* pp. 105–91.

72. For a discussion on the European labor movement during the interwar years see Giovanni Arrighi, "The Class Struggle in Twentieth Century Western Europe," paper presented at the Ninth World Congress of Sociology, Uppsala, Sweden, 14–19 Aug. 1978.

73. Irving Bernstein, *The Lean Years* (Boston, Mass.: Houghton Mifflin, 1972), p. 80.

74. For a more detailed discussion of the Socialist party and the Communist party and the IWW during the postwar years see Cannon, *First Ten Years*; James Weinstein, *The Decline of Socialism in America, 1912–1925,* rev. ed. (New Brunswick, N.J.: Rutgers University Press, 1984), pp. 177–339; idem, *Ambiguous Legacy: The New Left in American Politics* (New York: New Viewpoints, 1975), pp. 26, 43; Dubofsky, *We Shall Be All,* pp. 376–468.

75. Albert K. Steigerwalt, *The National Association of Manufacturers, 1895–1914* (Ann Arbor, Mich.: Bureau of Business Research, Graduate School of Business Administration, 1974), p. 12.

76. See Gabriel Kolko, *Main Currents in Modern American History* (New York: Harper & Row, 1976), p. 177. Although the NAM represented the interest of nonmonopoly capital, the association still maintained a membership that included those businessmen who would be associated more with monopoly capital. See also, Griffin, Wallace, and Rubin, "Capitalist Resistance."

77. Edwards, *Contested Terrain,* pp. 65–72.

78. Soule, *Prosperity Decade,* pp. 134–35.

79. Skowronek, *Building a New American State.*

80. Carl N. Degler, "American Political Parties and the Rise of the City: An Interpretation," *Journal of American History* 51, 1 (June 1964): 49; Skowronek, *Building a New American State,* pp. 167–76.

81. Gerald D. Nash, "Industry and the Federal Government, 1850–1933," *Current History* 48, 286 (June 1965): 327.

82. James L. Sundquist, *Dynamics of the Party System* (Washington, D.C.: Brookings Institution, 1973), pp. 175–77.

83. Aglietta, *Theory of Capitalist Regulation,* p. 134.

84. For an interesting analysis of the relationship between class struggle and the rationalization of production see James A. Geschwender, "Class Struggle, the Labor Process and Racial Stratification," paper presented at the annual meetings of the Society for the Study of Social Problems, Aug. 1979, Boston, Massachusetts.

85. Aglietta, *Theory of Capitalist Regulation,* p. 134.

86. Ibid., p. 94.

87. Ibid., p. 8.

88. Nicos Poulantzas, *State, Power, Socialism* (London: New Left Books, 1978), p. 137.

CHAPTER THREE. THE CRISIS AND ITS IMPACT ON LABOR AND CAPITAL

1. The epigraphs are from a memorandum to Governor Franklin D. Roosevelt from A. A. Berle, 15 Aug. 1932, Berle Papers, box 15, FDR Library, Hyde Park, N.Y.; and Berle to FDR, 4 Feb. 1933, Raymond Moley Collection, box 63, Hoover Institute on War, Revolution and Peace, Stanford University, Palo Alto, Calif.

2. See Charles P. Kindleberger, *The World in Depression, 1929–1939* (Berkeley: University of California Press, 1973), pp. 108–27; Bertil Ohlin, *The Course and Phases of World Economic Depression* (New York: Arno, 1972), pp. 187–89, 141–42; P. T. Ellsworth, *The International Economy* (New York: Macmillan, 1950), p. 501.

3. See John Weeks, *Capital and Exploitation* (Princeton, N.J.: Princeton University Press, 1981), pp. 187–217; and Maurice Dobb, *Studies in the Development of Capitalism* (New York: International, 1973), pp. 320–93, for a discussion of the general and specific dynamics of capitalist crises and the world economic crisis of the 1930s; see also Manuel Castells, *The Economic Crisis and American Society* (Princeton, N.J.: Princeton University Press, 1980), pp. 14–77.

4. David M. Gordon, Richard Edwards, and Michael Reich, *Segmented Work, Divided Workers: The Historical Transformation of Labor in the United States* (New York: Cambridge University Press, 1982), p. 129.

5. Erik Olin Wright, *Class, Crisis, and the State* (London: New Left Books, 1978), pp. 173–75.

6. Donald Winch, *Economics and Policy* (New York: Walker, 1969), p. 219.

7. Louis M. Hacker, *The Course of American Economic Growth and Development* (New York: John Wiley, 1970), pp. 300–301.

8. Robert Sobel, *The Age of Giant Corporations: A Microeconomic History of American Business, 1914–1970* (Westport, Conn.: Greenwood, 1972), p. 85.

9. Ibid., p. 86.

10. Jonathan R. T. Hughes, *The Governmental Habit: Economic Controls from Colonial Times to the Present* (New York: Basic, 1977), pp. 155–56.

11. Arthur M. Schlesinger, Jr., *The Crisis of the Old Order* (Boston, Mass.: Houghton Mifflin, 1957), p. 177.

12. Elliot A. Rosen, *Hoover, Roosevelt, and the Brains Trust* (New York: Columbia University Press, 1977), p. 65.

13. Sobel, *Age of Giant Corporations,* pp. 88–89.

14. Rosen, *Hoover, Roosevelt, and the Brains Trust,* pp. 62–63.

15. Ibid., p. 63.

16. Sobel, *Age of Giant Corporations,* pp. 89–90.

17. Rosen, *Hoover, Roosevelt, and the Brains Trust,* p. 64.

18. Sobel, *Age of Giant Corporations,* p. 93.

19. Broadus Mitchell, *Depression Decade: From New Era through New Deal, 1929–1941* (New York: Holt, Rinehart & Winston, 1962), pp. 77–78.

20. U.S. Bureau of the Census, *Historical Statistics of the United States, Colonial Times to 1970,* Bicentennial Edition, pt. 1 (Washington, D.C.: Government Printing Office, 1975), p. 135.

21. Roy Rosenzweig, "Organizing the Unemployed: The Early Years of the Great Depression, 1929–1933," *Radical America* 10, 4 (July–Aug. 1976): 38.

22. Bernard Bellush, *The Failure of the NRA* (New York: W. W. Norton, 1975), p. xiii.

23. Marjorie R. Clark and S. Fanny Simon, *The Labor Movement in America* (New York: W. W. Norton, 1938), p. 134.

24. Rosenzweig, "Organizing the Unemployed," p. 38. For a detailed account of the

organizations of the unemployed see Eleanor Nora Kahn, "Organizations of the Unemployed Workers as a Factor in the American Labor Movement" (Master's thesis, University of Wisconsin, 1934).

25. Daniel J. Leab, "United We Eat: The Creation and Organization of the Unemployed Councils in 1930," *Labor History* 8, 3 (Fall 1967): 301–2. There was a great effort in 1930 to build the Trade Union Unity League and to recruit workers for the "building up of revolutionary unions, on the basis of our program for struggle against capitalist rationalization." See Letter from Trade Union Unity League to All Party District Bureaux, 12 July 1930, Browder Papers, ser. 2, box 19, George Arents Research Library, Syracuse University, Syracuse, N.Y.

26. Irving Bernstein, *The Lean Years* (Boston, Mass.: Houghton Mifflin, 1972), pp. 426–27. The 6 Mar. 1930 unemployment demonstration in New York City called for unity between the employed and unemployed. In fact, the Communist party called for workers to strike on March 6 in solidarity with the unemployment demonstration. See Leaflet, Browder Papers, ser. 2, box 9.

27. Frances Fox Piven and Richard A. Cloward, *Regulating the Poor* (New York: Vintage, 1972), pp. 64ff.

28. Bernstein, *Lean Years,* p. 431.

29. Piven and Cloward, *Regulating the Poor,* p. 62.

30. See, e.g., Leab, "United We Eat," p. 308.

31. Bernstein, *Lean Years,* p. 428.

32. Piven and Cloward, *Regulating the Poor,* p. 63.

33. Bernstein, *Lean Years,* p. 433.

34. Piven and Cloward, *Regulating the Poor,* pp. 65ff.

35. Bernstein, *Lean Years,* pp. 433–34.

36. Rosenzweig, "Organizing the Unemployed," pp. 47–49.

37. Proposal Submitted for Adoption to the City Convention of the New York City Socialist Party Local, 26 and 27 Apr. 1930, Daniel Bell Collection, box 22, Tamiment Institute, New York, N.Y.

38. Rosenzweig, "Organizing the Unemployed," pp. 49–50.

39. See P. K. Edwards, *Strikes in the United States, 1881–1974* (Oxford, Eng.: Basil Blackwell, 1981), pp. 137–41.

40. *Historical Statistics of the United States,* p. 179.

41. See Bernstein, *Lean Years,* pp. 1–43 and 360–90.

42. *Party Organizer,* Jan. 1932.

43. Frances Fox Piven and Richard A. Cloward, *Poor People's Movements: How They Succeed, How They Fail* (New York: Pantheon, 1977), p. 109.

44. *Party Organizer,* Aug. 1931; Bernstein, *Lean Years,* pp. 360–90.

45. Schlesinger, *Crisis of the Old Order,* pp. 184–86.

46. See memo of the Central Committee of the Communist Party, 1930, Browder Papers, ser. 1, box 2.

47. *Party Organizer,* Mar.–July 1930.

48. See chart on Party Growth-Fluctuation, Browder Papers, ser. 2, box 3.

49. There is some evidence that Green wrote a 178-page document revealing Communist influence in the trade-union movement. See Browder Papers, ser. 2, box 19.

50. Bernstein, *Lean Years,* pp. 427–28.

51. Frank A. Warren, *An Alternative Vision: The Socialist Party in the 1930's* (Bloomington: Indiana University Press, 1974), p. 3.

52. Ibid., passim.

53. Schlesinger, *Crisis of the Old Order,* p. 207.

54. Letter from Clarence Senior, executive secretary of the Socialist Party of America to state and federation secretaries, 9 Feb. 1933, Daniel Bell Collection, box 22.

55. See Roy Rosenzweig, "Radicals and the Jobless: The Musteites and the Unemployed Leagues, 1932–1936," *Labor History* 16, 1 (Winter 1975): 52–77.

56. See Karel Denis Bicha, "Liberalism Frustrated: The League for Independent Political Action, 1928–1933," *Mid-America* 48, 1 (Jan. 1966): 19–28.

57. Cited by Robert Justin Goldstein in *Political Repression in Modern America, 1870 to the Present* (Cambridge, Mass.: Schenkman, 1978), p. 197.

58. For the most complete treatment of political repression during the early depression years see ibid., pp. 195–209.

59. H. V. Hodson, *Slump and Recovery, 1929–1937* (New York: Oxford University Press, 1938), p. 207.

60. Hal B. Lary and Associates, *The United States in the World Economy* (Washington, D.C.: U.S. Government Printing Office, 1943), p. 171.

61. Ibid., p. 172.

62. Ibid., p. 173.

63. Chamber of Commerce of the United States of America, *Nineteenth . . . Annual Report* (1931), p. 36, cited by Linda Brown in "Challenge and Response: The American Business Community and the New Deal, 1932–1934" (Ph.D. diss., University of Pennsylvania, 1972), p. 203.

64. Chamber of Commerce of the United States of America, *Referends, Nos. 5468, 1929–1934* (Washington, D.C.: Chamber of Commerce Archives), Special Bulletin, 18 Jan. 1932, cited by Brown in "Challenge and Response," p. 203.

65. Ellis W. Hawley, *The New Deal and the Problem of Monopoly* (Princeton, N.J.: Princeton University Press, 1966), p. 23.

66. James L. Sundquist, *Dynamics of the Party System* (Washington, D.C.: Brookings Institution, 1973), pp. 194–95.

67. David A. Shannon, *Between the Wars: America, 1919–1941* (Boston, Mass.: Houghton Mifflin, 1965), pp. 144–45.

68. For an interesting discussion of the development of a Democratic majority see Kristi Anderson, *The Creation of a Democratic Majority, 1928–1936* (Chicago: University of Chicago Press, 1979). Anderson argues that the creation of a Democratic majority was primarily due to a large pool of new voters who had no party identification.

69. James T. Patterson, *Congressional Conservatism and the New Deal* (Lexington: University of Kentucky Press, 1967), pp. 5–7.

70. For a discussion of capitalist ideology during the early depression years, see Yale R. Magrass, *Thus Spake the Moguls* (Cambridge, Mass.: Schenkman, 1981), pp. 1–45.

Chapter Four. The National Industrial Recovery Act as a State Solution to the Crisis

1. The epigraphs are from a memorandum to R. M. from A. A. Berle, Jr., 10 Nov. 1932, Berle Papers, box 15, FDR Library, Hyde Park, N.Y.; and Henry I. Harriman, president of the Chamber of Commerce of the United States, and William Green, president, American Federation of Labor, to Franklin D. Roosevelt 10 Feb. 1933, PPF 1483, FDR Library.

2. Berle-Faulkner memorandum, 19 May 1932, Raymond Moley Collection, box 1 (safe), Hoover Institute on War, Revolution, and Peace, Stanford University, Palo Alto, Calif.

3. Elliot Rosen argues that the Berle-Faulkner memorandum was "seminal in its impact on developments of the campaign and the tenor of the New Deal": see *Hoover, Roosevelt, and the Brains Trust* (New York: Columbia University Press, 1977), p. 206.

4. Memorandum for Judge Samuel I. Rosenman from Raymond Moley and Rexford G. Tugwell, 11 July 1932, Raymond Moley Collection, box 2 (safe).

5. Memorandum to Governor Franklin D. Roosevelt, 15 Aug. 1932, Berle Papers, box 15.

6. Memorandum to R. M. from A. A. Berle, Jr., 10 Nov. 1932, Berle Papers, box 15.

7. New Deal Diaries, 12 Jan. 1933, Tugwell Papers, box 15, FDR Library.

8. A. A. Berle to Raymond Moley, 12 Apr. 1933, Moley Collection, box 63.

9. Robert Lund to Louis McHenry Howe, 29 Mar. 1933, PPF 8246, FDR Library.

10. Labor Standards Memo, 6 Mar. 1933, Moley Collection, box 1 (safe).

11. See Ronald Radosh, "The Development of the Corporate Ideology of American Labor Leaders, 1914–1933" (Ph.D. diss., University of Wisconsin, 1967), passim; and Irving Bernstein, *The Lean Years* (Boston, Mass.: Houghton Mifflin, 1972), pp. 481–83.

12. William E. Leuchtenburg, *Franklin D. Roosevelt and the New Deal, 1932–1940* (New York: Harper & Row, 1963), p. 56.

13. Cited by Charles Roos in *NRA Economic Planning* (Bloomington, Ind.: Principa, 1937), p. 30.

14. Ellis W. Hawley, *The New Deal and the Problem of Monopoly* (Princeton, N.J.: Princeton University Press, 1966), p. 22.

15. See Robert F. Himmelberg, *The Origins of the National Recovery Administration* (New York: Fordham University Press, 1976), p. 196; Hawley, *New Deal and the Problem of Monopoly,* p. 22; Arthur M. Schlesinger, Jr., *The Coming of the New Deal* (Boston, Mass.: Houghton Mifflin, 1958), p. 95; Leuchtenburg, *Franklin D. Roosevelt and the New Deal,* p. 56.

16. U.S. Congress, Senate, *Thirty-Hour Work Week,* Hearings before the Subcommittee on the Judiciary, U.S. Senate, 72d Congress, 2d sess., on S. 5267, 5–19 Jan. 1933 (Washington, D.C.: Government Printing Office, 1933), pp. 1–23, cited by Leuchtenburg in *Franklin D. Roosevelt and the New Deal,* p. 56.

17. Himmelberg, *Origins of the National Recovery Administration,* p. 198.

18. Hawley, *New Deal and the Problem of Monopoly,* pp. 22–23.

19. Himmelberg, *Origins of the National Recovery Administration,* pp. 203–4.

20. See Louis Galambos, *Competition and Cooperation: The Emergence of a National Trade Association* (Baltimore, Md.: Johns Hopkins University Press, 1966), pp. 130–36; Roos, *NRA Economic Planning,* pp. 39–40; Leuchtenburg, *Franklin D. Roosevelt and the New Deal,* pp. 56–58; Himmelberg, *Origins of the National Recovery Administration,* p. 206.

21. Hawley, *New Deal and the Problem of Monopoly,* p. 25.

22. Henry I. Harriman to Franklin D. Roosevelt, 11 May 1933, POF 466, box 1, FDR Library.

23. Hawley, *New Deal and the Problem of Monopoly,* p. 25; Himmelberg, *Origins of the National Recovery Administration,* p. 206.

24. Robert Lund to Louis Howe, 29 Mar. 1933, PPF 8246, FDR Library.

25. Cited in Leuchtenburg, *Franklin D. Roosevelt and the New Deal,* p. 57.

26. Gabriel Kolko, *Main Currents in Modern American History* (New York: Harper & Row, 1976), p. 126.

27. Cited by Hawley in *New Deal and the Problem of Monopoly,* p. 26.

28. Ibid., p. 29.

29. Schlesinger, *Coming of the New Deal,* p. 99; Raymond S. Rubinow, *Section 7*

(a): Its History, Interpretation and Administration, record group 9, National Recovery Administration, National Archives, Washington, D.C.

30. James T. Patterson, *Congressional Conservatism and the New Deal* (Lexington: University of Kentucky Press, 1967), pp. 5–6.

31. Hawley, *New Deal and the Problem of Monopoly,* p. 30.

32. Ibid., p. 30.

33. Telegrams from capitalists who represented all fractions of the capitalist class were sent to the Senate Finance Committee between late May and early June, which expressed their particular position on the NIRA: see record group 46, box 52, United States Senate, 73d Cong., Senate, 73A-E5, HR 5755, records of the Senate, National Archives.

34. The position of capitalists over the proposed section 7a can be found in the telegrams and letters addressed to the Senate Finance Committee in late May and early June: see record group 46, boxes 52 and 53, United States Senate, 73A–E5, HR 5755, records of the Senate, National Archives.

35. U.S. Congress, Senate Finance Committee, Hearings before the Committee on Finance on S. 1712 and H.R. 5755, *National Industrial Recovery,* 73d Cong., 1st sess., 29 May 1933, pp. 283–301.

36. Ibid., 1 June 1933, pp. 388–89.

37. Kenneth Finegold and Theda Skocpol, "State, Party, and Industry: From Business Recovery to the Wagner Act in America's New Deal," in *Statemaking and Social Movements: Essays in History and Theory,* ed. Charles Bright and Susan Harding (Ann Arbor: University of Michigan Press, 1984), pp. 170–71.

38. Hawley, *New Deal and the Problem of Monopoly,* pp. 31–32.

39. The White House received letters showing concern regarding Communist infiltration of the unemployed and the importance of gathering more information on the matter. There is no indication, however, that Roosevelt or his aides took the Communist threat seriously. Nevertheless, it is significant that after Roosevelt signed the NIRA, he clearly stated that it was at root a reemployment bill. See OF 263, box 1, May and June 1933, FDR Library.

40. Hawley, *New Deal and the Problem of Monopoly,* pp. 50–51.

41. Leverett Lyon et al., *The National Recovery Administration* (Washington, D.C.: Brookings Institution, 1935), pp. 119–29.

42. Hawley, *New Deal and the Problem of Monopoly,* passim.

43. Kolko, *Main Currents,* p. 129.

44. See G. D. H. Cole, *Economic Planning* (London: Kennikat, 1971), p. 137; and Gerald D. Nash, "Industry and the Federal Government, 1850–1933," *Current History* 48, 286 (June 1965).

45. Hawley, *New Deal and the Problem of Monopoly,* p. 480.

46. Lewis Corey, *The Decline of American Capitalism* (New York: Covici, Friede, 1934), p. 100.

47. Lyon et al., *National Recovery Administration,* p. 546.

48. Corey, *Decline of American Capitalism,* pp. 100–103.

49. Hawley, *New Deal and the Problem of Monopoly,* pp. 58–59.

50. See Rubinow, *Section 7 (a),* pp. 67–78.

51. Hugh S. Johnson to Louis Howe, 17 Nov. 1933, Howe Papers, box 86, FDR Library.

52. Leuchtenburg, *Franklin D. Roosevelt and the New Deal,* p. 67.

53. See William H. Wilson, "How the Chamber of Commerce Viewed the NRA: A Re-examination," *Mid-America* 44, 2 (Apr. 1962): 95–108.

54. Memorandum for Gen. Hugh S. Johnson, 25 July 1933, OF 466, box 1, FDR Library.

55. See Schlesinger, *Coming of the New Deal,* pp. 136–51.

56. Himmelberg, *Origins of the NRA,* p. 212.

57. Hawley, *New Deal and the Problem of Monopoly,* pp. 135–36.

58. Paul K. Conkin, *The New Deal* (New York: Thomas Y. Crowell, 1967), pp. 36–37.

59. National Association of Manufacturers, "A Proposed Platform for Recovery 1934," record group 9, National Recovery Administration, National Industrial Recovery Board, general file, A. D. Whiteside, National Archives; and idem, "Unemployment Insurance Handbook," 1933 (pamphlet).

60. Chamber of Commerce of the United States of America, "Referendum No. 68: On the Report of the Special Committee on National Industrial Recovery Act, November 9, 1934," record group 9, National Recovery Administration, National Industrial Recovery Board, general file, A. D. Whiteside, National Archives.

61. Address of Robert L. Lund, president of the National Association of Manufacturers, before the Ohio State Chamber of Commerce, 24 Nov. 1933, PPF 8226, FDR Library.

62. Henry I. Harriman to Franklin Roosevelt, 24 Sept. 1934, OF 105, box 1, FDR Library.

63. "From the Report of Earl Browder," 7 July 1933, and Report of Earl Browder, 2 Apr. 1934, reprinted in "NRA from Within," International Pamphlets, no. 41, 1934.

64. Open letter from the American Workers Party-Provisional Organizing Committee, late 1933, organizational files, American Workers Party, Tamiment Institute, New York, N.Y.

65. In early 1934, the White House received petitions demanding a planned system of production and distribution, arguing that it would serve to prevent both waste and want: see OF 185, FDR Library.

66. See, e.g., National Planning Board, *Final Report, 1933–1934* (Washington, D.C.: Government Printing Office, 1934) and various addresses and memoranda, record group 187, Reports, Planning Board, Records of the National Resources Planning Board, National Archives.

67. Confidential Report to Hugh Johnson, of the National Recovery Administration, from A. A. Berle, July 1934, reprinted in Beatrice Bishop Berle and Travis Beal Jacobs, eds., *Navigating the Rapids, 1918–1971: From the Papers of Adolph A. Berle* (New York: Harcourt Brace Jovanovich, 1973), pp. 96–101.

68. Special and Supplementary Report to the president from Clarence Darrow and W. O. Thompson, 3 May 1934, POF 466F, box 47, FDR Library.

69. See Henry C. Luckey (congressman from Nebraska) to FDR, 15 Feb. 1935, PPF 777, FDR Library.

70. Hawley, *New Deal and the Problem of Monopoly,* pp. 111–27.

71. Ibid., pp. 127–29.

72. Robert Lund to Louis Howe, 29 Mar. 1933, PPF 8246, FDR Library.

73. See Frances Perkins to Howe, 29 Mar. 1933, Howe Papers, box 82, FDR Library.

74. See Howard J. Sherman, *Profits in the United States: An Introduction to a Study of Economic Concentration and Business Cycles* (Ithaca, N.Y.: Cornell University Press, 1968), p. 232.

75. Theda Skocpol and Kenneth Finegold, "State Capacity and Economic Intervention in the Early New Deal," *Political Science Quarterly* 97, 2 (Summer 1982): 259.

Chapter Five. The Monopoly Debate and Intracapitalist Conflict

1. The epigraphs are from To the president from Clarence S. Darrow, chairman, and W. O. Thompson, member of the board, "Special and Supplementary Report of the Report of the Review Board," National Recovery Act, 3 May 1934, POF 466E, box 47, FDR Library, Hyde Park, N.Y.; and W. O. Thompson to Honorable Franklin D. Roosevelt, 13 June 1934, POF 466E, FDR Library.

2. Nicos Poulantzas, "The Political Crisis and the Crisis of the State," in *Critical Sociology: European Perspective,* ed. J. W. Freiberg (New York: Irvington, 1970), pp. 376–77.

3. See Nicos Poulantzas, *Classes in Contemporary Capitalism* (London: New Left Books, 1975), pp. 144–45.

4. U.S. Congress, Temporary National Economic Committee, *Investigation of Concentration of Economic Power: Hearings,* pt. 1: *Economic Prologue* (Washington, D.C.: Government Printing Office, 1939), p. 195.

5. See ibid., Message from the President of the United States Transmitting Recommendations Relative to the Strengthening and Enforcement of Anti-Trust Laws, p. 188.

6. Broadus Mitchell, *Depression Decade: From New Era through New Deal, 1929–1941* (New York: Holt, Rinehart & Winston, 1962), pp. 257–58.

7. Henry C. Luckey to FDR, 15 Feb. 1935, PPF 777, FDR Library.

8. John F. Sinclair to FDR, National Recovery Review Board, 14 Apr. 1934, POF 466E, box 47, FDR Library.

9. Ellis W. Hawley, *The New Deal and the Problem of Monopoly* (Princeton, N.J.: Princeton University Press, 1966), pp. 95–96.

10. To the president from Clarence S. Darrow and W. O. Thompson, Review Board, National Recovery Act, 3 May 1934, POF 466E, box 47, FDR Library.

11. Ibid.

12. "Third Report to the President of the United States," National Recovery Review Board, 28 June 1934, POF 466E, box 48, FDR Library.

13. "Second Report to the President," National Recovery Review Board, 14 June 1934, Leon Henderson Papers, box 4, FDR Library.

14. Hawley, *New Deal and the Problem of Monopoly,* pp. 93–97.

15. W. O. Thompson to Honorable Franklin D. Roosevelt, 13 June 1934, POF 466E, box 47, FDR Library.

16. See Mitchell, *Depression Decade,* p. 257.

17. Hawley, *New Deal and the Problem of Monopoly,* pp. 104–7.

18. Ibid., pp. 109–10.

19. Mitchell, *Depression Decade,* pp. 257–68.

20. Hawley, *New Deal and the Problem of Monopoly,* pp. 406–7.

21. Ibid., p. 410.

22. Cited by Hawley in *New Deal and the Problem of Monopoly,* p. 411.

23. Robert Sobel, *The Age of Giant Corporations: A Microeconomic History of American Business, 1914–1970* (Westport, Conn.: Greenwood, 1972), p. 115.

24. Hawley, *New Deal and the Problem of Monopoly,* p. 413.

25. Sobel, *Age of Giant Corporations,* p. 115.

26. Hawley, *New Deal and the Problem of Monopoly,* pp. 416–18.

27. See "Memorandum of Suggestions: Investigation of Business Organization and Practices," A. A. Berle, Jr., 12 July 1938, Rosenman Papers, box 11, FDR Library.

28. For an enlightened discussion on the nature of competition between units of

capital see Michel Aglietta, *A Theory of Capitalist Regulation: The U.S. Experience* (London: New Left Books, 1979), pp. 273–327.

29. Sobel, *Age of Giant Corporations,* pp. 119–20.

30. Ibid., p. 117.

31. Hawley, *New Deal and the Problem of Monopoly,* p. 419.

32. John M. Blair, *Economic Concentration* (New York: Harcourt Brace Jovanovich, 1972), p. 67.

33. See Temporary National Economic Committee, *Investigation of Concentration of Economic Power,* monograph 17: *Problems of Small Business* (Washington, D.C.: Government Printing Office, 1941).

34. U.S. Congress, Temporary National Economic Committee, *Investigation of Concentration of Economic Power, Hearings,* pt. 1: *Economic Prologue* (Washington, D.C.: Government Printing Office, 1939) pp. 136–37.

35. U.S. Congress, Temporary National Economic Committee, *Investigation of Concentration of Economic Power,* pt. 31-A: *Supplemental Data Submitted to the Temporary National Economic Committee* (Washington, D.C.: Government Printing Office, 1949), pp. 18213–440.

36. Sidney Fine, *Sit-down: The General Motors Strike of 1936–1937* (Ann Arbor: University of Michigan Press, 1969), p. 21.

37. Sobel, *Age of Giant Corporations,* pp. 133–34.

38. U.S. Congress, Temporary National Economic Committee, *Investigation of Concentration of Economic Power,* pt. 31-A, p. 18257.

39. Ibid., p. 18423; and U.S. Congress, Temporary National Economic Committee, *Investigation of Concentration of Economic Power,* pt. 31: *A Study Submitted by the Federal Trade Commission* (Washington, D.C.: Government Printing Office, 1941), pp. 17745–60.

40. Harry Laidler, *Concentration in American Industry* (New York: Thomas Y. Crowell, 1931), pp. 348–49.

41. U.S. Congress, Temporary National Economic Committee, *Investigation of Concentration of Economic Power,* pt. 31-A, pp. 18286–423.

42. Sobel, *Age of Giant Corporations,* p. 152.

43. See David Lynch, *The Concentration of Economic Power* (New York: Columbia University Press, 1946), pp. 360–69.

44. Temporary National Economic Committee, *Investigation of Concentration of Economic Power: Final Report of the Executive Secretary* (Washington, D.C.: Government Printing Office, 1941), p. 26.

45. The classic study on the nature of competition and changes in the accumulation process is Arthur Robert Burns, *The Decline of Competition* (New York: McGraw-Hill, 1936). This book was quite influential among academic economists during the 1930s.

46. Ibid., p. 565.

47. Nicos Poulantzas, *State, Power, Socialism* (London: New Left Books, 1978), p. 133.

48. Temporary National Economic Committee, *Investigation of Concentration of Economic Power,* monograph 17: *Problems of Small Business* (Washington, D.C.: Government Printing Office, 1941), p. 139.

Chapter Six. Industrial Labor and the Struggle for Union Recognition

1. The epigraphs are from Sparrows Point Steel Worker to Gen. Hugh Johnson, 22 Oct. 1933, Records of the Labor Advisory Board, files of Wolman, National Recovery Administration, record group 9, National Archives, Washington, D.C.; memorandum for Mr. McIntyre from Keith Merrill regarding Minneapolis Truckers Strike, 24 May 1934, POF 407B, box 19, FDR Library, Hyde Park, N.Y.; and excerpts from a letter from Joseph M. Roush, salesman for Federal Laboratories, to his superior, referring to labor demonstration in San Francisco, 5 July 1934, cited in U.S. Congress, Senate, *Violations of Free Speech and Rights of Labor,* Hearings before the Committee on Education and Labor pt. 7, p. 2504.

2. By late 1933 it was quite clear to state administrators that Communists were becoming an increasingly critical force within working-class struggles. See, e.g., Eleanor Hickok to Harry Hopkins, 6 Aug. 1933, reprinted by Richard Lowitt and Maurine Beasley in *One Third of a Nation* (Urbana: University of Illinois Press, 1981), pp. 3–14.

3. Mike Davis, "The Barren Marriage of American Labour and the Democratic Party," *New Left Review* 124 (Nov.–Dec. 1980): 43. This article is by far the best analysis of the internal dynamics of the labor movement during the 1930s and World War II. Labor militancy, for Davis, is analyzed in relation to both the actual and the potential development of political consciousness within the industrial working class.

4. For an excellent theoretical account of the incorporation of trade unions into the national political-bargaining process, see Leo Panitch, "Trade Unions and the Capitalist State," *New Left Review* 125 (Jan.–Feb. 1981): 21–43. Panitch is basically concerned with theoretically analyzing the post–World War II aspects of the "political structure within advanced capitalism which integrates organized socio-economic producer groups through a system of representation and cooperative mutual interaction at the leadership level and mobilization and social control at the mass level" (p. 24).

5. Broadus Mitchell, *Depression Decade: From New Era through New Deal, 1929–1941* (New York: Holt, Rinehart & Winston, 1962), p. 271.

6. Ronald Radosh, "The Development of the Corporate Ideology of American Labor Leaders, 1914–1933" (Ph.D. diss., University of Wisconsin, 1967), p. 298.

7. Mitchell, *Depression Decade,* p. 272.

8. Cited by Lewis Corey in *The Decline of American Capitalism* (New York: Covici, Friede, 1934), p. 100.

9. Cited by Art Preis in *Labor's Giant Step* (New York: Pathfinder, 1972), p. 16.

10. U.S. Congress, Senate, *Violations of Free Speech and Rights of Labor,* Report of the Committee on Education and Labor, pt. 3: *The National Association of Manufacturers* (14 Aug. 1939), pp. 89–97.

11. Memorandum from Labor Advisory Board of Division VI to Members of the Staff, 23 July 1934, National Recovery Administration, Division of Review, office files of Leon C. Marshall, labor file, record group 9, National Archives.

12. For examples of letters and statements from workers and trade unionists expressing their discontent with the enforcement of section 7a and the benefits of the NIRA in general see National Recovery Administration, Labor Advisory Board, general file, record group 9, and National Labor Relations Board, National Labor Board, official correspondence, record group 25, National Archives; and POF 407 labor, 1933–35, box 1, FDR Library.

13. Public Hearing, group 1 on employment, abstract of speeches, vol. 1, 27 Feb. 1934, National Recovery Administration, records of Research and Planning Division,

miscellaneous office files of persons employed by the division, record group 9, National Archives.

14. The Blue Eagle was the symbol of compliance with the National Industrial Recovery Act. A flag bearing the symbol of the Blue Eagle was usually flown outside of enterprises that supported the efforts of the National Recovery Administration.

15. Bert Cochran, *Labor and Communism: The Conflict That Shaped American Unions* (Princeton, N.J.: Princeton University Press, 1977), p. 84.

16. Preis, *Labor's Giant Step,* p. 16.

17. See POF 407B, strikes-general 1933–1936, box 10, FDR Library, for more details with regard to the effect the strikes had on business activity. Many letters addressed to FDR from various businessmen indicated that Socialist and other radical elements were involved in the strikes and that unless something was done soon, the political career of FDR would be in jeopardy.

18. U.S. Bureau of the Census, *Historical Statistics of the United States, Colonial Times to 1970,* Bicentennial Edition, pt. 1 (Washington, D.C.: Government Printing Office, 1975), p. 179.

19. The relationship between the Communist party and the labor movement during the 1930s is an issue that is still debated among historians. Recent accounts of the relationship between the Communist party and the labor movement of the 1930s focus either on the relative positive impact of militant Communists on the labor movement or on mistakes that Communists made in trade-union work. Most, if not all, of the recent accounts focus on the degree to which Communists played a significant role in working-class history of the 1930s, as opposed to the standard works, which stress the undemocratic nature of the Communist party and how Communists were merely following directives from Moscow. For different views of the relationship between the Communist party and the labor movement, see, e.g., James R. Prickett, "Anti-Communism and Labor History," *Industrial Relations* 13, 3 (Oct. 1974): 219–27; idem, "Some Aspects of the Communist Controversy in the CIO," *Science and Society* 33, 3 (Summer–Fall 1969): 299–321; idem, "New Perspectives on American Communism and the Labor Movement," in *Political Power and Social Theory,* vol. 4, ed. Maurice Zeitlin and Howard Kimeldorf (Greenwich, Conn.: JAI, 1984), pp. 3–36; Walter Galenson, "Communists and Trade Union Democracy," *Industrial Relations* 13, 3 (Oct. 1974): 228–36; Nelson Lichtenstein, "The Communist Experience in American Trade Unions," *Industrial Relations* 19, 2 (Spring 1980): 119–30; Robert H. Zeiger, "Reply to Professor Lichtenstein," *Industrial Relations* 19, 2 (Spring 1980): 131–35; Roger R. Keeran, "Reply to Professor Lichtenstein," *Industrial Relations* 19, 2 (Spring 1980): 136–39; Martin Glaberman, "Vanguard to Rearguard," in *Political Power and Social Theory,* vol. 4, pp. 37–61; David Brody, "Radicalism and the American Labor Movement: From Party History to Social History," in *Political Power and Social Theory,* vol. 4, pp. 255–61; Harvey Klehr, "American Communism and the United Auto Workers: New Evidence on an Old Controversy," *Labor History* 24, 3 (Summer 1983): 404–13; idem, *The Heyday of American Communism: The Depression Decade* (New York: Basic, 1984); Harvey A. Levenstein, *Communism, Anticommunism, and the CIO* (Westport, Conn.: Greenwood, 1981).

20. See *Party Organizer,* 1933, for a more detailed account of the organizational tactics of the Communist party. The *Party Organizer* was an interparty journal, published between 1927 and 1937.

21. Paul Buhle, "Marxism in the United States, 1900–1940" (Ph.D. diss., University of Wisconsin, 1975), p. 211.

22. See Chart on the Party in the Factories, Browder Papers, ser. 2, box 3, George Arents Research Library, Syracuse University, Syracuse, N.Y.

23. Cochran, *Labor and Communism,* p. 75. There is considerable debate as to what the reasons were behind the change in policy. Cochran, e.g., argues that the change in policy was a direct order from Moscow and was the result of the United Front Period of the International Communist Movement. Keeran points out, however, that the dissolution of independent unions and the sending of party members into the American Federation of Labor foreshadowed the Comintern's adoption of the Popular Front in 1935. See Roger R. Keeran, *The Communist Party and the Auto Workers Union* (Bloomington: Indiana University Press, 1980), p. 4. I would argue that Cochran's view only partially explains the change in policy. The historically specific conditions of the American labor movement during the 1933–35 period would appear to be a more plausible explanation.

24. For an interesting discussion on the influence of Communists in CIO unions see Keeran, *Communist Party and the Auto Workers Union,* pp. 13–20; Cochran, *Labor and Communism,* passim.

25. For more detail on the extent of anti-Communist propaganda see POF 263, box 1, FDR Library; files on Communists in trade unions, AFL-CIO Library, Washington, D.C., general records of the Labor Department, chief clerk's file, record group 174, and records of Labor Advisory Board, files of Wolman, National Recovery Administration, record group 9, National Archives.

26. See chart on party growth—fluctuations, Browder Papers, ser. 2, box 3.

27. Robert J. Alperin, "Organization in the Communist Party, U.S.A., 1931–1938" (Ph.D. diss., Northwestern University, 1959), pp. 49–50.

28. James Robert Prickett, "Communists and the Communist Issue in the American Labor Movement, 1920–1950" (Ph.D. diss., University of California at Los Angeles, 1975), p. 35.

29. Alperin, "Organization in the Communist Party," p. 197.

30. Prickett, "Communists and the Communist Issue," pp. 37–42.

31. Alperin, "Organization in the Communist Party," pp. 54, 154, 159, 196.

32. Lichtenstein, "Communist Experience in American Trade Unions," p. 121.

33. See Robert Justin Goldstein, *Political Repression in Modern America, 1870 to the Present* (Cambridge, Mass.: Schenkman, 1978), pp. 209–44.

34. Irving Bernstein, *Turbulent Years* (Boston, Mass.: Houghton Mifflin, 1969), pp. 219–21.

35. Secret Service Report from Operative Haubner to Wm. G. Harper, operative in charge, 26 May 1934, POF 407B, box 27, FDR Library.

36. Sidney Lens, *The Labor Wars* (Garden City, N.Y.: Doubleday, 1973), p. 39.

37. Secret Service Report, 26 May 1934.

38. Prickett, "Communists and the Communist Issue," pp. 142–43.

39. Ibid., pp. 143–44.

40. Secret Service Report, 26 May 1934.

41. Bernstein, *Turbulent Years,* pp. 222–23.

42. Secret Service Report, 26 May 1934; Bernstein, *Turbulent Years,* pp. 223–24.

43. Preis, *Labor's Giant Step,* pp. 23–24.

44. *Party Organizer* 7, 1 (July 1934): 8–15.

45. Keeran argues that the American Workers party had greater influence on the walkout than did the Communist party. However, the Communist party did aid in generating strike support and major defiance of the court injunction. According to Keeran, Communist-party members helped organize picketing, and party women established a soup kitchen. The Communist party also held seven shop-gate meetings and approximately twelve strike-support rallies and issued sixteen different strike leaflets. Communist-

party and American-Workers'-party support for the defiance of the court order aided the walkout and saved the walkout from certain defeat. See Keeran, *Communist Party and the Auto Workers Union,* pp. 111–14.

46. Bernstein, *Turbulent Years,* p. 231.

47. Arthur M. Schlesinger, Jr., *The Coming of the New Deal* (Boston, Mass.: Houghton Mifflin, 1958), p. 386.

48. Lens, *Labor Wars,* p. 312.

49. Ibid., p. 312; Bernstein, *Turbulent Years,* p. 234.

50. Lens, *Labor Wars,* pp. 311–13; Bernstein, *Turbulent Years,* p. 236.

51. Lens, *Labor Wars,* p. 314.

52. Ibid., p. 315.

53. Bernstein, *Turbulent Years,* p. 239.

54. Schlesinger, *Coming of the New Deal,* pp. 288–89.

55. See, e.g., memorandum for Mr. McIntyre, 24 May 1934, POF 407B, box 19, FDR Library, for a sense of the anti-Communist propaganda being directed against the strike and being sent to the executive office. The informant in Minneapolis placed most of the "blame" for the violence and for the strike itself on "Communists."

56. *Party Organizer* 7, 1 (July 1934): 15–19; see also Farrell Dobbs, *Teamster Rebellion* (New York: Monad, 1972), passim.

57. See 1933—Early ILA Organization File, International Longshoremen's and Warehousemen's Union (ILWU) Archives, San Francisco, Calif.

58. Bernstein, *Turbulent Years,* p. 260.

59. See 1933—Albion Hall and Committee of 500—Basic Demands, July and November Conference, ILWU Archives.

60. Bernstein, *Turbulent Years,* pp. 261–63; report to FDR from Frances Perkins, 17 July 1934, POF 407B, box 25, FDR Library; and 9 May 1934 Strike Committee Minutes, 1934—Strike—Committee Minutes file, ILWU Archives.

61. Report to FDR from Frances Perkins, 17 July 1923.

62. Bernstein, *Turbulent Years,* pp. 269–72; Lens, *Labor Wars,* pp. 294–95.

63. Telegram to Mrs. Florence P. Kahn (House of Representatives), referred to Frances Perkins, secretary of labor, from R. P. Holliday (Hearst newspapers), 21 July 1934, Department of Labor, Office of the Secretary, Secretary Perkins, general subject file, 1933–40, Conciliation—Strikes, box 31, record group 174, National Archives.

64. Letter to Mr. Kerwin from William Green, 22 June 1934, ibid.

65. See POF 407B Strikes, Pacific Longshoremen's Strike, 1934, box 25, FDR Library.

66. The reasons to suspect that Bridges had close ties to, if he was not a member of, the Communist party are strengthened by the fact that in the Browder Papers, there are many correspondences regarding the eventual deportation hearings of Bridges as well as the complete text of his court case: see Browder Papers, ser. 2, box 2.

67. See 1934 Coast Strike—Personal Interviews, ILWU Archives, San Francisco, for personal accounts of the attacks of police on striking longshoremen.

68. Bernstein, *Turbulent Years,* p. 272.

69. Lens, *Labor Wars,* p. 297.

70. Ibid., pp. 298–99.

71. Roger Lapham to Frances Perkins, 15 and 14 July, Department of Labor, Office of the Secretary, Secretary Perkins, general subject file 1933–40, Conciliation—Strikes, box 32, record group 174, National Archives.

72. Cited by Lens in *Labor Wars,* pp. 300–301.

73. See 1934 Coast Strike—Personal Interviews, ILWU Archives.

74. Lens, *Labor Wars,* p. 303.

75. Statement of Lillian Symes, 1934 Coast Strike—Personal Interviews, ILWU Archives.

76. Report of the Board of Inquiry for the Cotton Textile Industry to the President, 20 Sept. 1934, POF 407B Cotton Textile Strike, box 19, FDR Library.

77. Ibid.

78. "Mechanization and Speed-Up: Their Effects on Employment," by Frances J. Gorman, international first vice-president, United Textile Workers of America, delivered at the Public Hearings on Employment Policy, conducted by the National Industrial Recovery Board in Washington, 30 Jan. 1935, National Recovery Board, Labor Advisory Board, personal files of Henry H. Collins, Jr., record group 9, National Archives.

79. Bernstein, *Turbulent Years,* pp. 300–303.

80. Charles D. Gray to Robert R. Reynolds, 7 Sept. 1934, Department of Labor, Office of the Secretary, Secretary Perkins, general subject file 1933–40, box 33, record group 174, National Archives.

81. Report of the Board of Inquiry for the Cotton-Textile Industry to the President, 20 Sept. 1934.

82. Bernstein, *Turbulent Years,* p. 309.

83. Lens, *Labor Wars,* pp. 304–6.

84. Bernstein, *Turbulent Years,* pp. 309–12.

85. Memorandum for the Attorney General from John Edgar Hoover, 15 Sept. 1934, POF 407B Cotton Textile Strike, box 19, FDR Library.

86. See General Records of the Department of Labor, chief clerk's files, record group 174, National Archives; Department of Labor, Office of the Secretary, Secretary Perkins, general subject file 1933–40, box 33, National Archives; and POF 407B Strikes, box 19, FDR Library.

87. Bernstein, *Turbulent Years,* pp. 311–15.

88. For a detailed account of the changes in ideological orientations of the AFL see Ruth L. Horowitz, *Political Ideologies of Organized Labor: The New Deal Era* (New Brunswick, N.J.: Transaction Books, 1978).

89. Lens, *Labor Wars,* pp. 323–24.

90. Len DeCaux, *Labor Radical* (Boston, Mass.: Beacon, 1970), p. 305.

91. For an illuminating analysis of the AFL and its position toward various state labor policies see Christopher L. Tomlins, *The State and the Unions: Labor Relations, Law, and the Organized Labor Movement in America, 1880–1960* (New York: Cambridge University Press, 1985), pp. 99–196.

92. Schlesinger, *Coming of the New Deal,* p. 395.

93. J. David Greenstone, *Labor in American Politics* (New York: Vintage, 1969), p. 41.

94. Memo for Secretary Morrison from Julius Pierce, 8 Mar. 1934, file on Communists in Trade Unions, AFL-CIO Library, Washington, D.C.

95. Confidential Report on Communists and Communist Activities within the Trade Union Movement, submitted to President Green, 11 Feb. 1935, file on Communists in Trade Unions, AFL-CIO Library.

96. Statement by Farrell Schnering to William Green, n.d., file on Communists in Trade Unions, AFL-CIO Library.

97. Report submitted to Franklin D. Roosevelt by Donald Richberg, chairman, National Industrial Recovery Board, 12, 13, 14, 20, 21, and 25 June 1935, POF 466 NRA container 26, FDR Library.

98. Mitchell, *Depression Decade,* pp. 283–86.

99. See Irving Bernstein, *The New Deal Collective Bargaining Policy* (New York:

Da Capo, 1975), pp. 84–128; and Harry A. Millis and Emily Clark Brown, *From the Wagner Act to Taft-Hartley* (Chicago: University of Chicago Press, 1950), pp. 3–29.

100. Bernstein, *New Deal Collective Bargaining Policy,* pp. 100–111.

101. Ibid., pp. 116–17.

102. William E. Leuchtenburg, *Franklin D. Roosevelt and the New Deal, 1932–1940* (New York: Harper & Row, 1963), p. 151.

103. See Rick Hurd, "New Deal Labor Policy and the Containment of Radical Union Activity," *Review of Radical Political Economics* 8, 3 (Fall 1976): 35–38.

104. Benjamin Stolberg, *The Story of the CIO* (New York: Viking, 1938), p. 18.

Chapter Seven. Industrial Unionization and the Political Scene

1. The epigraphs are from Communist Party leaflet, General Records of the Department of Labor, Office of the Secretary, record group 174, box 32, National Archives, Washington, D.C.; and memorandum to the Secretary from J. R. Steelman, 30 July 1937, ibid.

2. For an interesting account of the debates within the trade-union movement in 1936, see Arthur E. Suffern, "Craft vs. Industrial Union," *Current History* 44, 2 (May 1936): 97–104; and Walter Galenson, *The CIO Challenge to the AFL* (Cambridge, Mass.: Harvard University Press, 1960), passim.

3. Suffern, "Craft vs. Industrial Union," pp. 99–100.

4. These industrial unions included the coal miners' union, the typographical union, the amalgamated clothing workers' union, the textile workers' union, the oil-field, gas-well and refinery workers' union, the cap and millinery workers' union, and the mine, mill, and smelter workers' union.

5. Galenson, *CIO Challenge to the AFL,* pp. 3–74.

6. J. David Greenstone, *Labor in American Politics* (New York: Vintage, 1969), p. 45.

7. Bert Cochran, *Labor and Communism: The Conflict That Shaped American Unions* (Princeton, N.J.: Princeton University Press, 1977), pp. 95–96.

8. For a discussion of AFL resurgence in 1937/38 see Mike Davis, "The Barren Marriage of American Labour and the Democratic Party," *New Left Review* 124 (Nov.–Dec. 1980): 58–60.

9. Sidney Lens, *The Labor Wars* (Garden City, N.Y.: Doubleday, 1973), pp. 381–82.

10. Mike Davis, "Barren Marriage," p. 61.

11. A more detailed analysis of the relationship between organized labor and the Democratic party is discussed below.

12. U.S. Bureau of the Census, *Historical Statistics of the United States, Colonial Times to 1970,* Bicentennial Edition, pt. 1 (Washington, D.C.: Government Printing Office, 1975), p. 179.

13. Art Preis, *Labor's Giant Step* (New York: Pathfinder, 1972), p. 71.

14. See Beth A. Rubin, Larry J. Griffin, and Michael Wallace, "'Provided Only That Their Voice Was Strong': Insurgency and Organization of American Labor from NRA to Taft-Hartley," *Work and Occupations* 10, 3 (Aug. 1983): 325–47.

15. Irving Bernstein, *Turbulent Years* (Boston, Mass.: Houghton Mifflin, 1969), p. 500.

16. Lens, *Labor Wars,* p. 332.

17. Ibid., pp. 332–33.

18. See P. W. Chappell to H. L. Kerwin, 6 Nov. 1935, Department of Labor, Office of the Secretary, Secretary Perkins, record group 174, box 32.

19. Lens, *Labor Wars,* p. 335.

20. Telegram to Perkins from managing editor of *Akron* (Ohio) *Beacon Journal,* 16 Mar. 1936, Department of Labor, Office of the Secretary, Secretary Perkins, record group 174, box 32.

21. Lens, *Labor Wars,* p. 336; and Galenson, *CIO Challenge to the AFL,* pp. 266–69.

22. Cochran, *Labor and Communism,* pp. 105–7.

23. Frances Fox Piven and Richard A. Cloward, *Poor People's Movements: How They Succeed, How They Fail* (New York: Pantheon, 1977), p. 316.

24. See Sidney Fine, *Sit-down: The General Motors Strike of 1936–1937* (Ann Arbor: University of Michigan Press, 1970), pp. 199–230.

25. For accounts of the sit-down strikes see ibid. and Roger R. Keeran, *The Communist Party and the Auto Workers Union* (Bloomington: Indiana University Press, 1980), pp. 148–85.

26. James Robert Prickett, "Communists and the Communist Issue in the American Labor Movement, 1920–1950" (Ph.D. diss., University of California at Los Angeles, 1975), pp. 188–89.

27. During the period of the sit-down strikes, Roosevelt received many letters and telegrams from businessmen who stated that they were horrified by the sit-down strikes in the auto industry and could not understand why Roosevelt would even recognize the CIO as a legitimate union organization since, they argued, to defend the sit-down was to defy private property. See POF 407B Strikes, box 18, FDR Library, Hyde Park, N.Y.

28. Prickett, "Communists and the Communist Issue," pp. 299–301.

29. Keeran, *Communist Party and the Auto Workers Union,* pp. 183–85; and Fine, *Sit-down,* pp. 310–11.

30. Piven and Cloward, *Poor People's Movements,* pp. 140–41.

31. Memorandum of a conversation with Arthur H. Young, 3 Apr. 1934, National Recovery Administration, Division of Review, office files of Leon C. Marshall, labor file, record group 9, National Archives.

32. See J. F. Dewey to H. L. Kerwin, 13 May 1937, Department of Labor, Office of the Secretary, Secretary Perkins, record group 174, box 32, National Archives.

33. For a detailed account of the strike in the Republic plant in Chicago see Pierce Williams to Harry L. Hopkins, 26 June 1937, POF 407B Steel Strike, box 27, FDR Library.

34. Mike Davis, "Barren Marriage," p. 54; and James R. Green, *The World of the Worker* (New York: Hill & Wang, 1980), pp. 164–65. After the Memorial Day Massacre, Roosevelt did not criticize the actions of the Chicago Police Department and distanced himself from the plight of industrial workers.

35. Jerold S. Auerbach, *Labor and Liberty: The La Follette Committee and the New Deal* (New York: Bobbs-Merrill, 1966), p. 152.

36. U.S. Congress, Senate, *Violations of Free Speech and Rights of Labor,* Report of the Committee on Education and Labor, *Report on Industrial Espionage* (Washington, D.C.: Government Printing Office, 1937), p. 23.

37. U.S. Congress, Senate, Committee on Education and Labor, Hearings before a subcommittee on the *Violations of Free Speech and Rights of Labor,* 11 Feb. 1937, p. 1619.

38. Ibid., *Industrial Munitions,* p. 156.

39. Ibid., *Strikebreaking Services,* Jan. 1939, pp. 94–98.

40. Ibid., *Republic Steel Corporation,* p. 150.

41. Ibid., *Report on Industrial Espionage,* 1937, pp. 17–26.

42. Ibid., Preliminary Report of the Committee on Education and Labor, 8 Feb. 1937, p. 12.

43. Ibid., *Industrial Munitions,* pp. 41–66.

44. Ibid., *Strikebreaking Services,* Jan. 1939, pp. 106–7.

45. Ibid., *Republic Steel Corporation,* pp. 177–89.

46. Ibid., *The National Association of Manufacturers,* pp. 218–19.

47. See Claus Offe, *Disorganized Capitalism* (Cambridge, Mass.: MIT, 1985), pp. 184–99.

48. The Social Security Act of 1935 providing for unemployment compensation, old-age insurance, and retirement benefits; and the Fair Labor Standards Act of 1938, which provided for minimum wages and maximum hours, reflected the strategy of a uniform policy for industrial wage labor located throughout the United States. See Piven and Cloward, *Poor People's Movements,* pp. 146–47. For a detailed examination of the history of the Social Security Act see Edwin E. White, *The Development of the Social Security Act* (Madison: University of Wisconsin Press, 1969), pp. 192–240.

49. See, e.g., Kenneth Finegold and Theda Skocpol, "State, Party, and Industry: From Business Recovery to the Wagner Act in America's New Deal," in *Statemaking and Social Movements: Essays in History and Theory,* ed. Charles Bright and Susan Harding (Ann Arbor: University of Michigan Press, 1984), p. 161.

50. See Kristi Anderson, *The Creation of a Democratic Majority, 1928–1936* (Chicago: University of Chicago Press, 1979), passim.

51. Otis L. Graham, Jr., "The Democratic Party, 1932–1945," in *History of U.S. Political Parties,* vol. 3: *1910–1945,* ed. Arthur M. Schlesinger, Jr. (New York: Chelsea House, 1973), p. 145.

52. See Robert R. Alford, "The Role of Social Class in American Voting Behavior," in *Political Parties and Political Behavior,* ed. William J. Crotty, Donald M. Freeman, and Douglas C. Gatlin (Boston: Allyn & Bacon, 1966).

53. Arthur M. Schlesinger, Jr., "Labor's New Role: The 1936 Election," in *Labor and American Politics,* ed. Charles M. Rehmus, Doris B. McLaughlin, and Frederick H. Nesbitt (Ann Arbor: University of Michigan Press, 1978), pp. 159–61.

54. Carl N. Degler, *Out of Our Past* (New York: Harper & Row, 1959), pp. 395–99; John B. Kirby, *Black Americans in the Roosevelt Era* (Knoxville: University of Tennessee Press, 1980), passim.

55. Harvard Sitkoff, *A New Deal for Blacks* (New York: Oxford University Press, 1978), pp. 58–101; David A. Shannon, *Between the Wars: America, 1919–1941* (Boston, Mass.: Houghton Mifflin, 1965), p. 174.

56. Shannon, *Between the Wars,* p. 174.

57. Mike Davis, *Prisoners of the American Dream* (London: Verso, 1986), p. 96.

58. See Everett Carll, Jr., and Charles D. Hadley, *Transformations of the American Party System* (New York: W. W. Norton, 1978), pp. 59–65.

59. See Rianne Mahon, "Canadian Public Policy: The Unequal Structure at Representation," in *The Canadian State: Political Economy and Political Power,* ed. Leo Panitch (Toronto: University of Toronto Press, 1977), pp. 166–74.

60. Walter Galenson, "Labor and New Deal Politics, 1936–1940," in *Labor and American Politics,* pp. 161–65.

61. Greenstone, *Labor in American Politics,* pp. 49–50.

62. Davis, *Prisoners of the American Dream,* pp. 69–70.

63. Cochran, *Labor and Communism,* p. 237.

64. For an excellent discussion of the relationship between organized labor and the Democratic party during and after World War I see Davis, *Prisoners of the American Dream,* pp. 69–84.

65. Leslie Benson, *Proletarians and Parties* (New York: Methuen, 1978), pp. 182–83; Kenneth Waltzer, "The Party and the Polling Place: American Communism and an American Labor Party in the 1930s," *Radical History Review* 23 (Spring 1980): 104–29.

66. "Economic class struggle" refers to the contradiction between capitalist class practices that aim at generating surplus value and the realization of profits and working-class practices that aim at an increase in real wages. "Political class struggle" refers to the contradiction between capitalist-class practices that aim at the maintenance of the existing social relations of production and working-class practices that aim at the transformation of social relations of production. Political class struggle involves a level of organization and strategy that forms the basis of a class-unified movement capable of challenging the direct control of capital over the labor process and has as its specific objective a transformation of social relations of production and state power. Political repression and significant concessions made to the industrial working class during the 1930s helped to prevent a political class struggle.

67. Michel Aglietta, *A Theory of Capitalist Regulation: The U.S. Experience* (London: New Left Books, 1979), p. 364.

Chapter Eight. Foundations for a Restructuring of the Political and Economic Order

1. The epigraphs are from confidential memorandum, "The Problem of the Independent Regulatory Commission," by Robert E. Cushman, submitted to the President's Committee on Administrative Management, 15 Oct. 1936, Papers of the President's Committee on Administrative Management, box 5, FDR Library, Hyde Park, N.Y.; Bert E. Askern to FDR, 31 Mar. 1938, OF 285C, box 12, FDR Library; and "Some Accomplishments of the New Deal," memorandum from Rosenman giving information for a press release, n.d., Rosenman Papers, box 12, FDR Library.

2. Robert Justin Goldstein, *Political Repression in Modern America, 1870 to the Present* (Cambridge, Mass.: Schenkman, 1978), pp. 239–43.

3. Frances Fox Piven and Richard A. Cloward, *Poor People's Movements: How They Succeed, How They Fail* (New York: Pantheon, 1977), p. 165.

4. Goldstein, *Political Repression,* p. 244.

5. Starobin, for example, argues that the Communist party's reliance on the Soviet Union contributed to the declining influence of the Communist party on the American working class. See Joseph R. Starobin, *American Communism in Crisis, 1943–1957* (Cambridge, Mass.: Harvard University Press, 1972), passim.

6. For an excellent discussion of the union movement during World War II see Nelson Lichtenstein, *Labor's War at Home: The CIO in World War II* (New York: Cambridge University Press, 1982).

7. For an interesting discussion on the structural resistance to state regulation during the early part of the 1930s see Antonio Carlo, "The Crisis of the State in the Thirties," *Telos* 46 (Winter 1980–81): 62–80.

8. For an examination of reorganization see Charles G. Benda, "State Organization and Policy Formation: The 1970 Reorganization of the Post Office Department," *Politics and Society* 9, 2 (1979): 123–51.

9. For a discussion of different perceptions of monopoly growth see Theodore Rosenof, *Dogma, Depression, and the New Deal* (Port Washington, N.Y.: Kennikat, 1975), pp. 98–112.

10. See Bob Jessop, *The Capitalist State* (New York: New York University Press, 1982), pp. 164–65.

11. See James T. Patterson, *Congressional Conservatism and the New Deal* (Lexington: University of Kentucky Press, 1967); John M. Allswang, *The New Deal and*

American Politics (New York: John Wiley, 1978), pp. 113–31; Richard Polenberg, "The Decline of the New Deal, 1937–1940," in *The New Deal: The National Level,* ed. John Braeman, Robert H. Bremner, and David Brody (Columbus: Ohio State University Press, 1975), pp. 246–66.

12. See Barry Dean Karl, *Executive Reorganization and Reform in the New Deal* (Cambridge, Mass.: Harvard University Press, 1963), passim.

13. *Report of the President's Committee on Administrative Management, 1936,* p. 29, OF 285C, box 17, FDR Library.

14. See Margaret Weir and Theda Skocpol, "State Structures and the Possibilities for 'Keynesian' Responses to the Great Depression in Sweden, Britain, and the United States," in *Bringing the State Back In,* ed. Peter B. Evans, Dietrich Rueschemeyer, and Theda Skocpol (New York: Cambridge University Press, 1985), pp. 107–63.

15. Richard Polenberg, *Reorganizing Roosevelt's Government: The Controversy over Executive Reorganization, 1936–1939* (Cambridge, Mass.: Harvard University Press, 1966), pp. 3–6; see also statements from Hoover and from Wilson on the need for reorganization, in the Papers of the President's Committee on Administrative Management, box 6, FDR Library.

16. Polenberg, *Reorganizing Roosevelt's Government,* pp. 11–15.

17. Press release, 22 Mar. 1936, POF 285C, box 8, FDR Library.

18. Herbert Emmerich, *Federal Organization and Administrative Management* (University: University of Alabama Press, 1971), pp. 48–49.

19. Ibid., p. 50.

20. "Departmental Re-organization," Luther Gulick's original draft on reorganization for Report of Committee, n.d., Papers of the President's Committee on Administrative Management, box 6, FDR Library.

21. Confidential memorandum, "The Problem of the Independent Regulatory Commissions," Robert E. Cushman, 15 Oct. 1936, Papers of the President's Committee on Administrative Management, box 5, FDR Library.

22. *Report of the President's Committee on Administrative Management, 1936,* p. 31, OF 285C, box 17, FDR Library.

23. Otis L. Graham, Jr., *Toward a Planned Society: From Roosevelt to Nixon* (New York: Oxford University Press, 1976), pp. 59–63.

24. Polenberg, *Reorganizing Roosevelt's Government,* pp. 41–43.

25. Patterson, *Congressional Conservatism,* pp. 216–18.

26. Polenberg, *Reorganizing Roosevelt's Government,* pp. 42–51; Emmerich, *Federal Organization,* p. 57.

27. Polenberg, *Reorganizing Roosevelt's Government,* pp. 55–78.

28. See letters OF 285C, boxes 15 and 16 for letters opposing the bill and boxes 12, 13, and 14 for letters in favor of the bill, addressed to the White House, FDR Library.

29. Polenberg, *Reorganizing Roosevelt's Government,* p. 73.

30. Patterson, *Congressional Conservatism,* p. 22.

31. Polenberg, *Reorganizing Roosevelt's Government,* p. 154.

32. J.H.O. Research Co. to Honorable H. McIntyre, 20 Apr. 1938, OF 105, box 3, FDR Library.

33. Polenberg, *Reorganizing Roosevelt's Government,* pp. 88–89.

34. Ibid., pp. 90–99.

35. Ibid., pp. 139–40.

36. Graham, *Toward a Planned Society,* p. 62.

37. Polenberg, *Reorganizing Roosevelt's Government,* pp. 137–45.

38. Patterson, *Congressional Conservatism,* p. 224.

39. Grace M. Aister to FDR, 31 Mar. 1938, OF 285C, box 15, FDR Library.

40. Polenberg, *Reorganizing Roosevelt's Government,* pp. 162–66; and Patterson, *Congressional Conservatism,* pp. 225–26.

41. Polenberg, *Reorganizing Roosevelt's Government,* p. 175.

42. Ibid., pp. 181–85.

43. Emmerich, *Federal Organization,* p. 134.

44. Polenberg, *Reorganizing Roosevelt's Government,* pp. 187–88.

45. For a discussion of ideology and political power see Goran Therborn, *The Ideology of Power and the Power of Ideology* (London: New Left Books, 1980).

46. For an excellent theoretical account of the relationship between trade unions and the state apparatus see Leo Panitch, "Trade Unions and the Capitalist State," *New Left Review* 125 (Jan.–Feb. 1981): 21–43.

47. Manuel Castells, *The Economic Crisis and American Society* (Princeton, N.J.: Princeton University Press, 1980), p. 53.

48. Nicos Poulantzas, *Classes in Contemporary Capitalism* (London: New Left Books, 1975), pp. 142–43.

49. For a systematic account and analysis of the current economic crisis in the United States and its roots in the conditions provided for the resolution of the last economic crisis see Castells, *Economic Crisis and American Society,* passim.

BIBLIOGRAPHY

Government Records

Franklin D. Roosevelt Library, Hyde Park, N.Y.
Papers of the President's Committee on Administrative Management

National Archives, Washington, D.C.
Record group 9: National Recovery Administration
Record group 25: National Labor Relations Board
Record group 44: Office of Government Reports
Record group 46: United States Senate
Record group 174: Department of Labor
Record group 187: National Resources Planning Board

Manuscript Collections

Bancroft Library, University of California, Berkeley
Oleta O'Connor Yates Papers

Franklin D. Roosevelt Library, Hyde Park, N.Y.
Adolph A. Berle Papers
Stephen T. Early Papers
Katherine Pollack Ellickson Papers
Leon Henderson Papers
Louis M. Howe Papers
Franklin D. Roosevelt Papers (Official File, Personal File, Secretary's File)
Samuel L. Rosenman Papers
Rexford G. Tugwell Papers

George Arents Research Library, Syracuse University, Syracuse, N.Y.
Earl Browder Papers

Hoover Institution on War, Revolution and Peace, Stanford University, Stanford, Calif.
Raymond Moley Papers

Jackson Library of Business, Stanford University, Stanford, Calif.
Theodore John Kreps Collection

Tamiment Institute, New York University
Daniel Bell Files

Labor Files

AFL-CIO Library, Washington, D.C.
AFL-CIO Files (industrial unionism, CIO company unionism, Communists in trade unions, industrial unions)

International Longshoremen's and Warehousemen's Union Library, San Francisco, Calif.
International Longshoremen's Association Files

Tamiment Institute, New York University
American Workers Party Files
Workers Party of the U.S. Files

Government Publications and Documents

The Blue Eagle, vols. 1 and 2

The President's Committee on Administrative Management. *Report of the Committee with Studies of Administrative Management in the Federal Government.* Washington, D.C.: Government Printing Office, 1937.

Report of the Committee on Recent Economic Changes of the President's Conference on Unemployment: *Recent Economic Changes in the United States.* New York: McGraw Hill, 1929.

Report of the President's Research Committee on Social Trends: *Recent Social Trends in the United States.* New York: McGraw Hill, 1933.

Temporary National Economic Committee. *Investigation of Concentration of Economic Power.* Monographs 12, 13, 17, 21, 25, 26, 27, 29, 31, 42, Formal Report. Washington D.C.: Government Printing Office, 1941.

U.S. Bureau of the Census. *Historical Statistics of the United States, Colonial Times to 1970.* Bicentennial Edition, pt. 1. Washington, D.C.: Government Printing Office, 1975.

U.S. Congress. House of Representatives. House Ways and Means Committee. *National Industrial Recovery.* Hearings before the Committee on Ways and Means on H.R. 5664. 73d Cong., 1st sess., 1933.

U.S. Congress. Senate. *Thirty-Hour Work Week.* Hearings before a subcommittee of the Committee of the Judiciary, 74th Cong., 1st sess., 1935.

———. *Violations of Free Speech and Rights of Labor.* Hearings before a subcommittee of the Committee on Education and Labor, 1936–1940.

———. *Violations of Free Speech and Rights of Labor.* Report of the Committee on Education and Labor, 1937–1939.

U.S. Congress. Senate Finance Committee. *National Industrial Recovery.* Hearings before the Committee on Finance on S. 1712 and H.R. 5755, 73d Cong., 1st sess., 1933.

U.S. Congress. Temporary National Economic Committee. *Investigation of Concentration of Economic Power. Hearings. Pt. 1: Economic Prologue.* Washington, D.C.: Government Printing Office, 1939.

———. *Investigation of Concentration of Economic Power: Final Report and Recommendations of the Temporary National Economic Committee.* Washington, D.C.: Government Printing Office, 1941.

———. *Investigation of Concentration of Economic Power. Pt. 31: A Study Submitted*

by the Federal Trade Commission. Washington, D.C.: Government Printing Office, 1941.
———. *Investigation of Concentration of Economic Power. Pt. 31-A: Supplemental Data Submitted to the Temporary National Economic Committee.* Washington, D.C.: Government Printing Office, 1941.

BUSINESS AND POLITICAL PUBLICATIONS

Chamber of Commerce of the United States. "Administration of Codes." Mar. 1934.
Chamber of Commerce. Department of Manufacture Committee. "Labor Standards in Government." Nov. 1935.
National Association of Manufacturers. "Evidence for the Open Shop." 28 Feb. 1927.
———. "Unemployment Insurance Handbook." 1933.
National Association of Manufacturers of the United States of America. "Codes of Fair Competition." 18 Aug. 1933.
———. "Report of Committee on Open Shop." Oct. 1925.
———. "Who Wants the Wagner Act Amended?" Mar. 1939.
NRA from Within. International Pamphlets no. 4. 1934.
Party-Organizer. Vols. 3–7, 1930–34.

SECONDARY SOURCES

Abraham, David. *The Collapse of the Weimar Republic.* Princeton, N.J.: Princeton University Press, 1981.
Adams, Henry. *Harry Hopkins.* New York: G. P. Putnam's Sons, 1977.
Adams, Walter, and Horace Gray. *Monopoly in America.* New York: Macmillan Co., 1955.
Aglietta, Michel. "Phases of U.S. Capitalist Expansion." *New Left Review* 110 (July–Aug. 1978): 17–28.
———. *A Theory of Capitalist Regulation: The U.S. Experience.* London: New Left Books, 1979.
Alford, Robert R. "The Role of Social Class in American Voting Behavior." In *Political Parties and Political Behavior,* edited by William J. Crotty, Donald M. Freeman, and Douglas C. Gatlin. Boston, Mass.: Allyn & Bacon, 1966.
Alinsky, Saul. *John L. Lewis.* New York: G. P. Putnam's Sons, 1949.
Allswang, John M. *The New Deal and American Politics.* New York: John Wiley, 1978.
Alperin, Robert J. "Organization in the Communist Party, U.S.A., 1931–1938." Ph.D. diss., Northwestern University, 1959.
Althusser, Louis. "Ideology and Ideological State Structures." In *Lenin and Philosophy,* edited by Louis Althusser. New York: Monthly Review, 1971.
Amin, Samir. "Toward a Structural Crisis of World Capitalism." *Socialist Revolution* 5, 1 (Apr. 1975): 9–44.
Anderson, Kristi. *The Creation of a Democratic Majority, 1928–1936.* Chicago: University of Chicago Press, 1979.
Arndt, H. W. *The Economic Lessons of the Nineteen-Thirties.* New York: Augustus M. Kelly, 1965.
Aronowitz, Stanley. *False Promises.* New York: McGraw-Hill, 1973.

Arrighi, Giovanni. "The Class Struggle in Twentieth Century Western Europe." Paper presented at the Ninth World Congress of Sociology, Uppsala, Sweden, 14–19 Aug. 1978.

———. "A Crisis of Hegemony." In *Dynamics of Global Crisis,* edited by Samir Amin, Andre Gunder Frank, and Immanuel Wallerstein. New York: Monthly Review, 1982.

———. "Towards a Theory of Capitalist Crisis." *New Left Review* 111 (Sept.–Oct. 1978): 3–24.

Auerbach, Jerold S. "The Influence of the New Deal," *Current History* 48, 286 (June 1956): 334–65.

———. *Labor and Liberty: The La Follette Committee and the New Deal.* New York: Bobbs-Merrill, 1966.

———. "The La Follette Committee: Labor and Civil Liberties in the New Deal." *Journal of American History* 51, 3 (Dec. 1964): 435–59.

———. "New Deal, Old Deal, or Raw Deal: Some Thoughts on New Left Historiography." *Journal of Southern History* 35 (Feb. 1969): 18–30.

———. "Southern Tenant Farmers: Socialist Critics of the New Deal." *Labor History* 7, 1 (Winter, 1966): 3–18.

Bachrach, Peter, and Morton Baratz. "Decisions and Non-Decisions." *American Political Science Review* 57 (Sept. 1963): 632–42.

Baker, Ray Stannard. *The New Industrial Unrest: Reasons and Remedies.* New York: Doubleday, Page, 1920.

Barker, Colin. "A Note on the Theory of Capitalist States." *Capital and Class* 4 (Spring 1978): 118–26.

Bart, Philip; Theodore Bassett; William E. Weinstein; and Arthur Zipser, eds. *Highlights of a Fighting History: 60 Years of the Communist Party USA.* New York: International, 1979.

Bellush, Bernard. *The Failure of the NRA.* New York: W. W. Norton, 1975.

Benda, Charles G. "State Organization and Policy Formation: The 1970 Reorganization of the Post Office Department." *Politics and Society* 9, 2 (1979): 123–51.

Beney, Ada. *Wages, Hours, and Employment in the United States, 1914–1936.* New York: National Industrial Conference Board, 1936.

Bennett, David H. *Demagogues in the Depression: American Radicals and the Union Party, 1932–1936.* New Brunswick, N.J.: Rutgers University Press, 1969.

Benson, Leslie. *Proletarians and Parties.* New York: Methuen, 1978.

Berle, Adolf, and Gardiner Means. *The Modern Corporation and Private Property.* New York: Harcourt, Brace & World, 1967.

Berle, Beatrice Bishop, and Travis Beal Jacobs, eds. *Navigating the Rapids, 1918–1971: From the Papers of Adolf A. Berle.* New York: Harcourt Brace Jovanovich, 1973.

Bernstein, Barton J. "The Conservative Achievements of Liberal Reform." In *Towards a New Past,* edited by Barton J. Bernstein. New York: Vintage, 1969.

Bernstein, Irving. "The End of the Turbulent Years." In *The New Deal: The Critical Issues,* edited by Otis L. Graham, Jr. Boston, Mass.: Little, Brown, 1971.

———. *The Lean Years.* Boston, Mass.: Houghton Mifflin, 1972.

———. *The New Deal Collective Bargaining Policy.* New York: Da Capo, 1975.

———. *Turbulent Years.* Boston, Mass.: Houghton Mifflin, 1969.

Beuner, David. "The Democratic Party, 1910–1931." In *History of U.S. Political Parties,* vol. 3: *1910–1945,* edited by Arthur M. Schlesinger, Jr. New York: Chelsea House, 1973.

Bicha, Karel Denis. "Liberalism Frustrated: The League for Independent Political Action, 1928–1933." *Mid-America* 48, 1 (Jan. 1966): 19–28.

Bingham, Alfred M. *Insurgent America: Revolt of the Middle Classes.* New York: Harper, 1935.

Bingham, Alfred M., and Seldon Rodman, eds. *Challenge to the New Deal.* New York: Falcon, 1934.

Bird, Caroline. *The Invisible Scar.* New York: Longman, 1966.

Blair, John. *Economic Concentration.* New York: Harcourt Brace Jovanovich, 1972.

Block, Fred. "Beyond Relative Autonomy: State Managers as Historical Subjects." *Socialist Register,* 1980, pp. 227–42.

———. *The Origins of International Economic Disorder.* Berkeley: University of California Press, 1977.

———. "The Ruling Class Does Not Rule: Notes on the Marxist Theory of the State." *Socialist Revolution* 33 (May–June 1977): 6–28.

Blum, Albert A. "Labor and the Federal Government, 1850–1933." *Current History* 48, 286 (June 1965): 328–33.

Blum, John Morton. *From the Morgenthau Diaries: Years of Crisis, 1928–1938.* Boston, Mass.: Houghton Mifflin, 1959.

Blumberg, Barbara. *The New Deal and the Unemployed: The View from New York City.* Lewisburg, Pa.: Bucknell University Press, 1979.

Bodnar, John. "Immigration, Kinship, and the Rise of Working Class Realism in Industrial America." *Journal of Social History* 14, 1 (Fall 1980): 45–65.

Bone, Hugh H. "Political Parties in New York City." *American Political Science Review* 40, 2 (Apr. 1946): 272–88.

Bonn, M. J. *The Crisis of Capitalism in America.* New York: John Day, 1932.

Bonnet, Clarence E. *History of Employer's Associations in the United States.* New York: Vantage, 1957.

Bowles, Samuel, and Herbert Gintis. "The Crisis of Liberal Democratic Capitalism: The Case of the United States." *Politics and Society* 11, 1 (1982): 51–93.

Boyer, Richard O., and Herbert M. Morais. *Labor's Untold Story.* New York: United Electrical, Radio, and Machine Workers of America, 1955.

Brady, Robert A. *Business as a System of Power.* New York: Columbia University Press, 1943.

Braeman, John. "The New Deal and the 'Broker State': A Review of the Recent Scholarly Literature." *Business History Review* 46, 4 (Winter 1972): 409–29.

Braeman, John; Robert H. Bremner; and David Brody, eds. *The New Deal: The National Level.* Columbus: Ohio State University Press, 1975.

Braeman, John; Robert H. Bremner; and Everett Walters, eds. *Change and Continuity in Twentieth Century America.* Columbus: Ohio State University Press, 1964.

Brecher, Jeremy. *Strike!* San Francisco, Calif.: Straight Arrow Books, 1972.

Bridges, Amy. "Nicos Poulantzas and the Marxist Theory of the State." *Politics and Society* 4, 2 (1974): 161–90.

Brighton Labour Process Group. "The Capitalist Labour Process." *Capital and Class* 1 (Spring 1977): 3–26.

Brockie, Melvin D. "Theories of the 1937–1938 Crisis and Depression." *Economics Journal* 60, 238 (June 1950): 292–310.

Brody, David. "The Emergence of Mass Production Unionism." In *Change and Continuity in Twentieth Century America,* edited by John Braeman et al. Columbus: Ohio State University Press, 1964.

———. "The Expansion of the American Labor Movement: Institutional Sources of Stimulation and Restraint." In *The American Labor Movement,* edited by David Brody. New York: Harper & Row, 1971.

———. "Labor and the Great Depression: The Interpretive Prospects." *Labor History* 13, 2 (Spring 1972): 231–44.
———. "The New Deal and World War II." In *The New Deal: The National Level,* edited by John Braeman et al. Columbus: Ohio State University Press, 1975.
———. "Radicalism and the American Labor Movement: From Party History to Social History." In *Political Power and Social Theory,* vol. 4, edited by Maurice Zeitlin and Howard Kimeldorf. Greenwich, Conn.: JAI Press, 1984.
———. *Steelworkers in America.* New York: Harper & Row, 1969.
Brooks, Robert. *When Labor Organizes.* New Haven, Conn.: Yale University Press, 1937.
Brown, Linda. "Challenge and Response: The American Business Community and the New Deal, 1932–1934." Ph.D. diss., The University of Pennsylvania, 1972.
Buhle, Paul. "Marxism in the United States, 1900–1940." Ph.D. diss., University of Wisconsin, 1975.
Burawoy, Michael. "Terrains of Contest: Factory and State under Capitalism." *Socialist Review* 58 (July–Aug. 1981): 83–124.
Burch, Philip H., Jr. "The NAM as an Interest Group." *Politics and Society* 4, 1 (Fall 1973): 97–130.
Burns, Arthur Robert. *The Decline of Competition.* New York: McGraw-Hill, 1936.
Burns, Helen. *The American Banking Community and New Deal Banking Reforms, 1933–1935.* Westport, Conn.: Greenwood, 1974.
Cannon, James P. *The First Ten Years of American Communism.* New York: Pathfinder, 1962.
———. *The History of American Trotskyism.* New York: Pathfinder, 1972.
———. *The Left Opposition in the U.S., 1928–31.* New York: Monad, 1981.
Cantor, Milton. *The Divided Left: American Radicalism 1900–1975.* New York: Hill & Wang, 1978.
Carlo, Antonio. "The Crisis of the State in the Thirties." *Telos* 46 (Winter 1980/81): 62–80.
Castells, Manuel. *The Economic Crisis and American Society.* Princeton, N.J.: Princeton University Press, 1980.
Chambers, Whittaker. *Witness.* New York: Random House, 1952.
Chambers, William Nisbet. "The Concept of Party: An Analytical Model." In *Political Parties and Political Behavior,* edited by William J. Crotty, Donald M. Freeman, and Douglas C. Gatlin. Boston, Mass.: Allyn & Bacon, 1966.
Chandler, Alfred D., Jr. "The Structure of American Industry in the Twentieth Century: A Historical Overview." *Business History Review* 43, 3 (Autumn 1969): 255–97.
———. "The United States: Evolution of Enterprise." In *Cambridge Economic History of Europe,* vol. 7, pt. 2, edited by Peter Mathias and Michael Postan. New York: Cambridge University Press, 1978.
———. *The Visible Hand: The Managerial Revolution in American Business.* Cambridge, Mass.: Harvard University Press, 1977.
Chandler, Lester V. *America's Greatest Depression, 1929–1941.* New York: Harper & Row, 1970.
Chase, Stuart. *A New Deal.* New York: Macmillan, 1932.
Childs, Marquis. "They Hate Roosevelt." In *The New Deal: The Critical Issues,* edited by Otis L. Graham, Jr. Boston, Mass.: Little, Brown, 1971.
Chirot, Daniel. *Social Change in the Twentieth Century.* New York: Harcourt Brace Jovanovich, 1977.
Clark, Marjorie R., and S. Fanny Simon. *The Labor Movement in America.* New York: W. W. Norton, 1938.

Clarke, Simon. "Capital, Fractions of Capital and the State: Neo-Marxist Analyses of the South African State." *Capital and Class* 5 (Summer 1978): 32–77.
———. "Marxism, Sociology and Poulantzas' Theory of the State." *Capital and Class* 2 (Summer 1977): 1–31.
Cleaver, Harry. *Reading Capital Politically.* Austin: University of Texas Press, 1979.
Cochran, Bert. *Labor and Communism: The Conflict That Shaped American Unions.* Princeton, N.J.: Princeton University Press, 1977.
Cochran, Thomas C. *American Business in the Twentieth Century.* Cambridge, Mass.: Harvard University Press, 1957.
———. *The American Business System: A Historical Perspective, 1900–1955.* Cambridge, Mass.: Harvard University Press, 1972.
———. *Business in American Life.* New York: McGraw-Hill, 1972.
Cole, G. D. H. *Economic Planning.* London: Kennikat, 1971.
———. *A Guide through World Chaos.* New York: Alfred A. Knopf, 1932.
Colm, Gerhard. "Fiscal Policy." In *The New Economics: Keynes' Influence on Theory and Public Policy,* edited by Seymour Harris. New York: Alfred A. Knopf, 1947.
Conkin, Paul K. *The New Deal.* New York: Thomas Y. Crowell, 1967.
Conrad, David Eugene. *The Forgotten Farmer: The Story of Sharecroppers in the New Deal.* Urbana: University of Illinois Press, 1965.
Corey, Lewis. *The Decline of American Capitalism.* New York: Covici, Friede, 1934.
Cramer, Clarence. *American Enterprise: The Rise of U.S. Commerce.* London: Paul Elek, 1973.
Creamer, Daniel. *Capital and Output Trends in Manufacturing Industries.* New York: National Bureau of Economic Research, 1954.
Creamer, Daniel B. *Is Industry Decentralizing?* Philadelphia: University of Pennsylvania Press, 1935.
Crotty, William J.; Donald M. Freeman; and Douglas C. Gatlin, eds. *Political Parties and Political Behavior.* Boston, Mass.: Allyn & Bacon, 1966.
Cuff, Robert D. *The War Industries Board.* Baltimore, Md.: Johns Hopkins University Press, 1973.
Davis, Joseph S. *The World between the Wars, 1919–34: An Economist's View.* Baltimore, Md.: Johns Hopkins University Press, 1975.
Davis, Lance, and Robert E. Gallman. "Capital Formation in the United States during the Nineteenth Century." In *Cambridge Economic History of Europe,* vol. 7, pt. 2, edited by Peter Mathias and Michael Postan. New York: Cambridge University Press, 1978.
Davis, Mike. "The Barren Marriage of American Labour and the Democratic Party." *New Left Review* 124 (Nov.–Dec. 1980): 43–84.
———. *Prisoners of the American Dream.* London: Verso, 1986.
———. "Why the U.S. Working Class Is Different." *New Left Review* 123 (Sept.–Oct. 1980): 3–44.
de Brunhoff, Suzanne. *The State, Capital and Economic Policy.* London: Pluto, 1978.
DeCaux, Len. *Labor Radical.* Boston, Mass.: Beacon, 1970.
Degler, Carl N. "American Political Parties and the Rise of the City: An Interpretation." *Journal of American History* 51, 1 (June 1964): 41–59.
———. *Out of Our Past.* New York: Harper & Row, 1959.
———. "The Third Revolution." In *The New Deal: The Critical Issues,* edited by Otis L. Graham, Jr. Boston, Mass.: Little, Brown, 1971.
Dennis, Jack. "Trends in Public Support for the American Party System." *British Journal of Political Science* 5, 2 (Apr. 1975): 189–230.

Dennis, Peggy. *The Autobiography of an American Communist.* Berkeley, Calif.: Lawrence Hill, 1977.
Derber, Milton. *The American Idea of Industrial Democracy.* Chicago: University of Chicago Press, 1970.
———. "The New Deal and Labor." In *The New Deal: The National Level,* edited by John Braeman et al. Columbus: Ohio State University Press, 1975.
Derber, Milton, and Edwin Young. *Labor and the New Deal.* Madison: University of Wisconsin Press, 1957.
Divine, Robert A. *American Immigration Policy, 1924–1952.* New Haven, Conn.: Yale University Press, 1957.
Dobb, Maurice. *Studies in the Development of Capitalism.* New York: International Publishers, 1973.
Dobbs, Farrell. *Teamster Rebellion.* New York: Monad, 1972.
Dorfman, Joseph. *The Economic Mind in American Civilization.* New York: Viking, 1959.
Douglas, Paul H. *Real Wages in the United States, 1890–1926.* New York: Houghton Mifflin, 1930.
Dowd, Douglas F. "Accumulation and Crisis in U.S. Capitalism." *Socialist Revolution* 5, 2 (June 1975): 7–44.
———. *The Twisted Dream: Capitalist Development in the United States since 1776.* Cambridge, Mass.: Winthrop, 1974.
Dubofsky, Melvyn. *American Labor since the New Deal.* Chicago: Quadrangle, 1971.
———. *Industrialism and the American Worker, 1865–1920.* Arlington Heights, Ill.: AHR, 1975.
———. *We Shall Be All.* New York: Quadrangle, 1969.
Dubofsky, Melvyn, and Warren Van Tine. *John L. Lewis: A Biography.* New York: Quadrangle, 1977.
Duverger, Maurice. *Political Parties.* New York: John Wiley, 1963.
Edwards, P. K. *Strikes in the United States, 1881–1974.* Oxford, Eng.: Basil Blackwell, 1981.
Edwards, Richard. *Contested Terrain: The Transformation of the Workplace in the Twentieth Century.* New York: Basic, 1979.
Einzig, Paul. *The World Economic Crisis, 1929–1931.* London: Macmillan, 1932.
Eliel, Paul. *The Waterfront and General Strike, San Francisco.* San Francisco, Calif.: n.p., 1934.
Eliot, Charles W. "National Planning." Paper presented before the Graduate School of City Planning, Harvard University, 11 Jan. 1935.
Elliott, William Y. "The Economics of the Recovery Program." *American Political Review* 28, 3 (June 1934): 410–23.
Ellis, Edward Robb. *A Nation in Torment.* New York: Coward-McCann, 1970.
Ellsworth, P. T. *The International Economy.* New York: Macmillan, 1950.
Emmerich, Herbert. *Essays on Federal Reorganization.* University: University of Alabama Press, 1950.
———. *Federal Organization and Administrative Management.* University: University of Alabama Press, 1971.
Esping-Anderson, Gosta; Roger Friedland; and Erik Olin Wright. "Modes of Class Struggle and the Capitalist State." *Kapitalistate* 4/5 (1976): 186–220.
Fabricant, Solomon. *Employment in Manufacturing Industries, 1899–1937.* New York: National Bureau of Economic Research, 1942.
———. *The Output of Manufacturing Industries, 1899–1937.* New York: National Bureau of Economic Research, 1940.

———. *The Trend of Government Activity in the United States since 1900.* New York: National Bureau of Economic Research, 1952.
Faulkner, Harold. *American Economic History.* New York: Harper, 1924.
Faulkner, Harold U. *The Decline of Laissez-faire, 1897–1917.* New York: Holt, Rinehart & Winston, 1951.
Feis, Herbert. *1933: Characters in Crisis.* Boston, Mass.: Little, Brown, 1960.
Filene, Edward A. "Business Needs the New Deal." In *New Deal Thought,* edited by Howard Zinn. New York: Bobbs-Merrill, 1966.
Fine, Sidney. *The Automobile under the Blue Eagle.* Ann Arbor: University of Michigan Press, 1963.
———. *Sit-down: The General Motors Strike of 1936–1937.* Ann Arbor: University of Michigan Press, 1969.
Finegold, Kenneth, and Theda Skocpol. "State, Party, and Industry: From Business Recovery to the Wagner Act in America's New Deal." In *Statemaking and Social Movement: Essays on History and Theory,* edited by Charles Bright and Susan Harding. Ann Arbor: University of Michigan Press, 1984.
Firestone, John M. *Federal Receipts and Expenditures during Business Cycles, 1879–1958.* Princeton, N.J.: Princeton University Press, 1960.
Fite, Gilbert C. "Farmer Opinion and the Agricultural Adjustment Act, 1933." *Mississippi Valley Historical Review* 48, 4 (Mar. 1962): 656–73.
Foner, Philip S. *Organized Labor and the Black Worker, 1619–1973.* New York: Praeger, 1974.
Foster, William Z. *American Trade Unionism.* New York: International, 1947.
———. *History of the Communist Party of the United States.* New York: Greenwood, 1968.
Freeman, Josua. "Delivering the Goods: Industrial Unionism during World War II." *Labor History* 19, 4 (Fall 1978): 570–93.
Friedal, Frank. *FDR: Launching the New Deal.* Boston, Mass.: Little, Brown, 1973.
Friedlander, Peter. *The Emergence of a UAW Local, 1930–1939.* Pittsburgh, Pa.: University of Pittsburgh Press, 1975.
Friedman, Andrew L. *Industry and Labor: Class Struggle at Work and Monopoly Capitalism.* London: Macmillan, 1977.
Fusfeld, Daniel R. *The Economic Thought of Franklin D. Roosevelt and the Origins of the New Deal.* New York: Columbia University Press, 1956.
Galambos, Louis. *Competition and Cooperation: The Emergence of a National Trade Association.* Baltimore, Md.: Johns Hopkins University Press, 1966.
Galbraith, John Kenneth. *The Great Crash.* Boston, Mass.: Houghton Mifflin, 1954.
Galenson, Walter. *The CIO Challenge to the AFL.* Cambridge, Mass.: Harvard University Press, 1960.
———. "Communists and Trade Union Democracy." *Industrial Relations* 13, 3 (Oct. 1974): 228–36.
Galloway, George. *Planning for America.* New York: Henry Holt, 1941.
Gamble, A., and P. Walton. *Capitalism in Crisis: Inflation and the State.* London: Macmillan, 1976.
Garraty, John A. "Unemployment during the Great Depression." *Labor History* 17, 2 (Spring 1976): 133–59.
———. *Unemployment in History.* New York: Harper & Row, 1978.
Geschwender, James A. "Class Struggle, the Labor Process and Racial Stratification." Paper presented at the annual meetings of the Society for the Study of Social Problems, Boston, Mass., Aug. 1979.
Giddens, Anthony. *A Contemporary Critique of Historical Materialism.* Berkeley: University of California Press, 1981.

Glaberman, Martin. "Vanguard to Rearguard." In *Political Power and Social Theory,* vol. 4, edited by Maurice Zeitlin and Howard Kimeldorf. Greenwich, Conn.: JAI, 1984.

Glyn, Andrew, and Bob Sutcliffe. *Capitalism in Crisis.* New York: Pantheon, 1972.

Gold, David; Clarence Y. H. Lo; and Erik Wright. "Recent Developments in Marxist Theories of the Capitalist State." *Monthly Review* (Oct. 1975): 29–43.

———. "Recent Developments in Marxist Theories of the Capitalist State, Part 2." *Monthly Review* (Nov. 1975): 36–51.

Goldstein, Robert Justin. *Political Repression in Modern America, 1870 to the Present.* Cambridge, Mass.: Schenkman, 1978.

Goldston, Robert. *The Great Depression.* Greenwich, Conn.: Fawcett, 1968.

Gordon, David M.; Richard Edwards; and Michael Reich. *Segmented Work, Divided Workers: The Historical Transformation of Labor in the United States.* New York: Cambridge University Press, 1982.

Gordon, Max. "The Party and Polling Place: A Response." *Radical History Review* 23 (Spring 1980): 130–35.

Gordon, Rita Werner. "The Change in the Political Alignment of Chicago's Negroes during the New Deal." *Journal of American History* 56, 3 (Dec. 1969): 584–603.

Graham, Otis L., Jr. "The Democratic Party, 1932–1945." In *History of U.S. Political Parties,* vol. 3: *1910–1945,* edited by Arthur M. Schlesinger, Jr. New York: Chelsea House, 1973.

———. *Toward a Planned Society: From Roosevelt to Nixon.* New York: Oxford University Press, 1976.

———, ed. *The New Deal: The Critical Issues.* Boston, Mass.: Little, Brown, 1971.

Green, James R. *The World of the Worker.* New York: Hill & Wang, 1980.

Greenberg, Edward S. *Serving the Few: Corporate Capitalism and the Basis of Government Policy.* New York: John Wiley, 1974.

Greenstone, J. David. *Labor in American Politics.* New York: Vintage, 1969.

Griffin, Larry J.; Michael E. Wallace; and Beth A. Rubin. "Capitalist Resistance to the Organization of Labor before the New Deal: Why? How? Success?" *American Sociological Review* 51, 2 (Apr. 1986): 147–67.

Gross, James A. *The Making of the National Labor Relations Board.* Albany: State University of New York Press, 1974.

Grubbs, Donald H. *Cry from the Cotton: The Southern Tenant Farmers' Union and the New Deal.* Chapel Hill: University of North Carolina Press, 1971.

———. "Gardner Jackson, That 'Socialist' Tenant Farmers' Union, and the New Deal." *Agricultural History* 42, 2 (Apr. 1968): 125–37.

Gurko, Leo. *The Angry Decade.* New York: Dodd, Mead, 1947.

Haberler, Gottfried. *Prosperity and Depression.* Cambridge, Mass.: Harvard University Press, 1960.

———. *The World Economy, Money, and the Great Depression, 1919–1939.* Washington, D.C.: American Enterprise Institute for Public Policy Research, 1976.

Hacker, Louis M. *The Course of American Economic Growth and Development.* New York: John Wiley, 1970.

———. *A Short History of the New Deal.* New York: F. S. Crofts, 1935.

Hacker, Louis M., and Benjamin B. Kendrick. *The United States since 1865.* New York: F. S. Crofts, 1932.

Hamby, Alonzo L., ed. *The New Deal: Analysis and Interpretation.* New York: Weybright & Talley, 1970.

Hansen, Alvin. *Full Recovery or Stagnation?* New York: W. W. Norton, 1938.

Harbaugh, William H. "The Republican Party, 1893–1932." In *History of U.S. Political*

Parties, vol. 3: *1910–1945,* edited by Arthur M. Schlesinger, Jr. New York: Chelsea House, 1973.

Harris, Herbert. *American Labor.* New Haven, Conn.: Yale University Press, 1939.

Harris, Seymour E. *The New Economics: Keynes' Influence on Theory and Public Policy.* New York: Alfred A. Knopf, 1952.

Hawley, Ellis W. "The New Deal and Business." In *The New Deal: The National Level,* edited by John Braeman et al. Columbus: Ohio State University Press, 1975.

———. *The New Deal and the Problem of Monopoly.* Princeton, N.J.: Princeton University Press, 1966.

Hevener, John W. *Which Side Are You On?* Chicago: University of Chicago Press, 1978.

Hildebrand, George H. "The Economic Effects of Unionism." In *The New Deal: The Critical Issues,* edited by Otis L. Graham, Jr. Boston, Mass.: Little, Brown, 1971.

Himmelberg, Robert F. *The Origins of the National Recovery Administration.* New York: Fordham University Press, 1976.

Hobsbawn, Eric. "The Crisis of Capitalism in Historical Perspective." *Socialist Revolution* 30 (Oct.–Dec. 1976): 77–96.

Hodson, H. V. *Slump and Recovery, 1929–1937.* New York: Oxford University Press, 1938.

Hoffman, Charles. *The Depression of the Nineties.* Westport, Conn.: Greenwood, 1970.

Hofstadter, Richard. *The Age of Reform.* New York: Vintage, 1955.

———. *The American Political Tradition.* New York: Vintage, 1974.

———. *The Idea of a Party System.* Berkeley: University of California Press, 1972.

Holley, Donald. "The Negro in the New Deal Resettlement Program." *Agricultural History* 45, 3 (July 1971): 179–93.

Holloway, John, and Sol Picciotto. "Capital, Crisis and the State." *Capital and Class* 2 (Summer 1977): 76–101.

———. *State and Capital.* London: Edward Arnold, 1978.

Holt, James. "The New Deal and the American Anti-Statist Tradition." In *The New Deal: The National Level,* edited by John Braeman et al. Columbus: Ohio State University Press, 1975.

Hoover, Herbert C. "An Attempt to Revolutionize the American System of Life." In *The New Deal: The Critical Issues,* edited by Otis L. Graham, Jr. Boston, Mass.: Little, Brown, 1971.

Horowitz, Ruth L. *Political Ideologies of Organized Labor: The New Deal Era.* New Brunswick, N.J.: Transaction Books, 1978.

Howe, Irving; Lewis Coser; and Julius Jacobson. *The American Communist Party.* Boston, Mass.: Beacon, 1957.

Huberman, Leo. *The Labor Spy Racket.* New York: Monthly Review Press, 1966.

Hughes, Jonathan R. T. *The Governmental Habit: Economic Controls from Colonial Times to the Present.* New York: Basic, 1977.

Hunt, E. K. "A Neglected Aspect of the Economic Ideology of the Early New Deal." *Review of Social Economy* 29, 2 (Sept. 1971): 180–92.

Hurd, Rick. "New Deal Labor Policy and the Containment of Radical Union Activity." *Review of Radical Political Economics* 8, 3 (Fall 1976): 32–43.

Ickes, Harold L. "The Fundamental Political Issue Today Is Taxation." In *The New Deal: The Critical Issues,* edited by Otis L. Graham, Jr. Boston, Mass.: Little, Brown, 1971.

Industrial Relations Research Association. *Manpower in the United States.* New York: Harper, 1954.

Institute for Contemporary Studies. *Emerging Coalitions in American Politics.* San Francisco, Calif.: Institute for Contemporary Studies, 1978.

Institute of Economics of the Brookings Institution. *The Recovery Problem in the United States.* Washington, D.C.: Brookings Institution, 1936.

Isserman, Maurice. "Three Generations: Historians View American Communism." *Labor History* 26, 4 (Fall 1985): 517–45.

Jessop, Bob. "Accumulation Strategies, State Forms, and Hegemonic Projects." *Kapitalistate* 10/11 (1983): 89–111.

———. *The Capitalist State.* New York: New York University Press, 1982.

———. *Nicos Poulantzas: Marxist Theory and Political Strategy.* New York: St. Martin's, 1985.

———. "Recent Theories of the Capitalist State." *Cambridge Journal of Economics* 1 (Dec. 1977): 353–73.

Johnson, Arthur M. "Continuity and Change in Government-Business Relations." In *Change and Continuity in Twentieth Century America,* edited by John Braeman, Robert Bremner, and Everett Walters. Columbus: Ohio State University Press, 1964.

Kahn, Eleanor Nora. "Organizations of Unemployed Workers as a Factor in the American Labor Movement." Master's thesis, University of Wisconsin, 1934.

Karl, Barry Dean. *Executive Reorganization and Reform in the New Deal.* Cambridge, Mass.: Harvard University Press, 1963.

Keeran, Roger R. "Communist Influence in the Automobile Industry, 1920–1933: Paving the Way for an Industrial Union." *Labor History* 20, 2 (Spring 1979): 189–225.

———. *The Communist Party and the Auto Workers Union.* Bloomington: Indiana University Press, 1980.

———. "Reply to Professor Lichtenstein." *Industrial Relations* 19, 2 (Spring 1980): 136–39.

Keler, Jim. "A Veteran Communist Speaks: Akron Rubber Workers' Strikes of 1936." New York: Workers Press, 1975.

Kemler, Edgar. *The Deflation of American Ideals: An Ethical Guide for New Dealers.* Washington, D.C.: American Council on Public Affairs, 1941.

Kendrick, John W. *Productivity Trends in the United States.* Princeton, N.J.: Princeton University Press, 1961.

Kester, Howard. *Revolt among the Sharecroppers.* New York: Covici, Friede, 1936.

Keynes, John Maynard. *The End of Laissez-faire.* London: Hogarth, 1926.

Kimmel, Lewis H. *Federal Budget and Fiscal Policy, 1789–1958.* Washington, D.C.: Brookings Institution, 1959.

———. "Keynesian Theory, Public Opinion, and the New Deal." In *United States Economic History: Selected Readings,* edited by Harry N. Schieber. New York: Alfred A. Knopf, 1964.

Kindleberger, Charles P. *The World in Depression, 1929–1939.* Berkeley: University of California Press, 1973.

Kirby, John B. *Black Americans in the Roosevelt Era.* Knoxville: University of Tennessee Press, 1980.

Kirkendall, Richard S. "The Great Depression: Another Watershed in American History?" In *Change and Continuity in Twentieth Century America,* edited by John Braeman et al. Columbus: Ohio State University Press, 1964.

———. "The New Deal as Watershed: The Recent Literature." *Journal of American History* 54, 4 (Mar. 1968): 839–52.

———, ed. *The New Deal: The Historical Debate.* New York: John Wiley, 1973.

Kirkland, Edward C. *Industry Comes of Age.* New York: Holt, Rinehart & Winston, 1961.

Klare, Karl E. "Judicial Deradicalization of the Wagner Act and the Origins of Modern Legal Consciousness, 1937–1941." *Minnesota Law Review* 62, 3 (Mar. 1978): 265–339.

Klehr, Harvey. "American Communism and the United Auto Workers: New Evidence on an Old Controversy." *Labor History* 24, 3 (Summer 1983): 404–13.

———. *The Heyday of American Communism: The Depression Decade.* New York: Basic, 1984.

Klein, Lawrence R. *The Keynesian Revolution.* New York: Macmillan, 1966.

Kocka, Jurgen. *White Collar Workers in America, 1890–1940.* Beverly Hills, Calif.: Sage, 1980.

Kolko, Gabriel. *Main Currents in Modern American History.* New York: Harper & Row, 1976.

Kroos, Herman E. *Executive Opinion: What Business Leaders Said and Thought on Economic Issues, 1920's–1930's.* New York: Doubleday, 1970.

Kuczynski, Jurgen. *A Short History of Labour Conditions under Industrial Capitalism,* vol. 2: *The United States of America, 1789–1946.* New York: Barnes & Noble, 1973.

Kuznets, Simon. *National Income and Its Composition, 1919–1938.* New York: National Bureau of Economic Research, 1941.

Laclau, Ernesto. "The Specificity of the Political: The Poulantzas-Miliband Debate." *Economy and Society* 4 (1975): 87–110.

Ladd, Everett Carll, Jr., and Charles D. Hadley. *Transformation of the American Party System.* New York: W. W. Norton, 1975.

Laidler, Harry W. *Concentration of Control in American Industry.* New York: Thomas Y. Crowell, 1931.

Larrowe, Charles P. *Harry Bridges: The Rise and Fall of Radical Labor in the United States.* New York: Lawrence Hill, 1972.

Lary, Hal B., and Associates. *The United States in the World Economy.* Washington, D.C.: Government Printing Office, 1943.

Leab, Daniel J. "United We Eat: The Creation and Organization of the Unemployed Councils in 1930." *Labor History* 8, 3 (Fall 1967): 300–315.

League of Nations. *International Currency Experience: Lessons of the Inter-War Period.* Geneva: n.p., 1944.

Lebergott, Stanley. *The American Economy.* Princeton, N.J.: Princeton University Press, 1967.

———. *Manpower in Economic Growth: The American Record since 1800.* New York: McGraw-Hill, 1964.

Leiserson, Avery. *Parties and Politics.* New York: Alfred A. Knopf, 1958.

Lekachman, Robert. *Age of Keynes.* New York: Random House, 1966.

Lens, Sidney. *The Labor Wars.* Garden City, N.Y.: Doubleday, 1973.

Letwin, William, ed. *A Documentary History of American Economic Policy since 1789.* New York: Doubleday, 1961.

Leuchtenburg, William E. *Franklin D. Roosevelt and the New Deal, 1932–1940.* New York: Harper & Row, 1963.

———. *The Perils of Prosperity, 1914–1932.* Chicago: University of Chicago Press, 1958.

———, ed. *The New Deal: A Documentary History.* New York: Harper & Row, 1968.

Levenstein, Harvey A. *Communism, Anticommunism, and the CIO.* Westport, Conn.: Greenwood, 1981.

Levine, David P. "The Theory of the Growth of the Capitalist Economy." *Economic Development and Cultural Change* 24, 1 (Oct. 1975): 74–75.

Lewinson, Paul. *Race, Class, and Party.* New York: Russell & Russell, 1932.

Licht, Walter, and Hal Barron. "Labor's Men: A Collective Biography of Union Officialdom during the New Deal Years." *Labor History* 19, 4 (Fall 1978): 532–45.

Lichtenstein, Nelson. "Auto Worker Militancy and the Structure of Factory Life, 1937–1955." *Journal of American History* 67, 2 (Sept. 1980): 335–53.

———. "The Communist Experience in American Trade Unions." *Industrial Relations* 19, 2 (Spring 1980): 119–30.
———. *Labor's War at Home: The CIO in World War II.* New York: Cambridge University Press, 1982.
Liebes, Richard. "Longshore Labor Relations on the Pacific Coast, 1934–1942." Ph.D. diss., University of California, 1942.
Lipkowitz, Irving. *Monopoly and Big Business.* New York: League for Industrial Democracy, 1940.
Lipset, Seymour Martin. "Why No Socialism in the United States?" In *Sources of Contemporary Radicalism,* edited by Seweryn Bialer and Sophia Sluzar. Boulder, Colo.: Westview, 1977.
Lorwin, Lewis L., and A. F. Henrichs. *National Planning.* Washington, D.C.: National Resources Board, 1934.
Lowitt, Richard, and Maurine Beasley, eds. *One Third of a Nation.* Urbana: University of Illinois Press, 1981.
Lynch, David. *The Concentration of Economic Power.* New York: Columbia University Press, 1946.
Lynd, Staughton. *American Labor Radicalism.* New York: John Wiley, 1973.
Lyon, Leverett S., et al. *The National Recovery Administration: An Analysis and Appraisal.* Washington, D.C.: Brookings Institution, 1935.
McCoy, Donald R. *Angry Voices: Left-of-Center Politics in the New Deal Era.* New York: Kennikat, 1971.
———. *Coming of Age: The United States during the 1920's and 1930's.* New York: Penguin, 1977.
McFarland, C. K. *Roosevelt, Lewis, and the New Deal, 1933–1940.* Fort Worth: Texas Christian University Press, 1970.
MacIver, Robert M. "The Ambiguity of the New Deal." In *New Deal Thought,* edited by Howard Zinn. New York: Bobbs-Merrill, 1966.
McQuaid, Kim. "Competition, Cartelization, and the Corporate Ethic: General Electric's Leadership during the New Deal Era, 1933–40." *American Journal of Economics and Sociology* 36, 4 (Oct. 1977): 417–28.
———. "Young, Swope and General Electric's 'New Capitalism': A Study in Corporate Liberalism, 1920–33." *American Journal of Economics and Sociology* 36, 3 (July 1977): 323–34.
Magrass, Yale R. *Thus Spake the Moguls.* Cambridge, Mass.: Schenkman, 1981.
Mahon, Rianne. "Canadian Public Policy: The Unequal Structure of Representation." In *The Canadian State,* edited by Leo Panitch. Toronto: University of Toronto Press, 1977.
Mandel, Ernest. *Late Capitalism.* London: New Left Books, 1975.
Marglin, Stephen A. "What Do Bosses Do?" *Review of Radical Political Economics* 6, 2 (Summer 1974): 60–112.
Marshall, Leon C. *Hours and Wages Provisions in NRA Codes.* Washington, D.C.: Brookings Institution, 1935.
Martin, George. *Madam Secretary, Frances Perkins.* Boston, Mass: Houghton Mifflin, 1976.
Marx, Karl. *Capital,* vol. 1. New York: Vintage, 1977.
———. *Capital,* vols. 1–3. New York: International, 1973.
Marx, Karl, and Frederick Engels. *Selected Works.* New York: International, 1970.
Mattick, Paul. *The Economic Crisis and Crisis Theory.* White Plains, N.Y.: M. E. Sharpe, 1981.
Mayer, George. "The Republican Party, 1932–1952." In *History of U.S. Political Parties,* vol. 3: *1910–1945,* edited by Arthur M. Schlesinger, Jr. New York: Chelsea House,

1973.
Mayer, Stephen. "Adapting the Immigrant to the Line: Americanization in the Ford Factory, 1914–1921." *Journal of Social History* 14, 1 (Fall 1980): 67–82.
Meier, August, and Elliott Rudwick. *Black Detroit and the Rise of the UAW.* New York: Oxford University Press, 1979.
Meriam, Lewis, and Laurence F. Schmeckebier. *Reorganization of the National Government.* Washington, D.C.: Brookings Institution, 1939.
Miliband, Ralph. "The Capitalist State: Reply to Nicos Poulantzas." *New Left Review* 59 (Jan.–Feb. 1970): 53–60.
———. *Marxism and Politics.* New York: Oxford University Press, 1977.
———. "Poulantzas and the Capitalist State." *New Left Review* 82 (Nov.–Dec. 1973): 83–92.
———. *The State in Capitalist Society.* London: Quartet, 1973.
Millis, Harry A., and Emily Clark Brown. *From the Wagner Act to Taft-Hartley.* Chicago: University of Chicago Press, 1950.
Mills, C. Wright. *The New Men of Power.* New York: Augustus M. Kelly, 1971.
Milton, David. *The Politics of US Labor: From the Great Depression to the New Deal.* New York: Monthly Review, 1982.
Mitchell, Broadus. *Depression Decade: From New Era through New Deal, 1929–1941.* New York: Holt, Rinehart & Winston, 1962.
Montgomery, David. "The 'New Unionism' and the Transformation of Workers' Consciousness in America, 1909–22." *Journal of Social History* 7, 4 (Summer 1974): 509–29.
———. "Workers' Control of Machine Production in the Nineteenth Century." *Labor History* 17, 4 (Fall 1976): 485–509.
Montgomery, David, and Ronald Schatz. "Facing Layoffs." *Radical America* 4, 2 (Mar.–Apr. 1976): 15–27.
Mulder, Ronald. *The Insurgent Progressives in the Senate and the New Deal, 1933–1939.* New York: Garland, 1979.
Muste, A. J. "The Automobile Industry and Organized Labor." *New Frontiers* 4, 5 (Sept. 1936): 5–47.
Nadworney, Milton J. *Scientific Management and the Unions, 1900–1932.* Cambridge, Mass.: Harvard University Press, 1955.
Naison, Mark. *Communists in Harlem during the Depression.* New York: Grave, 1983.
———. "Harlem Communists and the Politics of Black Protest." *Marxist Perspectives* 1, 3 (Fall 1978): 20–50.
———. "Historical Notes on Blacks and American Communism: The Harlem Experience." *Science and Society* 42, 3 (Fall 1978): 324–43.
Nash, Gerald D. "Industry and the Federal Government, 1850–1933." *Current History* 48, 286 (June 1965): 321–27.
———. *United States Oil Policy, 1890–1964.* Pittsburgh, Pa.: University of Pittsburgh Press, 1968.
National Industrial Conference Board. *Economic Conditions in Foreign Countries, 1932–1933.* New York, 1933.
———. *A Picture of World Economic Conditions.* New York: n.p., 1928.
National Planning Board. *A Plan for Planning.* Washington, D.C.: Government Printing Office, 1934.
National Resources Committee. *The Structure of the American Economy.* New York: Augustus M. Kelley, 1966.
Nelson, Daniel. *Managers and Workers: Origins of the New Factory System in the United States, 1880–1920.* Madison: University of Wisconsin Press, 1975.

———. *Unemployment Insurance: The American Experience, 1915–1935.* Madison: University of Wisconsin Press, 1969.

North, Douglas C. "Was the New Deal a Social Revolution?" In *The New Deal: The Critical Issues,* edited by Otis L. Graham, Jr. Boston, Mass.: Little, Brown, 1971.

Nutter, G. Warren, and Henry Adler Einhorn. *Enterprise Monopoly in the United States, 1899–1958.* New York: Columbia University Press, 1969.

O'Connor, James. "Capital Accumulation, Economic Crisis, and the Mass Worker." *Social Praxis* 6, 1–2 (1979): 5–18.

———. *The Fiscal Crisis of the State.* New York: St. Martin's, 1973.

Offe, Claus. *Disorganized Capitalism.* Cambridge, Mass.: MIT Press, 1985.

———. "Structural Problems of the Capitalist State." In *German Political Studies,* vol. 1: *1974,* edited by Klaus von Beyme. Beverly Hills, Calif.: Sage, 1974.

———. "The Theory of the Capitalist State and the Problem of Policy Formation." Unpublished manuscript, May 1974.

———, and Volker Ronge. "Theses on the Theory of the State." *New German Critique* 6 (Fall 1975): 139–47.

Ogburn, William F., ed. *Social Change and the New Deal.* Chicago: University of Chicago Press, 1934.

Ohlin, Bertil. *The Course and Phases of the World Economic Depression.* New York: Arno, 1972.

Ostrogorski, M. *Democracy and the Organization of Political Parties,* vol. 2: *The United States.* Chicago: Quadrangle, 1964.

Palloix, Christian. "The Labor Process: From Fordism to Neo-Fordism." In *The Labor Process and Class Strategies.* London: Conference of Socialist Economists, 1976.

Panitch, Leo. "Trade Unions and the Capitalist State." *New Left Review* 125 (Jan.–Feb. 1981): 21–43.

Parmet, Herbert S. *The Democrats.* New York: Oxford University Press, 1976.

Patterson, Ernest Minor. "The United States and the World Economy." In *Economic Essays in Honour of Gustav Cassel.* New York: Augustus M. Kelley, 1967.

Patterson, James T. *Congressional Conservatism and the New Deal.* Lexington: University of Kentucky Press, 1967.

Patterson, Robert T. *The Great Boom and Panic, 1921–1929.* Chicago: Henry Regnery, 1965.

Pelling, Henry. *American Labor.* Chicago: University of Chicago Press, 1960.

Pells, Richard H. *Radical Visions and American Dreams: Cultural and Social Thought in the Depression Years.* New York: Harper & Row, 1973.

Perkins, Van L. "The AAA and the Politics of Agriculture: Agricultural Policy Formulation in the Fall of 1933." *Agricultural History* 39, 4 (Oct. 1965): 220–29.

———. *Crisis in Agriculture: The Agricultural Adjustment Administration and the New Deal, 1933.* Berkeley: University of California Press, 1969.

Peterson, Brian. "Working Class Communism: A Review of the Literature." *Radical America* 5 (Jan.–Feb. 1971): 37–61.

Piven, Frances Fox, and Richard A. Cloward. *Poor People's Movements: How They Succeed, How They Fail.* New York: Pantheon, 1977.

———. *Regulating the Poor.* New York: Vintage, 1972.

Polenberg, Richard. "The Decline of the New Deal, 1937–1940." In *The New Deal: The National Level,* edited by John Braeman et al. Columbus: Ohio State University Press, 1975.

———. *Reorganizing Roosevelt's Government: The Controversy over Executive Reorganization, 1936–1939.* Cambridge, Mass.: Harvard University Press, 1966.

———, ed. *Radicalism and Reform in the New Deal.* Reading, Mass.: Addison-Wesley, 1972.

Potter, Jim. *The American Economy between the World Wars.* New York: John Wiley, 1974.

Poulantzas, Nicos. "The Capitalist State: A Reply to Miliband and Laclau." *New Left Review* 95 (Jan.–Feb. 1976): 63–83.

———. *Classes in Contemporary Capitalism.* London: New Left Books. 1975.

———. *La Crise de l'état.* Paris: Presses Universitaires de France, 1976.

———. *The Crisis of the Dictatorships.* London: New Left Books, 1976.

———. "The Current Transformation of the State, the Political Crisis and the Crisis of the State." *Socialism in the World* 1 (1977): 239–73.

———. *Fascism and Dictatorship.* London: New Left Books, 1974.

———. "The Political Crisis and the Crisis of the State." In *Critical Sociology: European Perspectives,* edited by J. W. Freidberg. New York: Irvington, 1979.

———. *Political Power and Social Classes.* London: New Left Books, 1973.

———. "The Problem of the Capitalist State." *New Left Review* 58 (Nov.–Dec. 1969): 67–78.

———. *State, Power, Socialism.* London: New Left Books, 1978.

Preis, Art. *Labor's Giant Step.* New York: Pathfinder, 1972.

Prickett, James Robert. "Anti-Communism and Labor History." *Industrial Relations* 13, 3 (Oct. 1974): 219–27.

———. "Communists and the Communist Issue in the American Labor Movement, 1920–1950." Ph.D. diss., University of California at Los Angeles, 1975.

———. "New Perspectives on American Communism and the Labor Movement." In *Political Power and Social Theory,* vol. 4, edited by Maurice Zeitlin and Howard Kimeldorf. Greenwich, Conn.: JAI, 1984.

———. "Some Aspects of the Communist Controversy in the CIO." *Science and Society* 33 (Summer–Fall 1969): 299–321.

Przeworski, Adam. "Material Bases of Consent: Economics and Politics in a Hegemonic System." In *Political Power and Social Theory,* vol. 1, edited by Maurice Zeitlin. Greenwich, Conn.: JAI, 1980.

———. "Proletariat into a Class: The Process of Class Formation from Karl Kautsky's *Class Struggle* to Recent Controversies." *Politics and Society* 7, 4 (1977): 343–401.

Quadagno, Jill. "Two Models of Welfare State Development: A Reply to Skocpol and Amenta." *American Sociological Review* 50, 4 (Aug. 1985): 575–78.

———. "Welfare Capitalism and the Social Security Act of 1935." *American Sociological Review* 49, 5 (Oct. 1984): 632–47.

Radical History Review. "Once upon a Shop Floor: An Interview with David Montgomery." *Radical History Review* 23 (Spring 1980): 37–53.

Radosh, Ronald. "The Development of the Corporate Ideology of American Labor Leaders, 1914–1933." Ph.D. diss., University of Wisconsin, 1967.

———. "The Myth of the New Deal." In *A New History of Leviathan,* edited by Ronald Radosh and Murray N. Rothbard. New York: E. P. Dutton, 1972.

Rauch, Basil. *The History of the New Deal, 1933–1938.* New York: Creative Age, 1944.

Rees, Albert. *New Measures of Wage-Earner Compensation in Manufacturing, 1914–1957.* New York: National Bureau of Economic Research, 1960.

———. *Real Wages in Manufacturing, 1890–1914.* Princeton, N.J.: Princeton University Press, 1961.

Rees, Goronwy. *The Great Slump: Capitalism in Crisis, 1929–33.* London: Weidenfeld & Nicolson, 1970.

Rehmus, Charles M; Doris B. McLaughlin; and Frederick H. Nesbitt, eds. *Labor and American Politics.* Ann Arbor: University of Michigan Press, 1978.

Riehberg, Donald R. *The Rainbow.* New York: Doubleday, Doran, 1936.

Rogin, Leo. "The New Deal: A Survey of the Literature." *Quarterly Journal of Economics* 49 (May 1935): 325–55.

Roos, Charles. *NRA Economic Planning.* Bloomington, Ind.: Principa, 1937.

Rosen, Elliot A. *Hoover, Roosevelt, and the Brains Trust.* New York: Columbia University Press, 1977.

———. "Roosevelt and the Brains Trust: An Historiographical Overview." *Political Science Quarterly* 87, 4 (Dec. 1972): 531–57.

Rosenof, Theodore. *Dogma, Depression, and the New Deal.* Port Washington, N.Y.: Kennikat, 1975.

Rosenzweig, Roy. "Organizing the Unemployed: The Early Years of the Great Depression, 1929–1933." *Radical America* 10, 4 (July–Aug. 1976): 37–60.

———. "Radicals and the Jobless: The Musteites and the Unemployed Leagues, 1932–1936." *Labor History* 16, 1 (Winter 1975): 52–77.

———. "Socialism in Our Time: The Socialist Party and the Unemployed, 1929–1936." *Labor History* 20, 4 (Fall 1979): 485–504.

Rostow, W. W. *The World Economy: History and Prospects.* Austin: University of Texas Press, 1978.

Rothbard, Murray N. *America's Great Depression.* New York: D. Van Nostrand, 1963.

Rubin, Beth A.; Larry J. Griffin; and Michael Wallace. "'Provided Only That Their Voice Was Strong': Insurgency and Organization of American Labor from NRA to Taft-Hartley." *Work and Occupations* 10, 3 (Aug. 1983): 325–47.

Saposs, David J. "The American Labor Movement since the War." *Quarterly Journal of Economics* 49 (1935): 236–54.

Schlesinger, Arthur M., Jr. *The Coming of the New Deal.* Boston, Mass.: Houghton Mifflin, 1958.

———. *The Crisis of the Old Order.* Boston, Mass.: Houghton Mifflin, 1957.

———. *The New Deal in Action.* New York: Macmillan, 1940.

———. *The Politics of Upheaval.* Boston, Mass.: Houghton Mifflin, 1960.

———. "Sources of the New Deal." In *The New Deal: The Critical Issues,* edited by Otis L. Graham, Jr. Boston, Mass.: Little, Brown, 1971.

———, ed. *History of U.S. Political Parties,* vol. 3: *1910–1945.* New York: Chelsea House, 1973.

Schumpeter, Joseph A. *Business Cycles.* New York: McGraw-Hill, 1939.

Schwarz, Harvey. *The March Inland: Origins of the ILWU Warehouse Division, 1934–1938.* Los Angeles, Calif.: Institute of Industrial Relations, UCLA, 1978.

Seidman, Joel. *American Labor from Defense to Reconversion.* Chicago: University of Chicago Press, 1953.

Shaikh, Anwar. "An Introduction to the History of Crisis Theories." In *U.S. Capitalism in Crisis.* New York: Union for Radical Political Economists, 1978.

Shannon, David A. *Between the Wars: America, 1919–1941.* Boston, Mass.: Houghton Mifflin, 1965.

———. *The Great Depression.* Englewood Cliffs, N.J.: Prentice-Hall, 1960.

Shannon, Fred Albert. *America's Economic Growth.* New York: Macmillan, 1940.

Sherman, Howard J. *Profits in the United States: An Introduction to a Study of Economic Concentration and Business Cycles.* Ithaca, N.Y.: Cornell University Press, 1968.

Shively, W. Phillips. "A Reinterpretation of the New Deal Realignment." *Public Opinion Quarterly* 35, 4 (Winter 1971–72): 621–24.

Shover, John L. "The Communist Party and the Midwest Farm Crisis of 1933." *Journal of American History* 51, 2 (Sept. 1964): 248–66.
Simon, Rita James, ed. *As We Saw the Thirties.* Urbana: University of Illinois Press, 1969.
Simons, Henry C. *A Positive Program for Laissez-faire.* Chicago: University of Chicago Press, 1934.
Sitkoff, Harvard. *A New Deal for Blacks.* New York: Oxford University Press, 1978.
Skocpol, Theda. "Political Response to Capitalist Crisis: Neo-Marxist Theories of the State and the Case of the New Deal." *Politics and Society* 10, 2 (1980): 155–201.
———. *States and Social Revolutions.* New York: Cambridge University Press, 1979.
Skocpol, Theda, and Edwin Amenta. "Did Capitalists Shape Social Security?" *American Sociological Review* 50, 4 (Aug. 1985): 572–75.
Skocpol, Theda, and Kenneth Finegold. "State Capacity and Economic Intervention in the Early New Deal." *Political Science Quarterly* 97, 2 (Summer 1982): 255–78.
Skowronek, Stephen. *Building a New American State: The Expansion of National Administrative Capacities, 1877–1920.* New York: Cambridge University Press, 1982.
Slichter, Sumner. *The Challenge of Industrial Relations.* Ithaca, N.Y.: Cornell University Press, 1947.
———. *Economic Growth in the United States.* New York: Free Press, 1966.
———. *Union Policies and Industrial Management.* Washington, D.C.: Brookings Institution, 1941.
Sloan, Laurence, et al. *Two Cycles of Corporation Profits.* New York: Harper, 1936.
Smith, Geoffrey S. *To Save a Nation.* New York: Basic, 1973.
Snowman, Daniel. *America since 1920.* New York: Harper & Row, 1968.
Sobel, Robert. *The Age of Giant Corporations: A Microeconomic History of American Business, 1914–1970.* Westport, Conn.: Greenwood, 1972.
Sohn-Rethel, Alfred. *Intellectual and Manual Labour.* London: Macmillan, 1978.
Solomons, John. "The Marxist Theory of the State and the Problem of Fractions: Some Theoretical and Methodological Remarks." *Capital and Class* 7 (Spring 1979): 141–47.
Sombart, Werner. *Why Is There No Socialism in the United States?* White Plains, N.Y.: M. E. Sharpe, 1976.
Soule, George. *Prosperity Decade: From War to Depression, 1917–1929.* New York: Rinehart, 1947.
Starobin, Joseph R. *American Communism in Crisis, 1943–1957.* Cambridge, Mass.: Harvard University Press, 1972.
Steigerwalt, Albert K. *The National Association of Manufacturers, 1895–1914.* Ann Arbor, Mich.: Bureau of Business Research, Graduate School of Business Administration, 1964.
Stein, Herbert. *The Fiscal Revolution in America.* Chicago: University of Chicago Press, 1969.
Steindhl, Josef. *Maturity and Stagnation in American Capitalism.* New York: Monthly Review Press, 1952.
Steiner, George A. *Government's Role in Economic Life.* New York: McGraw-Hill, 1953.
Sternscher, Bernard. *Rexford Tugwell and the New Deal.* New Brunswick, N.J.: Rutgers University Press, 1964.
———, ed. *The Negro in Depression and War: Prelude to Revolution, 1930–1945.* Chicago: Quadrangle, 1969.
Stolberg, Benjamin, and Warren Jay Vinton. *The Economic Consequences of the New Deal.* New York: Harcourt, Brace, 1935.
Suffren, Arthur E. "Craft vs. Industrial Unions." *Current History* 44, 2 (May 1936): 97–104.

Sugar, Maurice. *The Ford Hunger March.* Berkeley, Calif.: Meiklejohn Civil Liberties Institute, 1980.
Sundquist, James L. *Dynamics of the Party System.* Washington, D.C.: Brookings Institution, 1973.
Svennilson, Ingvar. *Growth and Stagnation in the European Economy.* Geneva: United Nations, 1954.
Sweezy, Paul M. "Competition and Monopoly." *Monthly Review* 33, 1 (May 1981): 1–16.
———. *The Theory of Capitalist Development.* New York: Monthly Review Press, 1970.
Taft, Philip. *The A.F.L. from the Death of Gompers to the Merger.* New York: Harper, 1959.
Taylor, Albion Guilford. *Labor Policies of the National Association of Manufacturers.* New York: Arno, 1973.
Tedlow, R. S. "NAM and Public Relations during the New Deal." *Business History Review* 50, 1 (Spring 1976): 25–45.
Terkel, Studs. *Hard Times: An Oral History of the Great Depression.* New York: Avon, 1970.
Therborn, Goran. *The Ideology of Power and the Power of Ideology.* London: New Left Books, 1980.
———. "The Rule of Capital and the Rise of Democracy." *New Left Review* 103 (May–June 1977): 3–14.
———. *What Does the Ruling Class Do When It Rules?* London: New Left Books, 1978.
———. "Why Some Classes Are More Successful Than Others." *New Left Review* 138 (Mar.–Apr. 1983): 37–55.
Tomlins, Christopher L. "AFL Unions in the 1930's: Their Performance in Historical Perspective." *Journal of American History* 65, 4 (Mar. 1979): 1021–42.
———. *The State and the Unions: Labor Relations, Law, and the Organized Labor Movement in America, 1880–1960.* New York: Cambridge University Press, 1985.
Tronti, Mario. "Workers and Capital." *Telos* 14 (Winter 1972): 25–62.
Trout, Charles H. *Boston: The Great Depression and the New Deal.* New York: Oxford University Press, 1977.
Tugwell, Rexford G. *The Brains Trust.* New York: Viking, 1968.
———. *Roosevelt's Revolution.* New York: Macmillan, 1977.
Twentieth Century Fund, Inc. *Labor and the Government.* New York: McGraw-Hill, 1935.
VenKataramani, M. S. "Some Aspects of Life and Politics in the United States of America in 1932." *International Review of Social History* 3 (1958): 366–84.
Vogel, David. "Why Businessmen Distrust Their State: The Political Consciousness of American Corporate Executives." *British Journal of Political Science* 8 (Jan. 1978): 45–78.
Volpe, Paul A. *The International Financial and Banking Crisis, 1931–1933.* Washington, D.C.: Catholic University of America Press, 1945.
Wallerstein, Immanuel. "Crisis as Transition." In *Dynamics of Global Crisis,* edited by Samir Amin, Giovanni Arrighi, Andre Gunder Frank, and Immanuel Wallerstein. New York: Monthly Review Press, 1982.
———. "Cyclical Rhythms and Secular Trends of the Capitalist World Economy: Some Premises, Hypotheses and Questions." Paper prepared for the Colloquium on Crisis in the World Economy, Past and Present, Starnberg, Germany, 7–9 Aug. 1978.
Waltzer, Kenneth. "The Party and the Polling Place: American Communism and an American Labor Party in the 1930's." *Radical History Review* 23 (Spring 1980): 104–29.
Warren, Frank A. *An Alternative Vision: The Socialist Party in the 1930's.* Bloomington: Indiana University Press, 1974.

Waterfront Worker, Dec. 1932–Apr. 1936.
Weeks, John. *Capital and Exploitation.* Princeton, N.J.: Princeton University Press, 1981.
Weiner, Richard P. *Cultural Marxism and Political Sociology.* Beverly Hills, Calif.: Sage, 1981.
Weinstein, James. *Ambiguous Legacy: The New Left in American Politics.* New York: New Viewpoints, 1975.
Weir, Margaret, and Theda Skocpol. "State Structures and the Possibilities for 'Keynesian' Responses to the Great Depression in Sweden, Britain, and the United States." In *Bringing the State Back In,* edited by Peter B. Evans, Dietrich Rueschemeyer, and Theda Skocpol. New York: Cambridge University Press, 1985.
White, Graham J. *FDR and the Press.* Chicago: University of Chicago Press, 1979.
Williams, William Appleman. *America Confronts a Revolutionary World, 1776–1976.* New York: William Morrow, 1976.
———. *The Contours of American History.* New York: New Viewpoints, 1973.
Williamson, Harold. *The Growth of the American Economy.* Englewood Cliffs, N.J.: Prentice-Hall, 1946.
Wilson, Joan Hoff. *American Business and Foreign Policy, 1920–1933.* Boston, Mass.: Beacon, 1973.
Wilson, William H. "How the Chamber of Commerce Viewed the NRA: A Re-examination." *Mid-America* 44, 2 (Apr. 1962): 95–108.
Winch, Donald. *Economics and Policy.* New York: Walker, 1969.
Witte, Edwin E. *The Development of the Social Security Act.* Madison: University of Wisconsin Press, 1963.
Wolfe, Alan. *The Limits of Legitimacy.* New York: Free Press, 1977.
Wolters, Raymond. *Negroes and the Great Depression: The Problem of Economic Recovery.* Westport, Conn.: Greenwood, 1970.
———. "Section 7a and the Black Worker." *Labor History* 103 (Summer 1969): 459–74.
Wood, Ellen Meiksins. "The Separation of the Economic and Political in Capitalism." *New Left Review* 127 (May–June 1981): 66–95.
Wright, Erik Olin. *Class, Crisis, and the State.* London: New Left Books, 1978.
Yaffe, David. "Modern Marxian Theory of Crisis, Capital, and the State." *Economy and Society* 2 (1973): 186–232.
Zeiger, Robert H. "Reply to Professor Lichtenstein." *Industrial Relations* 19, 2 (Spring 1980): 131–35.
———. "Toward a History of the CIO: Bibliographical Report." *Labor History* 26, 4 (Fall 1985): 487–516.
Zeitlin, Maurice. "On Class, Class Conflict and the State: An Introduction Note." In *Classes, Class Conflict, and the State,* edited by Maurice Zeitlin. Cambridge, Mass.: Winthrop, 1980.
Zinn, Howard, ed. *New Deal Thought.* New York: Bobbs-Merrill, 1966.

INDEX